P9-CQU-917

The Kingfisher Book of the Universe

The Kingfisher Book of the Universe

NEW YORK

Authors David Lambert, Martin Redfern
Senior Editor Clive Wilson
Editors Rebecca Fry, Charlotte Hurdman
Design Jacqueline Palmer, Traffika Publishing Ltd.
Picture Research Veneta Bullen, Jane Lambert
Pre-Press Manager Caroline Jackson
DTP Coordinator Nicky Studdart
Indexer Hilary Bird

KINGFISHER
Larousse Kingfisher Chambers Inc.
95 Madison Avenue
New York, New York 10016

First published in 2001

2 4 6 8 10 9 7 5 3 1

1TR/1200/TWP/(MAR)/130SMA

LIBRARY OF CONGRESS CATALOGING-IN-PUBLICATION DATA
Lambert, David, 1932–
The Kingfisher book of the universe / by David Lambert and Martin Redfern.—1st ed.
p. cm.
Includes index.
ISBN 0-7534-5327-4
1. Earth sciences—Juvenile literature. 2. Solar system—Juvenile literature.
[1. Earth sciences. 2. Solar system.] I. Redfern, Martin, 1954– II. Title.

QE29 .L36 2001
550—dc21 00-048154

Color separations by Newsele
Printed in Singapore

CONTENTS

THE SOLAR SYSTEM

STARS

OUT IN SPACE, BACK IN TIME

COSMIC QUESTIONS

REFERENCE

Birth of the Earth

Five billion years ago, there was no planet Earth and no Sun. But the Universe was already in full swing and many generations of stars had already created the atomic building blocks—hydrogen, carbon, oxygen, and others—that would later make up the planets. In a spiral arm of what is now our galaxy, clouds of these atoms started to condense, pulled together either by gravity or by shock waves from distant explosions. As they contracted, they began to rotate, forming a swirling disk at the heart of which lay a small, young star. And so the Sun began its life.

△ *Every culture has developed its own story of the creation. This illustration from the Luther Bible (1530) shows God making the world and the Universe.*

Heat and dust

As the young Sun warmed, it blew a wind of energetic particles through the dusty disk, driving the remaining gases outward to form the giant planets Jupiter and Saturn. Other dust grains accumulated into rocky lumps which bumped into each other, sometimes joining together. Slowly, the remaining material was swept up into a few large planets. One of these was the beginnings of the Earth.

Fire and brimstone

The new Earth was a hot young planet, warmed by atoms spewed out by an earlier generation of stars and by its own gravity. It suffered heavy bombardment from large asteroids and comets which rained down upon it, melting its surface. One of these impacts was so large that it created the Moon.

◁ *Hindu theory sees the Universe as an egg, from which Brahma emerged before splitting himself into two people.*

The collision of an asteroid with e Earth threw up so much rock that it entually combined to form the Moon.

Hard core

As iron-rich minerals were drawn toward its center, the young Earth started to accumulate a great core of molten iron. This core now makes up 35 percent of the mass of the Earth—the remainder is made up of less dense, silicate rocks. As it grew, the molten core churned around, generating electric currents. These gave the planet its first magnetic field, which acted as a shield, protecting the Earth from radiation from space.

Living planet

Heat escaping from the core kept the surrounding mantle of silicate rock hot. Although this was solid, it flowed slowly, rather as ice in a glacier does, carrying heat to the surface in convection currents. Meanwhile, as the core continued to form, gases were rising to the surface, contributing to the early atmosphere. What had been born was not a dead lump of rock, but a living, dynamic new planet.

▽ *The Earth is one of nine planets, along with numerous moons, asteroids, and comets, that circle the Sun. The Sun itself is a minute dot on a spiral arm of the Milky Way, one of many similar galaxies in the Universe.*

Spaceship Earth

If an alien spaceship approached our Solar System and began scanning the planets for signs of life, it would soon detect that one planet was special. The Earth's atmosphere is different from that of all the other planets—it contains plenty of oxygen but very little carbon dioxide. Closer examination would also reveal a protective layer of ozone, and traces of the pigment chlorophyll on land and in the sea—confirmation of the existence of life. The alien space probe might even pick up the incessant babble of radio and television transmissions, suggesting that the Earth's life is intelligent.

△ Satellite sensors tuned to detect the pigment chlorophyll in plankton and plants were used to build up this image of life on land and in the sea.

Third rock from the Sun

The Earth is one of three planets that must have started their lives under similar conditions. Venus is about the same size as the Earth, but a little nearer to the Sun. Mars is slightly smaller and farther away. All three began with water vapor and carbon dioxide in their atmospheres. During their lifetimes, the Sun has warmed. On Venus, this gave rise to a runaway greenhouse effect that boiled away any water. On Mars, the free-flowing water froze or escaped into space. Today, the surface temperature of Venus is over 750°F (400°C), while that of Mars is typically −150°F (−100°C).

▽ Infrared sensors reveal growth of new vegetation on the volcanic island of Fogo, near West Africa. The blue is surrounding sea, white the clouds, and red the vegetation.

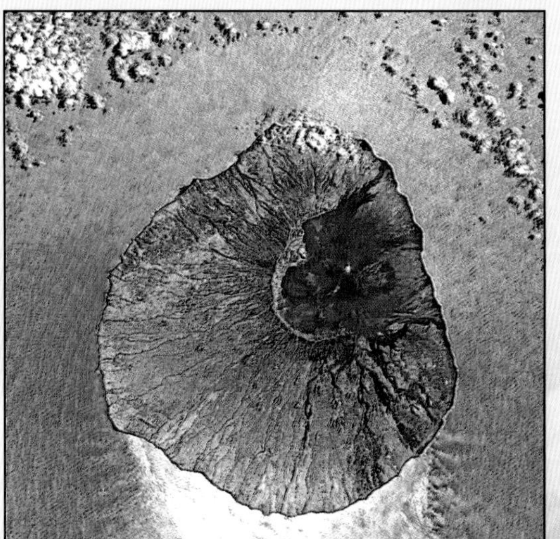

A living planet

Only on the Earth can life survive. The planet is a delicate ecosystem, maintained in a precarious balance between freezing and overheating. Yet, somehow, that balance has been maintained for billions of years, even while the Sun's heat has steadily increased. Many scientists now believe that the custodian of the planet is life itself. Thanks to life, the Earth's climate has not been disrupted by the warming Sun. Bacteria and algae, as well as plants, have consumed the carbon dioxide blanket that once enveloped the planet and liberated the oxygen. In this way, they have sustained a perfect atmosphere for life to flourish—at least so far. This concept is termed Gaia, after the ancient Greek mother Earth goddess.

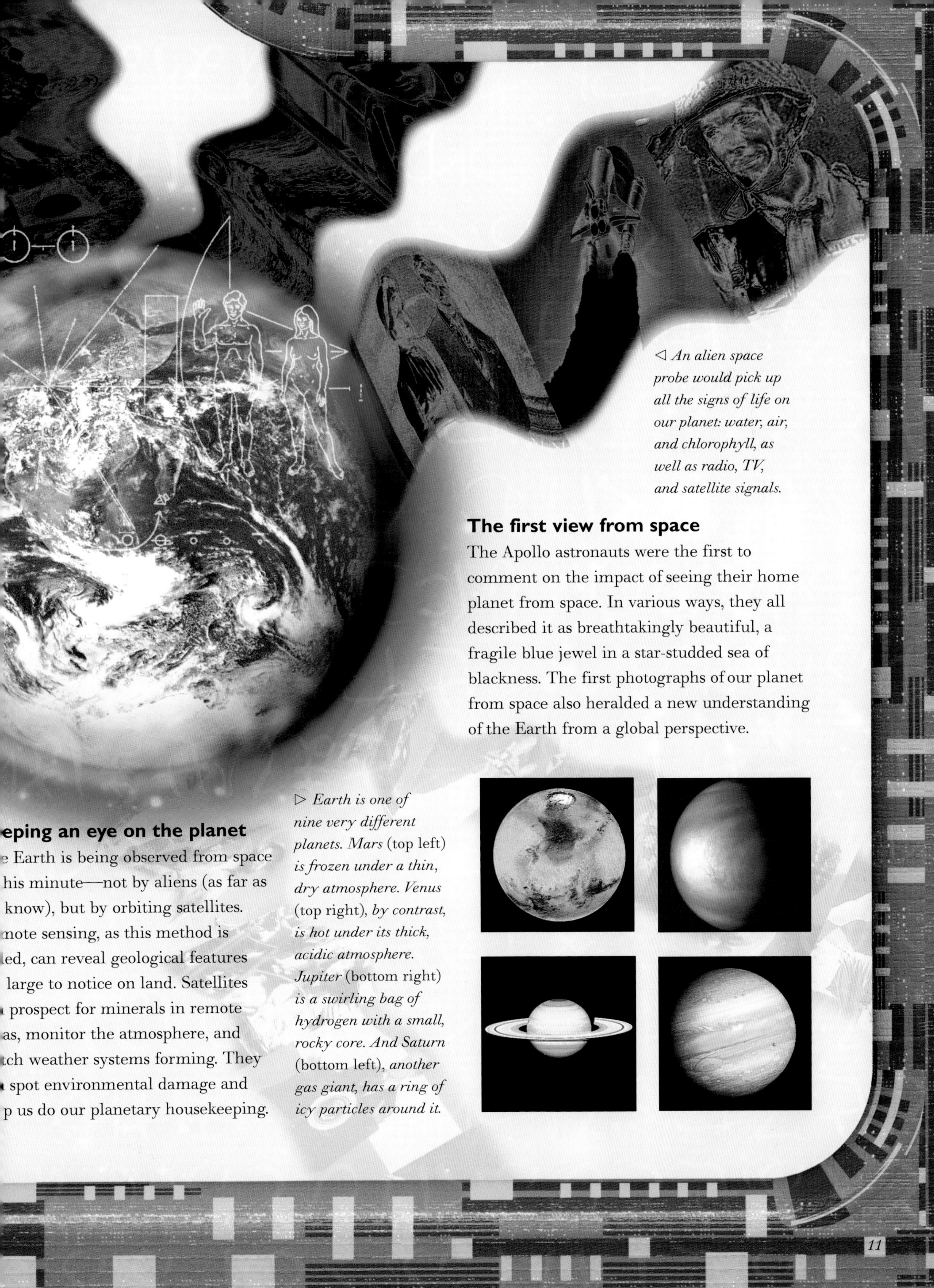

◁ *An alien space probe would pick up all the signs of life on our planet: water, air, and chlorophyll, as well as radio, TV, and satellite signals.*

The first view from space

The Apollo astronauts were the first to comment on the impact of seeing their home planet from space. In various ways, they all described it as breathtakingly beautiful, a fragile blue jewel in a star-studded sea of blackness. The first photographs of our planet from space also heralded a new understanding of the Earth from a global perspective.

eping an eye on the planet

e Earth is being observed from space his minute—not by aliens (as far as know), but by orbiting satellites. mote sensing, as this method is led, can reveal geological features large to notice on land. Satellites prospect for minerals in remote as, monitor the atmosphere, and tch weather systems forming. They spot environmental damage and p us do our planetary housekeeping.

▷ *Earth is one of nine very different planets.* Mars (top left) *is frozen under a thin, dry atmosphere.* Venus (top right), *by contrast, is hot under its thick, acidic atmosphere.* Jupiter (bottom right) *is a swirling bag of hydrogen with a small, rocky core. And* Saturn (bottom left), *another gas giant, has a ring of icy particles around it.*

Sky and Sea

From a single swirling cloud of gas and dust, the Sun and planets emerged about 4.5 billion years ago. At first, the young Earth may have had a thick atmosphere of hydrogen, similar to that of Jupiter. But if it did, it was very soon swept away as the new Sun began to shine. Volcanoes on the hot Earth were belching out gas and steam, but that too may have evaporated in the heat, or been stripped away by the solar wind and constant bombardment by asteroids. The Earth probably then resembled Jupiter's moon Io, with little atmosphere and a rash of volcanoes renewing its surface. Slowly, the atmosphere and oceans that we know today emerged.

△ *Comets brought water to the Earth in their icy cores, and volcanoes released gases into the atmosphere.*

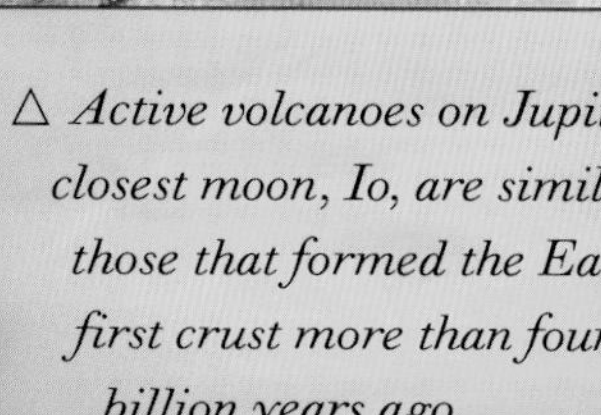

△ *Active volcanoes on Jupit closest moon, Io, are simil those that formed the Ear first crust more than four billion years ago.*

w the sea fell from the sky

› sky we know today probably came out of the ground, . the sea must have fallen from the sky. Volcanoes were stantly adding nitrogen and carbon dioxide to the new ıosphere. And the Earth's oceans were created by icy ıets returning from the outer Solar System and raining vn on the Earth's surface. Even today, many thousands ons of water fall to Earth from space every year.

e changing air

en it was first formed, the Earth's atmosphere had oxygen—only a lethal mixture of hydrogen, methane, monia, and hydrogen cyanide. It must have been the 'st case of pollution in history! But the hydrogen ıped to space and ultraviolet radiation from the Sun ke µdown the larger molecules, leaving a mixture of 'ogen and carbon dioxide. Only when life emerged . photosynthesis began did oxygen first appear on Earth—about 3.4 billion years ago. It probably produced by organisms called cyanobacteria, still found today in colonies known as stromatolites.

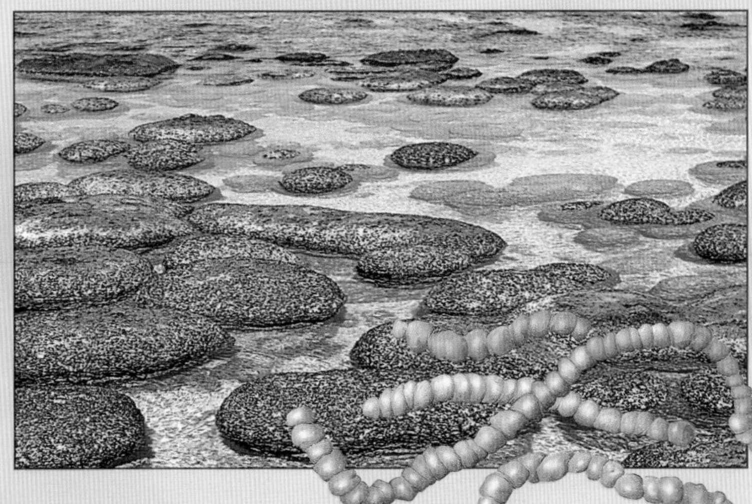

△ *Colonies of billions of cyanobacteria, known as stromatolites, grow in Shark Bay, Western Australia. Ancient stromatolites may have released the first oxygen on Earth.*

△ *Filaments of many tiny algal cells probably once filled the oceans, releasing oxygen into the young atmosphere.*

A climate for life

By two billion years ago, the levels of oxygen were rising as fast as algae filled the oceans. To produce the oxygen, the algae were consuming the carbon dioxide blanket that had kept the Earth warm. But the planet did not freeze, as the Sun was also warming steadily. The two kept pace with each other, maintaining a suitable climate for life.

Mantle Mysteries

The Earth is an engine driven by heat. The atmosphere, and to some extent the ocean is powered by heat from the Sun, but the solid bulk of the Earth is driven by heat from within. The plan is still cooling down from its violent formation. It is also generating heat today from its iron core, which is growing at a rate of 1,000 tons per second. The heat needs to escape somehow, but rock is a good insulator. Although the Earth's thick, rocky mantle is solid, it slowly convects, flowing like thick oatmeal cooking on a hot stove carrying heat to volcanoes on the surface. Just like oatmea a scum builds up on the surface—the Earth's crust.

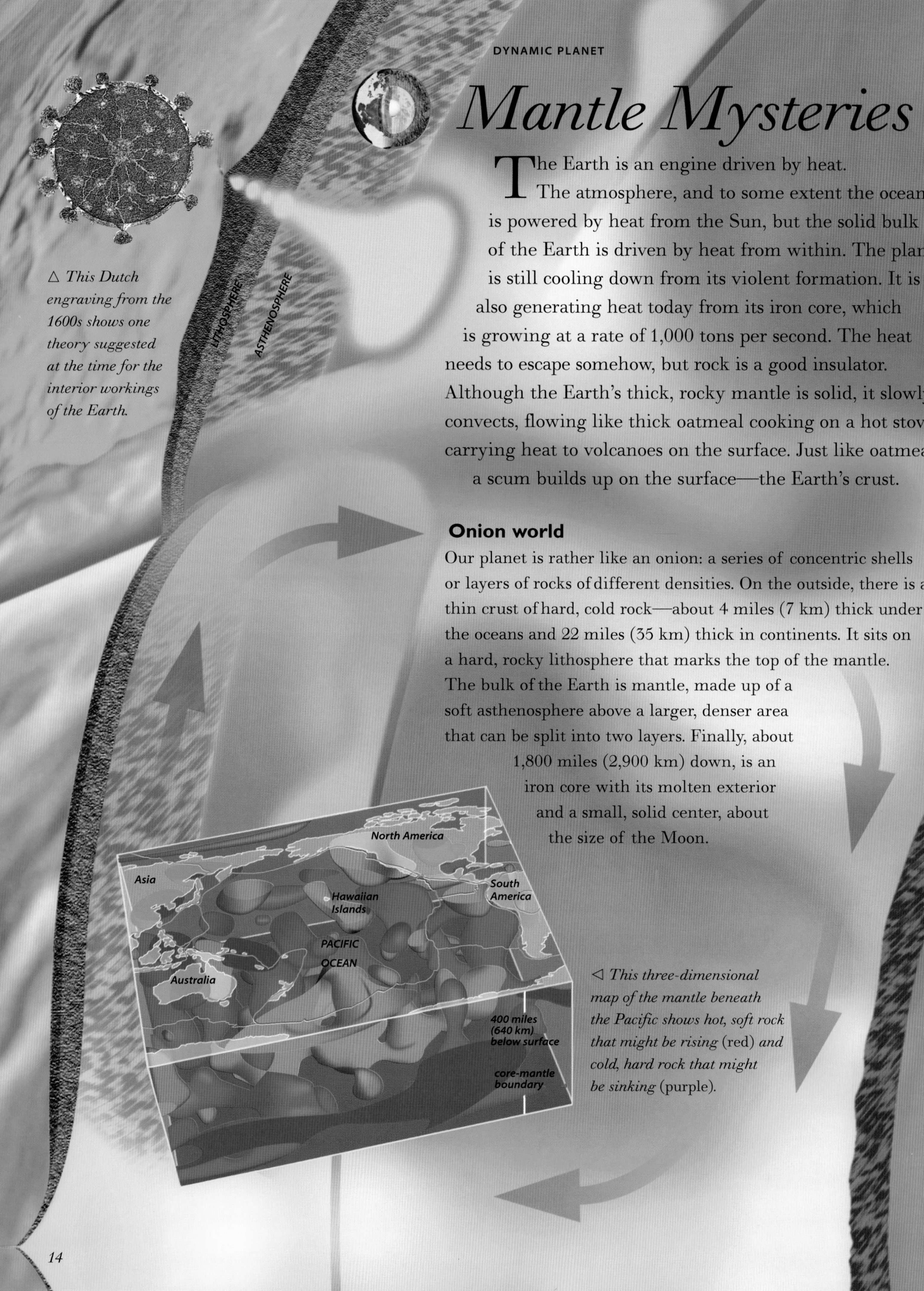

△ *This Dutch engraving from the 1600s shows one theory suggested at the time for the interior workings of the Earth.*

Onion world

Our planet is rather like an onion: a series of concentric shells or layers of rocks of different densities. On the outside, there is a thin crust of hard, cold rock—about 4 miles (7 km) thick under the oceans and 22 miles (35 km) thick in continents. It sits on a hard, rocky lithosphere that marks the top of the mantle. The bulk of the Earth is mantle, made up of a soft asthenosphere above a larger, denser area that can be split into two layers. Finally, about 1,800 miles (2,900 km) down, is an iron core with its molten exterior and a small, solid center, about the size of the Moon.

◁ *This three-dimensional map of the mantle beneath the Pacific shows hot, soft rock that might be rising* (red) *and cold, hard rock that might be sinking* (purple).

dless cycle

e Earth is constantly changing. New terial is being added to the surface, only be worn away and removed again. Hot k is rising up from the Earth's mantle, ile slabs of cold rock are sinking back vn into it. The entire rock cycle owered by heat from within l sunshine from above, he Earth constantly ews its surface.

▷ *Lava erupting on the Earth's surface may contain rock that has risen from the very base of the mantle, having begun its journey many hundreds of millions of years before.*

OUTER CORE

Lumps and bumps

As we travel over the surface of the Earth, we see all sorts of ifferent features. There are continents l oceans, mountains and valleys. some places the rocks are hard and ıse, in others they are soft and light. nilarly, deeper down, within the mantle l core, there are differences from place place, including lumps and bumps l temperature variations.

Secrets of the Earth's interior

About 420 miles (670 km) down in the Earth's mantle, there is a boundary. Old, cold slabs of ocean lithosphere descend toward it. Hot, soft rock rises from it, toward volcanic hotspots on the surface. Beneath it, the hot rocks also circulate. But does the whole mantle circulate, or is heat passed between the upper and lower mantle, without getting mixed up together? The answer could be that both are true. Material sinking in the upper mantle comes to a halt at the boundary, and spreads out for hundreds of millions of years before avalanching on through the lower mantle, almost to the top of the core.

Though made of solid k, the mantle is slowly ulating. Boundaries ome depths cause hot or cold rock read out before neying on.

INNER CORE

◁ *In the center of the Earth is a solid iron core about the size of the Moon. Around it is a slowly churning molten iron outer core. Electric currents circulating in it generate the planet's magnetic field.*

Changing Continents

As mantle rocks slowly circulate, they bring lighter rocks to the Earth's surface like a scum. This has built up to form the continents, the planet's great landmasses. As with icebergs, there is much more to a continent than you can see. Continental crust can be 20 or 25 miles (30 or 40 km) thick, compared to oce crust which is only about 4 miles (7 km) thick. Although it is ha to find ocean crust older than 400 million years, the continents have been slowly accumulating since the Earth's surface solidifie Part of Australia, for example, is more than 3 billion years old.

△ *This granite boulder, known as the Devil's Marble, is in northern Australia. Granite is made from ancient sediments that have melted at great depths and risen to the surface.*

Flotsam and jetsam

For billions of years, the continents have been tossed about on the mantle. Where they have crashed into one another, mountain ranges have formed. Where they have been pulled apart, oceans have opened up. When hot mantle rock rises under a continent, it can inject layers of volcanic rock, stretching the continent.

The rise of granite

As continental rocks pile up, the base of the continent gets buried deeper and deeper. As it descends, it heats up and the rocks at the base begin to melt and rise toward the surface. Huge bubbles of molten rock bake the surrounding rock, which cools slowly, forming crystals. Eventually, the surrounding rock wears away to reveal a new material—granite.

▷ *A technician from the U.S. Geological Survey checks a "creep" meter on the San Andreas Fault in California. It is sensitive enough to detect Earth movements as thin as human hair.*

ew crust
ns along mid-ocean
ges and moves aside, creating the
ocean crust that pushes continents apart and
s down beneath them, forming volcanic mountain ranges.

△▷ About 200 million years ago, almost all the land formed a single supercontinent. Since then, the Earth's face has changed dramatically, and will continue to do so.

▽ Seismic waves, produced by the 26-ton Vibroseis *truck, bounce off faults or hard layers in the rocks and are picked up by detectors.*

*he Devil's Tower in Wyoming is a volcanic plug. First, molten
solidified in the vent of a volcano. Then, the softer flanks
he volcano later eroded away, leaving the plug exposed.*

e continental waltz

ou look at the coastlines of the continents you
l notice what seems like a remarkable coincidence—
y seem to fit roughly together. Africa, for example,
ts into South America as if the Atlantic Ocean were
there. Align the edges of the continental shelves
her than their present-day coastlines, and the fit
etter still. This, geologists believe, is how the
tinents were placed 100 million years ago, before
Atlantic opened up. Run the clock back farther
l and you will find that 200 million years ago
re was a single supercontinent, known as Pangaea.
plit apart, opening up a new sea called the Tethys.

Under the Sea

△ Twenty Thousand Leagues Under the Sea *was written in 1870 by French science-fiction writer Jules Verne. It tells of a powered submarine,* Nautilus, *whose crew discovers weird and wonderful creatures at the bottom of the sea. One hundred years later, fiction became fact.*

More than 70 percent of our planet's surface is covered by oceans. Their average depth is more than 13,100 feet (4,000 m)—far too deep for sunlight to reach the ocean floor. Yet it is in the oceans that one of the mos important clues to how the Earth works has been found. In the 1960s, as the ocean floors began to be surveyed by sonar, magnetometers, and submersibles, it soon became clear that there is a system of ridges running down the middle of the world's oceans. This system is the longest continuous mountain chain on the planet—a network 43,500 miles (70,000 km) long, like the seam on a baseball. As oceanographers have discovered, the ridges are quite literally the seams of the planet—and the boundaries of creation.

Volcanoes beneath the waves

Mid-ocean ridges are peppered with active volcanic vents, from which dense, black basalt oozes like toothpaste into round lumps called pillow lava. The eruptions usually are not violent, but sometimes are accompanied by small earthquakes.

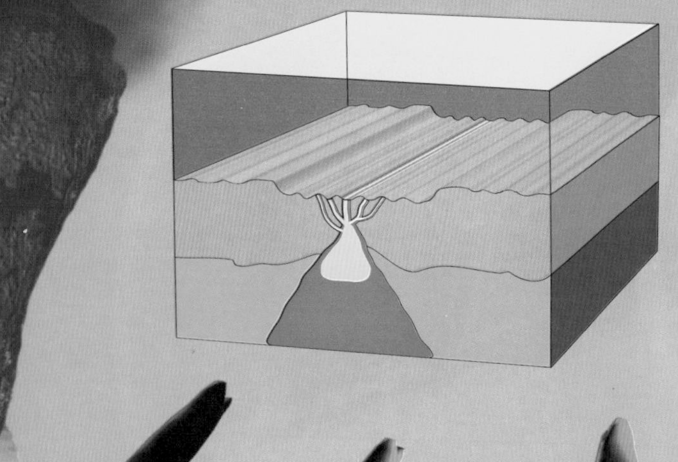

◁ *A mid-ocean ridge is the dividing point between two pieces of the Earth's crust. Hot magma from deep within the mantle forces its way up through the crack, continually creating new ocean crust.*

Black smokers

Water sometimes seeps into the volcanoe where it dissolves minerals and then rise out of hydrothermal vents known as bla smokers. The water can be as hot as 400–600°F (200°–300°C), but it does not boil because of the enormous pressure.

Life around the vents

Amazingly, a whole ecosystem of organisms has been discovered around such vents. Bacteria which take energy from sulfur provide food for giant tube worms, clams, fish, and blind white shrimp.

Recycling the ocean floor

If mid-ocean ridges are constantly spewing out new sea floor, does this mean that the Earth is expanding? The answer is no—the old ocean crust is sinking into the mantle. As the ocean crust cools, it becomes more dense and either dives into an ocean trench or under a continent, throwing up volcanic islands or mountain chains as it goes.

△ *This magnetic map reveals the symmetry of the rocks on either side of the Mid-Atlantic Ridge, where rising magma has pushed the continents apart.*

◁ *The sulfur and dissolved minerals released at hydrothermal vents allow creatures to exist without sunlight.*

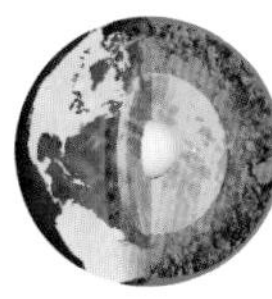

Earth Revealed

A journey to the center of the Earth was once a dream of science fiction. Today, it is possible in science fact. Humans can only burrow a few thousand feet underground in the deepest mines. Bore holes can only drill within the crust of the Earth—to date the deepest hole is just over 7 miles (12 km.) Science, however, can take us beyond the crust and deep into the planet. Using observations from the surface and from satellites in space, together with laboratory simulations, geologists now have a clear understanding of how the Earth works.

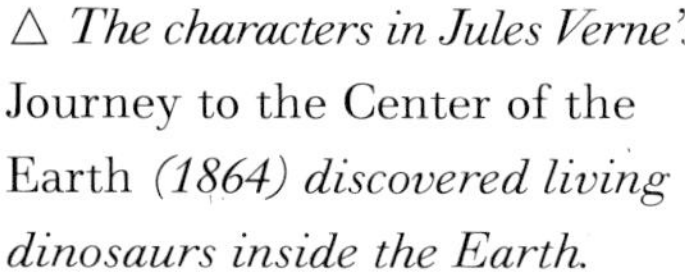

△ *The characters in Jules Verne's* Journey to the Center of the Earth *(1864) discovered living dinosaurs inside the Earth.*

▽ *The satellite* LAGEOS II *reveals variations in the Earth's gravity caused by different rock densities.*

△ *By squeezing a tin sample of rock betwee the polished faces of t diamonds, it is possibl recreate the pressures the center of the Earth*

Squashed Earth

The Earth is slightly squashed—its diameter at the equator is about 24 miles (38 km) greater than at the poles. This is because the planet is spinning, forcing material out toward the equator. Overall, however, the Earth is very smooth. If the planet were scaled down to the size of a 3-foot (1-m) ball, the difference between the highest mountains and the deepest valleys would be less than a quarter inch.

Free-fall

When Isaac Newton saw an apple fall, he realized that the force of gravity was pulling objects toward the center of the Earth. What he did not know was that apples fall slightly faster in some parts of the world than others—although you could not measure the difference using apples! Satellites, however, can measure the variations. The gravitational pull of a region of dense rock will make a satellite speed up. Over a region of lower gravity, it will slow down

Split-second timing

The Earth is slowing down. We know from daily growth lines in fossil shells that, 180 million years ago, there were about 400 days in the year and a day lasted only 22 hours. This slowing down is caused mainly by energy lost as the Moon's gravity pulls on the Earth. There are also variations, of billionths of a second, that take place over days and hours. These are caused partly by currents in the core.

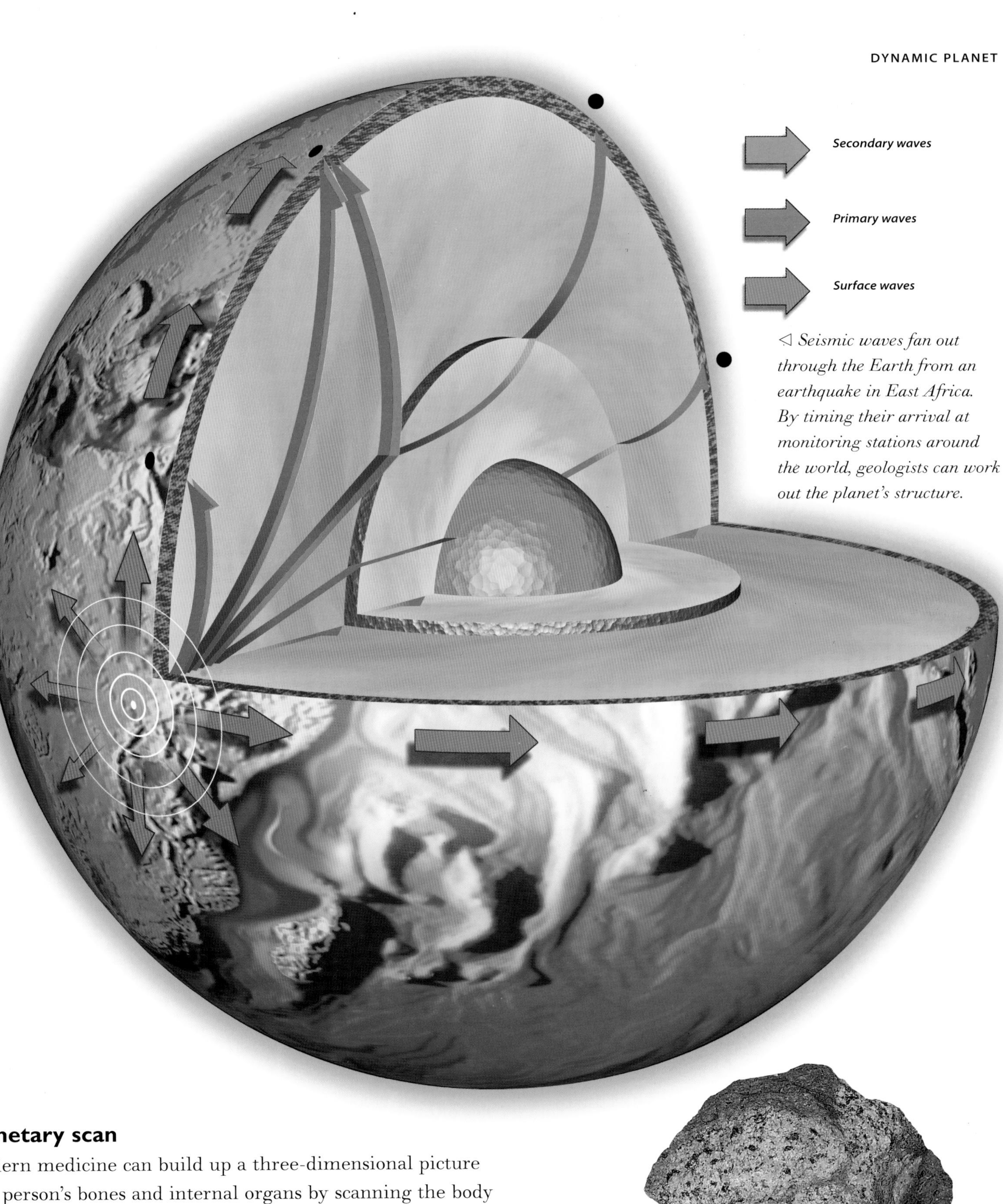

◁ *Seismic waves fan out through the Earth from an earthquake in East Africa. By timing their arrival at monitoring stations around the world, geologists can work out the planet's structure.*

anetary scan

odern medicine can build up a three-dimensional picture a person's bones and internal organs by scanning the body th x rays or magnetism. A similar process can be applied to Earth. Instead of x rays or magnetism, geologists use seismic ves from earthquakes and nuclear bomb tests. The waves move ickly through hard, dense rock, but more slowly through soft k. Computers then build up a detailed picture of the planet sed on the routes the waves take through the Earth.

△ *This dense rock, made of the mineral olivine, is a sample of the mantle. It was brought to the surface in a volcanic eruption.*

DYNAMIC PLANET

The Living Core

By tracking the paths of seismic waves as they travel through the Earth after an earthquake, geologists have discovered some surprisin facts about the planet's core. It seems to have a liquid outer layer that is churning like cement in a mixer at a speed of several sixteenths of an inc per second. And right at the Earth's center may be a crystal the size of the Moon! The pressure is so great at such depths that the only substance tha could behave in like this is iron, perhaps with traces of nickel, sulfur, oxygen, and silica. But geologists are puzzled by the discovery of a crusty boundary between the molten outer core and the mantle rocks above. Wh is this upside-down landscape 1,800 miles (2,900 km) beneath our feet?

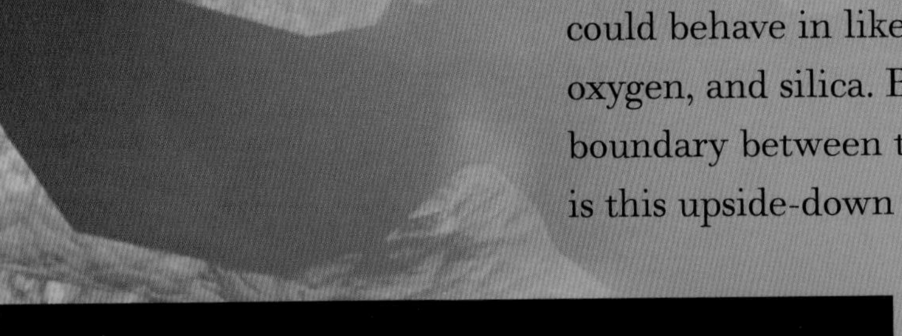

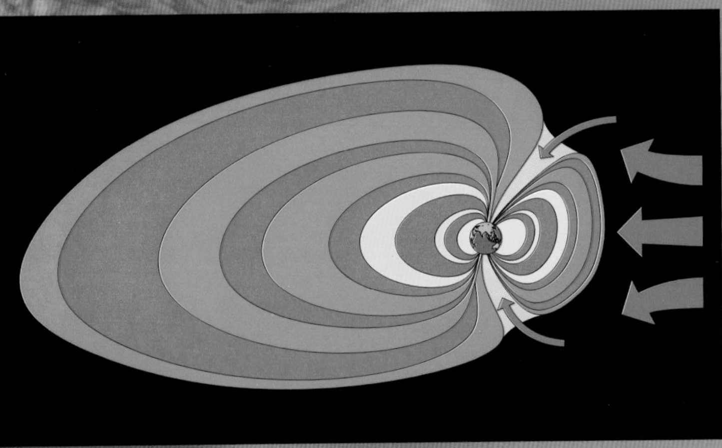

△ The Earth's magnetic field is rooted in the core, but reaches far out into space. It envelops the Earth and protects us from harmful radiation and particles, especially those emitted by the Sun.

Lost oceans

This mysterious boundary is not continuous—in some places it is 120 miles (200 km) thick and in others completely absent. It could be an iron and silicate scum that has risen like continents to the top of the core. Or, more likely, it is the final resting-place of old, cold ocea crust that has sunk down through the mantle—a lost oc

Upside-down mountains

The result is a subterranean landscape with mountains and valleys that dwarf any found on the surface of the Earth. Beneath Alaska is a liquid mountain taller than Mount Everest, and under the Philippines is a valley in the core that is twice the depth of the Grand Canyon.

△ *As charged particles from space stream in along magnetic lines over the poles, they strike the atoms and molecules in the Earth's upper atmosphere and cause spectacular light shows called auroras.*

lagnetic dynamo

he Earth's magnetic ɜld originates in the outer re. It is far too hot down there r a permanent magnet. Instead, the ɜld is generated by electric currents in e churning metal. Like any magnet, e Earth has two poles—North and South. t present they lie in the Arctic and Antarctic, ıt evidence in the rocks shows that they have versed positions many times in Earth's history.

rozen in time

ıe inner core is about the size of the Moon, and owing! Iron is freezing onto it at the rate of about 00 ton per second. Yet only about 4 percent of the total re has frozen in 4.5 billion years. This change to a solid leases a lot of heat, which combines with radioactive ecay to keep the outer core churning, the magnetic ɜld working, and the mantle moving.

If we could pull the mantle away from the core, a strange bterranean landscape of valleys and mountains would be visible the mantle's underside. The outer core—a liquid metal furnace, urning at temperatures of 9,000°F (5,000°C)—pushes against se features, and affects Earth's rotation and magnetism.

Eruption!

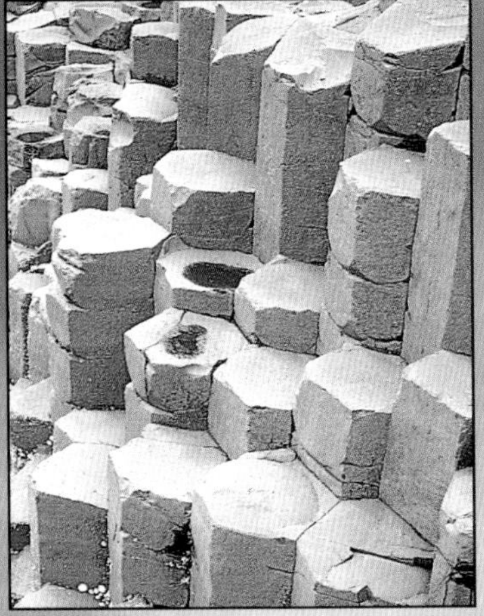

Chains of volcanoes encircle the globe. Dotted along the edges of the plates that make up the Earth's crust, they are evidence that the interior of our planet is hot and active. When two continents move apart, material from the Earth's mantle rises to fill the gap. As the rock rises and the pressure drops, it partly melts to form liquid basalt. Like toothpaste from a tube, this lava emerges in huge quantities from fissures and vents—volcanoes—under the newly forming ocean. Occasionally the ridges where the ocean crust is growing rise to the surface to form islands—Iceland is one example. Fresh volcanic land makes a rich and fertile home, but it can also be a risky place to live.

△ *The Giant's Causeway in Northern Ireland was formed from volcanic basalt, which erupted as Europe split from North America 60 million years ago. The lava cooled to form these hexagonal columns, each up to 1.6 feet (0.5 m) across.*

An explosive history

The relatively sudden eruption of vast quantities of basalt must have taken place many times during the history of the Earth. There is evidence of other such events on the floor of the Pacific and sometimes on land, for example in Siberia and Argentina.

Sticky lava

When lava is rich in silica, it is sticky and does not flow easily. This causes the pressure in the volcano to build up, until erupts in a violent explosion of superhea steam, ash, and molten rock. This kind of volcano is the most dangerous, and the hardest to predict.

Types of volcano

It is tempting to try to classify volcanoes according to the way they erupt, but the geological record shows that any one volcano can change during its history. It may begin fairly gently, producing runny basalt at first. Over time it will build up and gradually become unstable. Eventually it will start to crack and fall in on itself, and this causes explosive eruptions of viscous, silica-rich lava.

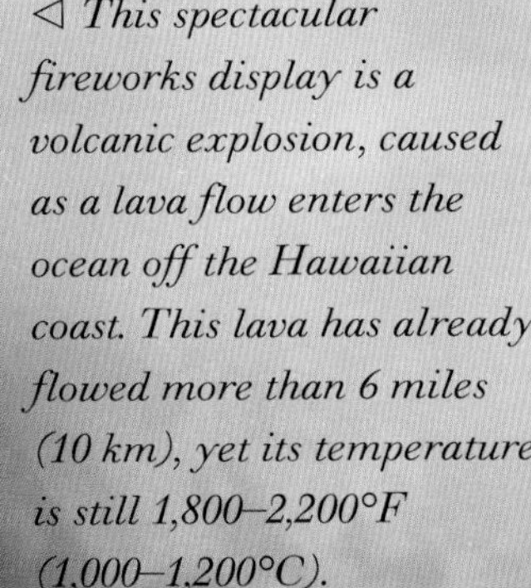

◁ *This spectacular fireworks display is a volcanic explosion, caused as a lava flow enters the ocean off the Hawaiian coast. This lava has already flowed more than 6 miles (10 km), yet its temperature is still 1,800–2,200°F (1,000–1,200°C).*

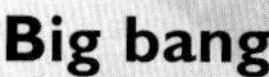

Big bang

The biggest volcanic eruption in recent history occurred on the island of Krakatoa, Indonesia. The volcano had been silent since 1680 and the crater was plugged with solidified lava. Then, on August 27, 1883, the volcano exploded, blowing the entire island into the sky. Tidal waves up to 130 feet (40 m) high resulted—hundreds of villages were destroyed and around 36,000 people died.

△ *This eight-legged robot was developed to explore other planets. But it has also been used on the Earth to collect samples of gas and rock from volcanoes too hazardous for humans.*

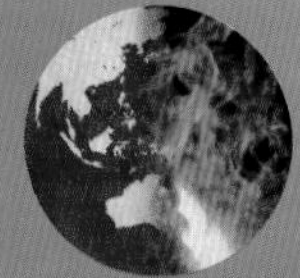

Anatomy of a Volcano

Mount Etna is one of the most active volcanoes on the Earth. It has erupted at least 40 times in the last 20 years and shows no signs of stopping. Towering 10,800 feet (3,300 m) above the Mediterranean in the east of Sicily, the volcano has four summit craters. During an eruption, some of these craters can fill with red-hot lava. Seen from the airplanes that pass overhead, they look like giant eyes in the night. Scientists have walked over every inch of the volcano with a variety of instruments. Seismographs measure the slightest shaking of the Earth, while gravity meters and magnetometers measure the gravitational pull of rocks and their magnetic effects underground. Finally, scientists survey and measure how the mountain swells and contracts as the lava rises and falls within it.

△ Carrying whatever they can, the population of a Sicilian village flees ahead of an advancing lava flow in this illustration from 1910.

▽ During the 1971 eruption of Mount Etna, a stream of lava slowly advanced down the slopes and engulfed the volcano observatory.

Underground plumbing

From all these measurements, it is clear that molten rock collects in a wide, flat chamber about 12 miles (20 km) beneath Etna and rises up a single pipe. Toward the top, perhaps 3,300 feet (1,000 m) beneath the summit, the pipe splits, leading to four different summit craters and various other cracks and fissures. There is always molten rock at some depth in the central pipe, and this gives off bubbles of sulfurous gas, as if the volcano is breathing.

◁ During the 1983 eruption of Mount Etna, lava surrounded the Sapienza Hotel. The flow moved slowly enough to allow people to be evacuated, and the building survived.

Story of an eruption

The 1971 eruption of Mount Etna began like many othe before and since. Magma in the central pipe reached th top of one of the summit craters, sending a fiery fountai of lava and hot rocks into the air. Lava then began to cre downhill at a slow walking pace. Then, about two mont later, a minor earthquake opened up several vents lowe down the mountain, draining magma away from the summit toward villages. Luckily, no one was hurt.

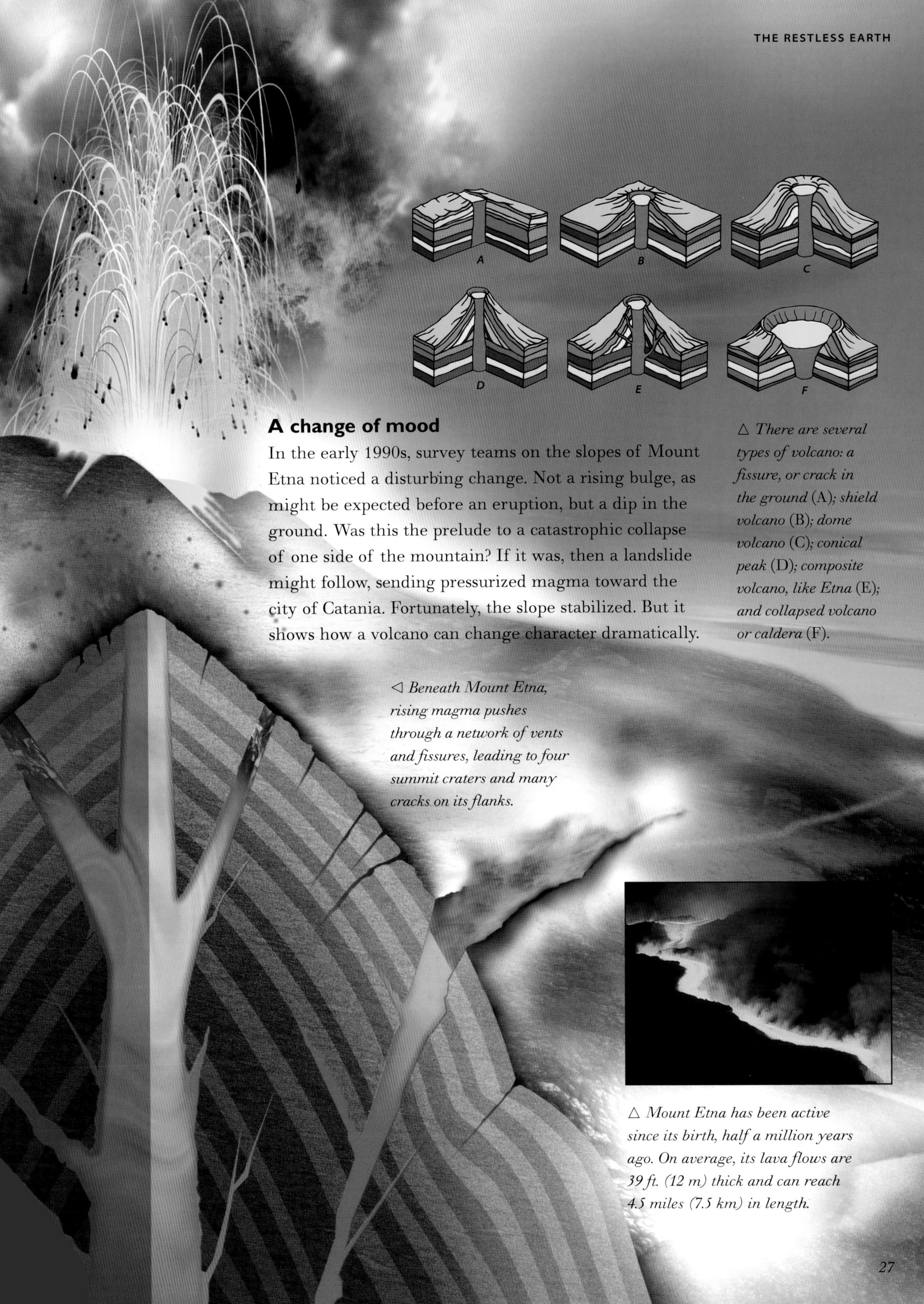

△ *There are several types of volcano: a fissure, or crack in the ground* (A)*; shield volcano* (B)*; dome volcano* (C)*; conical peak* (D)*; composite volcano, like Etna* (E)*; and collapsed volcano or caldera* (F).

A change of mood

In the early 1990s, survey teams on the slopes of Mount Etna noticed a disturbing change. Not a rising bulge, as might be expected before an eruption, but a dip in the ground. Was this the prelude to a catastrophic collapse of one side of the mountain? If it was, then a landslide might follow, sending pressurized magma toward the city of Catania. Fortunately, the slope stabilized. But it shows how a volcano can change character dramatically.

◁ *Beneath Mount Etna, rising magma pushes through a network of vents and fissures, leading to four summit craters and many cracks on its flanks.*

△ *Mount Etna has been active since its birth, half a million years ago. On average, its lava flows are 39 ft. (12 m) thick and can reach 4.5 miles (7.5 km) in length.*

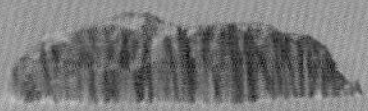

Hotspots

△ *This is a statue of the Hawaiian fire goddess, Pele, who is said to live in the crater of Kilauea.*

Around the Pacific Ocean is the Ring of Fire—a circle of volcanoes that marks the boundaries of the Pacific plate. But not all volcanoes lie on plate boundaries. In the middle of the Pacific Ocean is the biggest volcano of all—Hawaii. The island sits on top of a hotspot—a spring of rising magma that has burst through the Earth's crust from the mantle below. The hotspot has been in the same place for millions of years. But during that time, the Pacific plate has moved slowly to the northwest, passing over the top of the hotspot and creating a string of volcanic islands. The oldest of these was active more than 20 million years ago. The youngest is a submarine volcano called Loihi, lying beneath the waves, southeast of Hawaii.

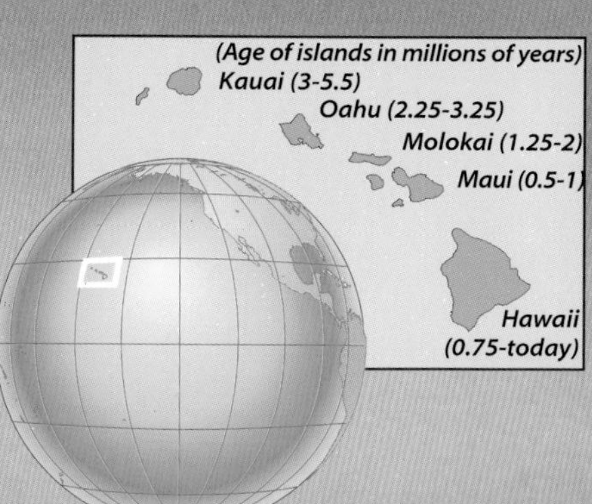

△ *The slow, northwesterly journey of the huge Pacific plate can be seen in the increasing ages of the islands as they move away from the hotspot.*

◁ *A night view reveals lava erupting along a fissure on the flanks of Kilauea and pouring into the sea.*

△ *Hawaii is entirely volcanic, with the peaks of Mauna Kea and Mauna Loa towering to 13,800 feet (4,200 m). Kilauea is one of the world's most active volcanoes.*

An Hawaiian eruption

Hawaiian volcanoes have their roots at a depth of 30 miles (50 km) or more. Lava rises in a pipe that broadens into a storage area a few thousand feet beneath the volcano. Tourists flock to Kilauea, the most active crater on the main island, to see an eruption. This usually begins with a curtain of fire, as gas sprays up lava along a fissure. Then the runny basalt builds a cone around a single vent. Sometimes, lava crosses roads, and streams toward the sea.

Cooking a continent

There are many hotspots on the Earth. Some are beneath continents. Yellowstone National Park in Wyoming is one example. Here, the continent is too thick for volcanic forces to break through, but heat still escapes, leading to the famous sulfurous hot springs and geysers of the park. Another hotspot under East Africa is slowly cooking the continent. It has already created the Great Rift Valley of East Africa, but one day it may split the continent in half.

'he chain of islands
'ching away to the northwest of
vaii represents eruptions of the past.
he Pacific plate moves northwest,
'rries the islands away from
volcanic activity.

△ *Many lava types can be found on Hawaii. The distinctive ropy texture of pahoehoe lava* (top left) *forms as scum on the surface as a flow crinkles up. Aa lava* (bottom left) *has a rough surface. Very hot, fluid lava* (top right) *can flow at a running pace. And basalt erupting underwater cools quickly to form pillow lava* (bottom right).

◁ *A new volcano, called Loihi, is rising beneath the sea. From ocean floor to surface is 10,000 feet (3,000 m); Loihi has 3,000 feet (900 m) to grow before it becomes an island in its own right.*

Opening an ocean

Geological evidence suggests that, before the Atlantic Ocean opened, the crust of Europe was stretched by a hotspot in the mantle underneath, and an ocean was nearly created farther east of where the Atlantic lies today. It is this process that formed the North Sea and helped to mature the oil deposits within it. When the Atlantic finally did open, about 60 million years ago, it may have been caused partly by the immense power of another hotspot.

Blowing Its Top

When old ocean crust dives down under a continent, it carries water with it. The rocks heat up, begin to melt, and magma rises. Bu the water turns it all into a giant pressure-cooker, waiting to blow its steam valve. On April 2, 1991, a nun walked into the Philippine Institute of Volcanology and, begging their pardon, pointed out that the mountain behind her village had just blown up. Mount Pinatubo had lain dormant for 600 years and was covered with lush vegetation. The first Earth tremors were followed by a plum of ash and gas, rising several miles into the sky. A rapid response force from the U.S. Volcano Disast Assistance Program rushed to the Philippines to monitor the eruption and warn the hundreds of thousands of people at risk.

△ *When Mount Pinatubo in the Philippines blew its top in June 1991, about 0.5 cubic miles (2 cubic km) of rock were turned to dust and sent high into the atmosphere, darkening the sky. Some dust spread around the world, creating spectacular sunsets and affecting the climate. But most rained down on nearby towns, leaving a thick layer of ash over everything.*

Ring around the Earth

Two months later, a mighty explosion shot steam and ash more than 19 miles (30 km) into the sky above Mount Pinatubo. Nearly 300 peopl died, but had there been no early warnings or evacuation, the death tol would have been catastrophic. Following the eruption, a cloud of volca ash spread out around the Earth, blotting out enough sunlight to lower global temperatures by about a degree over the next three years.

▽ *Super-hot pyroclastic flows of gas and lava raced down the flanks at 60 mph (100 km/h), sending those people not already evacuated racing for safety. Here, journalists flee from a giant cloud of noxious gases and dust.*

leven years earlier

ıe of the reasons why scientists could react so quickly to Mount natubo lay on the other side of the Pacific, in Washington State. even years earlier, in March 1980, Mount St. Helens had also begun ıshing steam and ash. Residents and loggers were evacuated and ologists flocked to the site. Instead of erupting out of the summit ater, a bulge began to appear in the northern flank. It grew to over 0 feet (100 m) high and, at one stage, was rising by 7 feet (2 m) a day.

ırning avalanche

8:30 in the morning of May 18, 1980, two sightseers watched as e entire bulge fell away during a mild earthquake. The lid was off e pressure-cooker! The volcano exploded sideways, sending a mixture superheated gas, steam, and ash racing along a valley at more than 90 ph (150 km/h). In all, 0.2 cubic miles (1 cubic km) of rock disappeared m the top of Mount St. Helens. The two sightseers escaped with ir lives, although 57 people died during the eruption.

▷ *Until May 18, 1980, Mount St. Helens was a serene volcanic peak. But the pressure beneath was mounting.*

▷ *After the eruption, the mountain was 1,300 feet (400 m) lower; 540 million tons of ash and lava had erupted.*

▷ *As far as 19 miles (30 km) from the volcano, trees were stripped of branches, flattened like matchsticks, or swept away.*

◁ *Molten magma inside Mount St. Helens pushed a bulge out on one side of the volcano. When that collapsed, hot magma shot out sideways in what is known as a pyroclastic eruption.*

△ *When heavy rain follow an eruption—as happened the Philippines in 1995—d and ash turn to rivers of m adding to the disaster.*

△ *In A.D. 79, hot ash from Mount Vesuvius buried thousands of citizens in Pompeii. Casts of their bodies remain.*

Volcanoes and Peopl

Few people have ever seen the birth of a volcano. One exception is a Mexican farmer called Dionisio Pulido. On February 5, 1943, while h was preparing a cornfield for planting near his home in Paricutin, Pulido noticed that a strange pit in the corner of a field had a crack running acr it from which gas was escaping. When glowing rocks were hurled out and nearby trees caught fire, he hurriedly departed. A day later there was a cinder cone 165 feet (50 m) high. After a year this had risen to 1,065 feet (325 m), and eruptions of lava had covered two villages, leaving only a church tower rising above them. But this case is unusual. Most active volcanoes have been in existence for thousands of years, and lie in easily identifiable and comparatively small areas of the world. Yet, people have always lived in their shadows and many still die in their eruptions every y

△ *Later eruptions of Mount Vesuvius have been less violent. This 1700s painting shows sightseers enjoying the pyrotechnic display.*

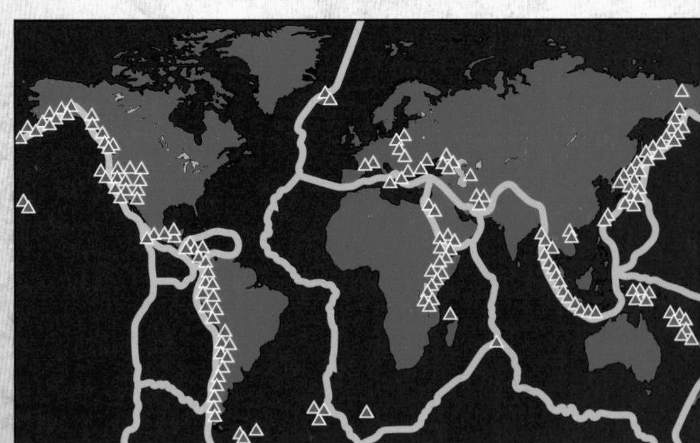

▷ *This map of recent volcanic eruptions shows how many volcanoes lie along plate margins, where one plate is diving beneath another. Others occur where the crust is splitting, or over a hotspot in the Earth's mantle.*

When Mount Pelée, on the Caribbean island of Martinique, an to give out sulfurous fumes in 1902, people in the port of Pierre did not evacuate because of local elections. A month later, entire city and its population of 29,000 were destroyed (top right), *rt from a condemned prisoner awaiting execution in his cell. On ntserrat* (right), *over 30 residents have died in eruptions since 5 because they would not leave their homes.*

mpeii revisited

e excavated remains of the crouched and huddled zens of Pompeii are a grim reminder of the speed with ich a volcano can overwhelm a population. In A.D. 79, 5-foot (20-m) thick blanket of burning ash and dust m Mount Vesuvius buried about 16,000 people. Were same to happen today, three million people in and und the Italian city of Naples would be at risk.

angerous waters

e and water are a dangerous combination. lcanic peaks are often covered in snow and the ulting mudflows or lahars can be more damaging than eruption itself. At Nevado del Ruiz in Columbia in 85, 22,000 people died as a 130-foot (40-m) high wave mud burst down a canyon above the town of Armero.

opping volcanoes

ere is no stopping a volcanic eruption—but the wer can be redirected, away from humans. In Iceland 1973, water was pumped into lava erupting from lgafell, causing it to solidify before reaching the harbor d village. And in Sicily in 1983, explosives were used to ert a lava flow from Etna away from tourist facilities.

△ *Volcano-watching can be an extremely hazardous profession. Here, a volcanologist in protective clothing ventures to within metres of lava fountaining from a fissure in Iceland.*

Earthquake!

The surface of the Earth is paved with slabs of crust, floating on dense, soft rocks of the mantle. But each slab is constantly on the move, as oceans open or disappear and continents drift like great ships on the mantle. Sometimes, one piece of crust dives down beneath another, or it grates alongside and gets stuck. Most spectacularly, two pieces may crash head-on. Where these mighty slabs meet, stresses gradually build up under the ground, and whole networks of cracks, known as faults, can appear. As the pieces suddenly slip into a new position, years of strain are released as an earthquake.

△ *As the tension created by two plates rubbing together is released, shock waves ripple outward from the hypocenter (A), causing an earthquake. The epicenter (B) is the point above where the waves hit the surface.*

Tracking continents

The drifting continents can be tracked by flashing laser beams from them to orbiting satellites and measuring how long the beams take to reflect back to the ground. Typically, continents move at the same pace as your fingernails grow—an inch or so every year.

▽ *A nearby earthquake measuring ove 7 on the Richte scale will dama the foundations buildings, ruptur pipes, tear cracks in roads, and even topple skyscrapers.*

▽ *The surface of the Earth may roll and heave for many days following a quake, as aftershocks reverberate through the rocks.*

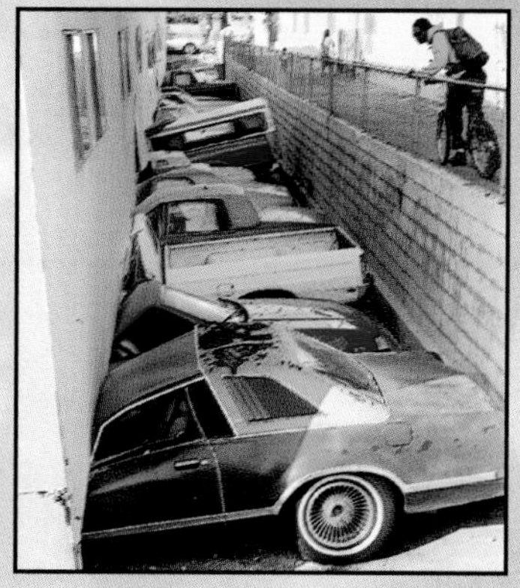

◁ *A row of cars in a basement parking lot in Northridge, California is squashed as the building collapses in 1994 during a quake measuring 6.8 on the Richter scale.*

◁ *The San Andreas Fault stretches like a giant scar across the Carrizo Plain between Los Angeles and San Francisco.*

The most famous crack in the world

Californians are used to living with the possibility of earthquakes. Their state is split north to south by a huge crack in the Earth's surface—the San Andreas Fault. To the west of the fault lies the Pacific plate which is moving northward, grating past the great North American plate.

rthquake intensity

rthquakes can be measured on two scales. The Richter le measures the energy of the ground waves produced an earthquake. The Mercalli scale monitors physical ects on the surface. At the bottom end of both scales, tremors are scarcely noticeable. At 5 on the Mercalli le, doors swing open and liquids spill. By 8, masonry rts crumbling, roads crack, and walking is difficult.

Changing places

The motion across the San Andreas Fault adds up to 1 inch (34 mm) per year, although it is far from smooth. Geological evidence shows that the fault moves during some quakes by up to 39 feet (12 m) at a time. In 1906, San Francisco was devastated by such a quake. At the present rate of movement, in 10 million years' time, Los Angeles will be as far north as San Francisco is today.

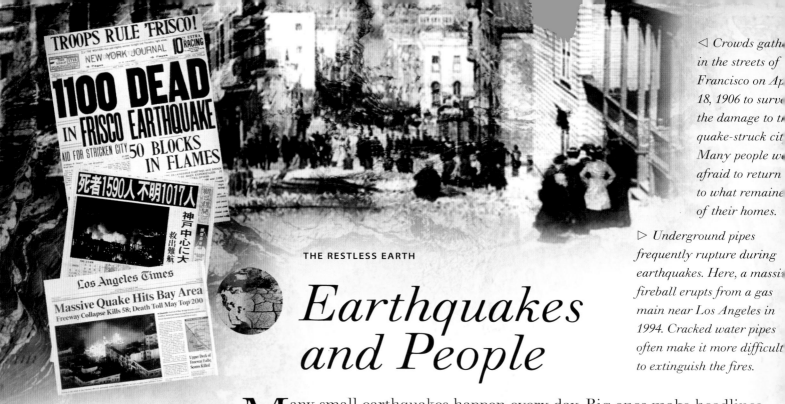

Earthquakes and People

◁ *Crowds gath[er] in the streets of [San] Francisco on Ap[ril] 18, 1906 to surv[ey] the damage to t[he] quake-struck cit[y]. Many people we[re] afraid to return to what remaine[d] of their homes.*

▷ *Underground pipes frequently rupture during earthquakes. Here, a massi[ve] fireball erupts from a gas main near Los Angeles in 1994. Cracked water pipes often make it more difficult to extinguish the fires.*

△ *Devastating earthquakes this century include the San Francisco quake in 1906, the Japanese Kobe quake in 1995, and the San Francisco quake in California in 1989.*

▽ *A giant crane lifts cars and debris from under the toppled Hanshin expressway in Kobe, western Japan, on January 18, 1995.*

Many small earthquakes happen every day. Big ones make headlines a few times a year, and every so often an earthquake kills tens of thousands of people. No one knows precisely when a quake will happen, but we do have a good idea where. Some high-risk places, such as California and Japan, are as well prepared as they can be. They have strict building co[des,] a well-educated public, and the emergency services are constantly on alert. In Japan, some skyscrapers have heavy weights in the roof that can be move[d] quickly to cancel out the shaking due to a quake. But in many earthquake-prone areas of Asia and South America, buildings are still poorly designed and there are few resources available to cope with a major earthquake.

▽ *This aerial view of Kobe reveals t[he] devastation caused by the quake wh[ich] measured 6.9 on the Richter scale. B[lack] smoke rises above burning buildings. Fires can often cause more damage than the earthquakes that start them.*

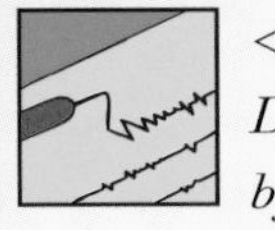

◁ **Richter below 3.0/Mercalli I**
Detected by seismographs but not by people. Over 500,000 each year.

◁ **Richter 3.0-3.4/Mercalli II**
Detected by instruments and a few people. Delicate objects may shake.

◁ **Richter 3.5-4.0/Mercalli III-IV**
Obvious shaking felt indoors, walls creak, hanging items swing.

◁ **Richter 4.1-4.8/Mercalli V**
Felt by most people. Some windows may crack and loose objects fall over.

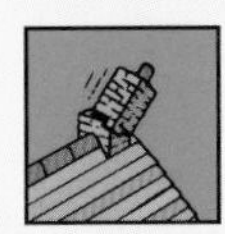

◁ **Richter 4.9-6.0/Mercalli VI-VII**
Felt by all. Furniture moves. People run outdoors. Some chimneys topple.

◁ **Richter 6.1-7.0/Mercalli VIII-IX**
General panic. Some houses collapse, roads crack, and pipes rupture.

◁ **Richter 7.1-8.1/Mercalli X-XI**
Large cracks open up in the ground, landslides, few buildings remain.

◁ **Richter over 8.1/Mercalli XII**
Total destruction. The ground rises and falls in waves.

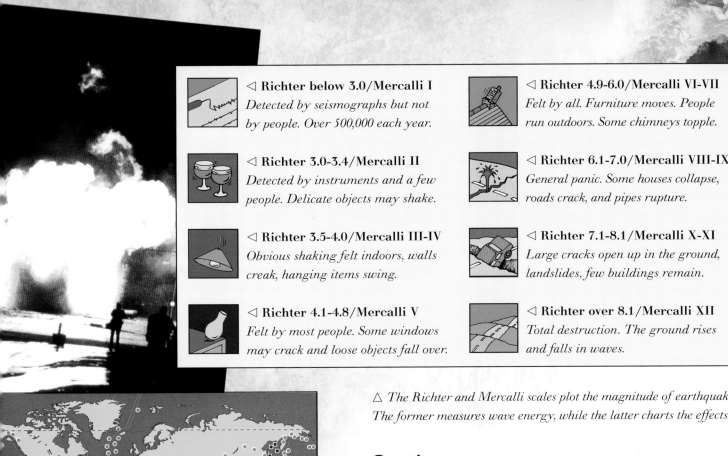

△ *The Richter and Mercalli scales plot the magnitude of earthquakes. The former measures wave energy, while the latter charts the effects.*

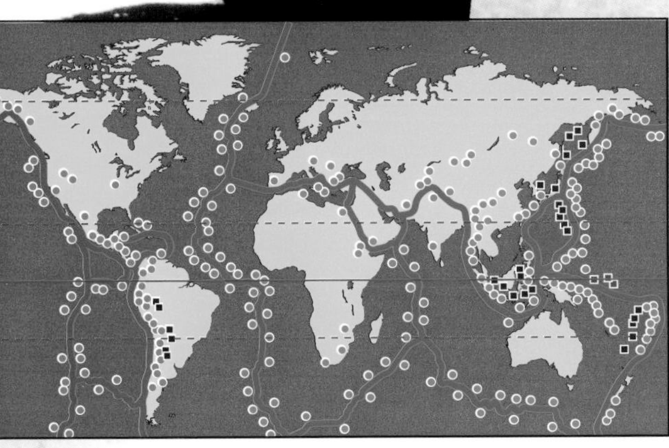

arthquake zones cluster along plate boundaries, making ssible to predict the location of earthquakes.

safe as houses

ether a building falls down in an earthquake depends he strength and duration of the quake, and also on the lding's design. In small buildings, flexible materials are ter than rigid ones, and lightweight structures kill fewer ple when they fall. The most dangerous buildings are de of brick or stone, or have poor-quality, reinforced crete frames. They are often found in poorer countries.

e! Fire!

e of the greatest dangers during an earthquake is fire. h in San Francisco in 1906 and Yokohama in 1923, re people died in fires than in the quakes themselves. e fires start, they are often fueled by cracked gas pipes. San Francisco, "smart pipes" are being developed that omatically shut off sections where a break is detected.

Creating waves

By the time the San Andreas Fault reaches South America, it lies 120 miles (200 km) out at sea. This should be good news for the people living along the coast, but in May 1960, several big earthquakes along the fault line created 3-foot (1-m)-high ripples in the ocean. As they traveled toward land, they grew to 30-foot (10-m)-high *tsunami*, or tidal waves. Three such waves hit the Chilean city of Valdiva, toppling buildings and tossing ships out of the harbor.

Urban dilemmas

When an earthquake strikes, the safest place to be is in flat, open countryside. The worst thing to do is panic. Nowadays, most people live in towns or cities, where falling glass and masonry outside can pose a real threat, so it is safer to stay indoors under strong structures such as stairwells.

◁ *During the 1989 San Francisco quake, the flexible structure of the Golden Gate Bridge kept it standing, while more rigid bridges collapsed under the strain.*

Prediction and Prevention

△ *This is the very first earthquake detector, made in China, A.D. 132. Earth tremors caused one of the balls to fall into a frog's mouth.*

Long before the age of scientific instruments, people watched for early warnings of earthquakes. The Chinese still look out for traditional warning signs such as strange animal behavior or sudden changes of water levels in wells. Using such indicators, the city of Haicheng was evacuated in 1975, hours before a massive earthquake, saving hundreds of thousands of lives. A year later 240,000 people died in Tangshan, where no warnings were given. There are many signs of an imminent quake, but the most reliable indicator may be the pattern of seismic waves that travel through the ground.

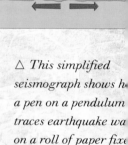

△ *This simplified seismograph shows h[ow] a pen on a pendulum traces earthquake wa[ves] on a roll of paper fix[ed] firmly to the ground.*

High stakes!

Most big earthquakes are preceded by foreshocks. But nobody knows whether a minor earth tremor is an isolated event or the prelude to a major quake. From historical records, a big earthquake may be predicted in the next 100 years—putting the chance of it occurring tomorrow at 1 in 36,500. However, the detection of minor tremors—suppose there are 10 of these a year—shortens the odds of a big quake in the next 24 hours to 1 in 1,000.

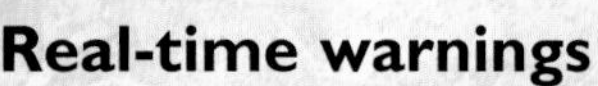

△ *These Chinese government posters warn people of the strange animal behavior to watch out for before an earthquake.*

Real-time warnings

Predicting earthquakes is difficult. But detecting them is easy. This fact was turned to an advantage in California in 1989. Following the San Francisco earthquake, rescue workers were trying to free motorists trapped beneath a section of the Nimitz freeway. Debris was unstable and any aftershocks potentially devastating. At the quake's focus, almost 60 miles (100 km) away, sensors were set to transmit a warning at the speed of light, so it would reach the scene 25 seconds ahead of the shock waves, which travel at the speed of sound. This gave people time to scramble clear.

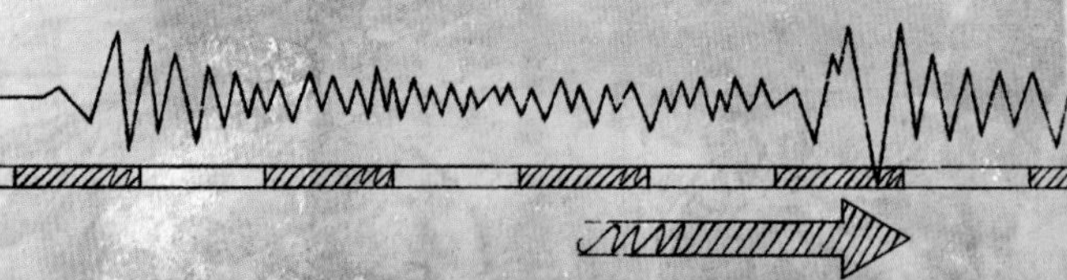

▽ *Tokyo school children, in firepro[of] headgear, emerge from their classroo[m] during a quake dril[l]*

◁ *John Milne designed the first practical seismograph when he lived in Japan. On retiring, with his Japanese wife, to Britain in 1895, he set up the world's first seismic monitoring headquarters.*

P-waves

S-waves

Love waves

Rayleigh waves

▷ *There are two types of body wave produced in an earthquake—Primary (P-waves) and Secondary (S-waves). These travel from the focus under the ground to the surface by either compressing and stretching, or shearing from side to side. Love waves and Rayleigh waves are L-waves, which cause surface effects.*

ding the joints

one can stop the relentless drift of the continents, and results in earthquakes. But it may be possible to stop ig earthquake by causing lots of little ones. The longer active fault line goes without a quake, the bigger the ke is likely to be when it happens. So if a fault line can kept moving, a big quake may be avoided. The idea is to ricate faults, and this has been tested on a small scale at old desert oil field in the U.S. By pumping water down ndoned oil wells, minor earth tremors were triggered, not in the places expected. This makes it unlikely that one will try this trick in a densely populated area.

▷ *Laser beams shine out from this hilltop monitoring station near Parkfield, California. Timing the flashes as they bounce off a network of 18 reflectors on the other hills can reveal shifts of less than .01 inches over 1 mile.*

Mountains

△ *These Jurassic limestone rocks at Stair Hole, in England, are the result of Africa's collision with Europe 18 million years ago.*

The mighty continents are forever colliding with one another, but like any well-designed vehicle, they have crumple zones that buckle under pressure. Although made of hard rock, the layers in the continental plates fold on impact like a rucked blanket, rising from the Earth's surface to form mountains. These collisions take place over millions of years, as if being played out in extremely slow motion. As each layer piles onto the next, the mountains grow into great ranges.

△ *Standing 15,770 feet (4,808m) high, Mount Blanc in the French Alps shows the huge amount of rock that can be thrown up by an intercontinental collision.*

Mountains in the making

The continents are still slowly colliding, and the newest ranges continue to rise. Just 18 millon years ago, Africa drove Italy into Europe, creating the Alps. The Himalayas rose 5 million years ago during India's collision with Asia, and are still rising. This range contains Everest, which at 29,021 feet (8,848m) is the world's highest mountain.

The birth of the Himalayas

Around 65 million years ago, huge volcanic eruptions caused the Indian subcontinent to split away from the other southern continents and head north, pushing the great Tethys Ocean ahead of it. The dense ocean floor was pushed under Asia, while the lighter seabed sediment was scooped up and squeezed between the continents, rising up to become part of the Himalayan range.

cient collisions

e Himalayas and the Alps are the results of the most ent mountain-building activity. But there is plenty evidence for more ancient continental collisions too. rth America's Appalachian chain, eastern Greenland, highlands of northern Scandinavia, and parts of tland were once joined in a huge range, the result of a crash that took place over 250 million years ago.

Completing the cycle

What goes up must come down, as the saying goes, and the Earth's crust records the history of a constant battle between the uplift of mountain-building and the forces of weathering and gravity. Little by little, the mountains crumble, and carried by rivers and glaciers, the sediment returns to the oceans. There it settles, only to be scooped up again several hundred million years later as a new mountain range is formed. And so the cycle continues.

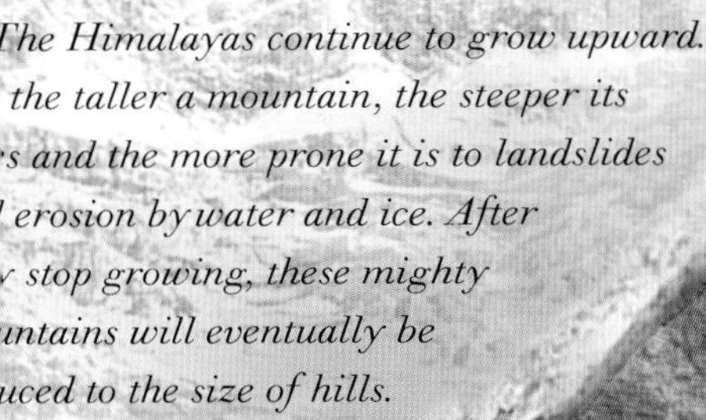

The Himalayas continue to grow upward. the taller a mountain, the steeper its s and the more prone it is to landslides erosion by water and ice. After stop growing, these mighty untains will eventually be uced to the size of hills.

△ *The Indian subcontinent moved north 35 to 45 million years ago (1). Ocean sediments were scooped up, and the ocean crust was forced under Tibet (2). The continents finally met 5 million years ago, creating the Himalayas (3).*

The Wind

If left to itself, the air in the Earth's atmosphere would not change in pressure or temperature. But it is not left to itself. The Earth revolves, the Sun rises and sets, ocean currents warm or cool the air, clouds gather and scatter, and mountains block the way. All this powers the atmosphere like a giant dynamo. As pockets of air become warm and expand, their pressure increases. This fuels winds which then blow to regions of lower pressure. At times, a wind can become so intense that it spins itself into a tornado or carves up the surface of the planet.

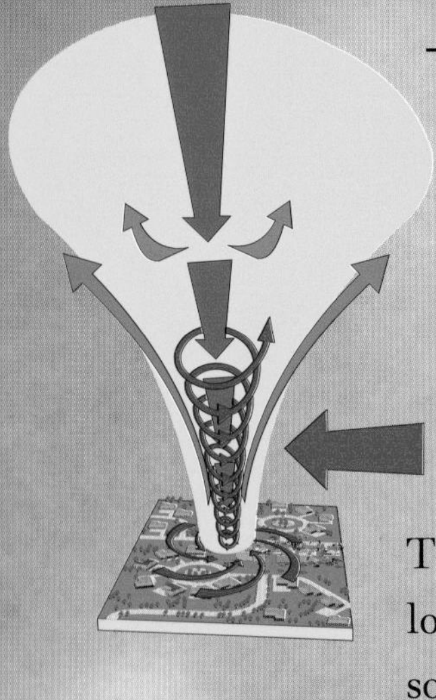

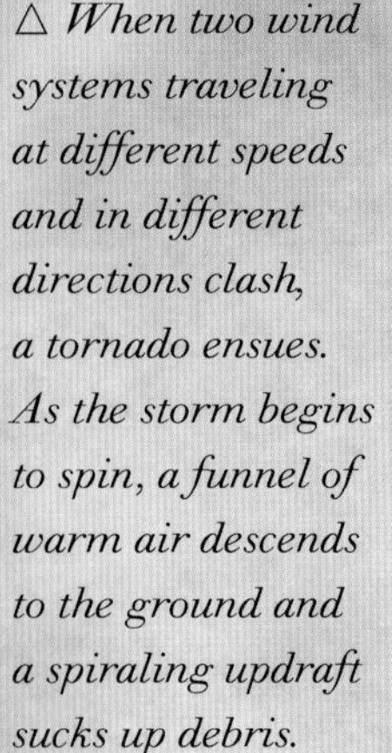

△ When two wind systems traveling at different speeds and in different directions clash, a tornado ensues. As the storm begins to spin, a funnel of warm air descends to the ground and a spiraling updraft sucks up debris.

△ This isolated farmhouse near Dalhart, Texa[s] was photographed in 1938. By then, many far[ms] had been abandoned as wind stripped away ov[er] cultivated soil, turning the fields into a dust bo[wl].

Carved with sand

Air by itself may not seem like a powerful force, but when the wind whips up sand, it can cut like a chisel. Desert landscapes are almost entirely sculpted by wind. As well as carving rocks, the wind can pile sand up into dunes hundreds of feet high, which slowly engulf villages and grasslands.

Dust bowl

Away from desert sands, the soil is usually held fast by vegetation. But careless farming practices can change all that. In the U.S. Midwest, it took centuries for prairie plants to evolve that could withstand the region's droughts and strong winds. Yet, within decades of the arrival of settlers, new crops and overgrazing had created a vast dust bow[l]

Twister!

The most violent of all windstorms are tornadoes. They can reach speeds of 300 mph (480 km/h), yet can last for only 30 seconds and strike in a small area. They usually form inside thunderclouds, as fast-moving warm air meets slower-moving cold air. Cars, houses, and even people may be picked up like toys in the vortex and flung far away.

Bryce Canyon National ·k in Utah is a jagged, ·d-eroded landscape. ·at columns of rock ·e been carved over ·e by windblown sand, ·ing needles of harder ·k behind.

Tearing across the states

"Tornado Alley" in the U.S. Midwest earned its name because hundreds of tornadoes strike the area each year as hot, humid air from the Gulf of Mexico hits cold, dry, polar air from Canada. In April 1965, 37 tornadoes tore through six states for nine hours, killing 271 people and injuring 3,000.

The Weather

While the climate is all about the broad changes that occur from season to season and year to year in different regions of the world, the weather concerns local variations, from day to day and hour to hour. Left to itself, the Earth would have no weather at all. But, of course, it is not left to itself. The world's weather is the product of a global, solar-powered heat engine. Constantly warmed by the Sun, especially near the equator, air is pushed around the planet, and it is this movement that creates weather. The world has three major circulation cells—systems where hot air continuously rises, then cools and descends. The first of these, the Hadley cell, is located over the equator. The hot air rises from this central band, moves to the north and south, then loses heat and drops. The second cell is found over the Tropics and the third over polar zones.

△ *A satellite wind-speed map of the Pacific shows (blue) slow, (pink and purple) medium-speed, and (red and orange) over 27 mph (44 km/h) winds.*

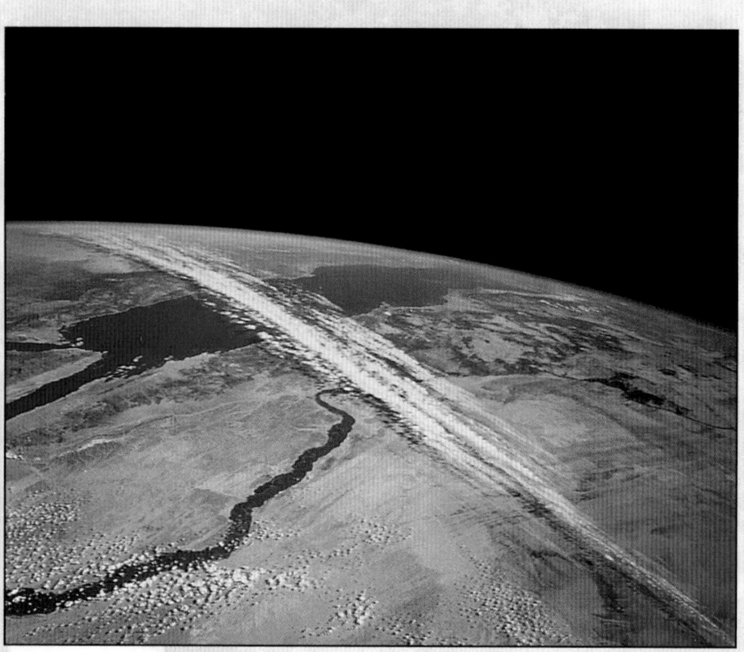

△ *High in the atmosphere, where there is no friction with the surface of the Earth, jet streams blow around the rotating globe. This jet stream is shown by a line of high-altitude cirrus clouds.*

The front line

Weather is governed by regions of low or high pressure that form when masses of cold and warm air meet. When warm air rises, it leaves a low-pressure hole, which is then filled by cold air. This is called a cold front. As the warm air rises, it cools. The water vapor it holds condenses into clouds and the system starts to rotate. Each of these stages brings different weather.

Land and sea

The land and the sea have a major influence on the weather. When warm air passes over the ocean, it picks moisture. If the warm air rises above the land during th day, it will draw in air from the sea, creating sea breeze Then, as the air moves inland, it passes over mountains or hills, where it is cooled. This causes clouds to form a eventually, the moisture falls as rain or snow. In Asia, th monsoon is caused by hot air rising over the Himalayas.

Modern meteorology uses readings from an ·ernational network of land-based weather stations, ·nospheric balloons, and space satellites. Research aircraft ·h as this C130, nicknamed Snoopy, *can fly into storm ·uds and measure conditions at the heart of the storm.*

·hen the wind blows

·metimes in late summer, when tropical sea ·mperatures are at their highest, hundreds of storm ·stems come together and rotate in a great low-pressure ·stem known as a hurricane. As the wind speed picks ·, a hurricane will tend to move away from the equator, ·thering force and whipping up high waves in the sea ·til it meets the coast, often with devastating results.

·ackyard forecasting

·nyone can forecast the weather. Simply look at what ·t of day it is today and predict exactly the same for ·norrow. In mid-latitudes, you will be right about · percent of the time. But, of course, you will never ·edict the times when the weather changes. To do that, ·u need to observe the weather on one day in thousands · different places, understand the processes at work, and ·culate all the interactions that are likely to take place.

Predicting the unpredictable

Meteorologists enlist the help of supercomputers to forecast the weather. Using data from weather stations around the world, they can calculate what will happen up to ten days ahead. Even so, they are often wrong. This is because of tiny, unpredictable changes that eventually have dramatic effects somewhere else in the world.

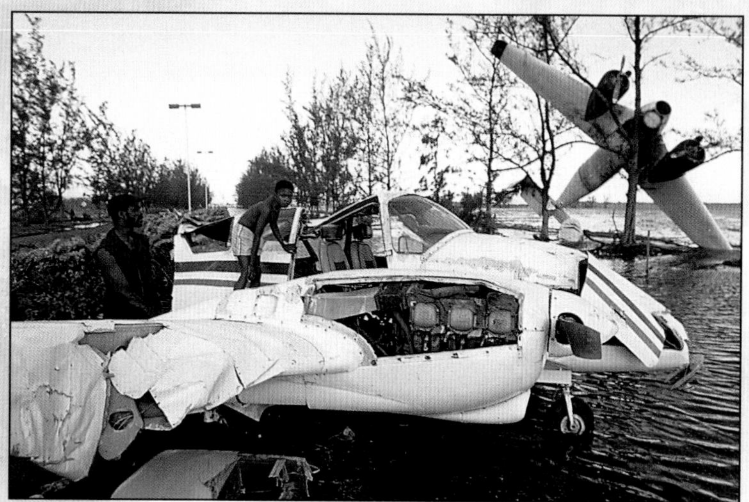

△ *These light aircraft were overturned and tossed into trees by powerful winds of over 100 mph (160 km/h) during Hurricane Gilbert, which struck Kingston, Jamaica, in September 1988.*

Weird Weather

△ *This is one of many buildings in the French Pyrenees damaged when hailstones the size of tennis balls fell in June 1991.*

The weather must be the most widely discussed natural phenomenon on Earth. Usually, people are complaining about the cold, heat, drought, or rain. In fact, our climate is remarkably constant and hospitable when compared to the extremes of heat and cold on Venus and Mars, or the 1,100 mph (1,800 km/h) per hour winds on Saturn. Most of the Earth's surface spends its time at a few degrees above the freezing point of water. Without that constancy, life would not be so easy. Even so, the Earth's weather does throw up some strange, varied, and often beautiful phenomena.

The clear light of day

Light waves of all colors shine from the Sun, but air molecules scatter blue light the most, so the sky appears to be blue. When the Sun sets, its light travels through the lower dusty atmosphere, which scatters more red light, making the sky look red. Light also travels at different speeds through air of different temperatures. Where cold air hangs above a layer of hot air, the light is bent and a heat haze is created. Occasionally, this will also magnify the image of a distant scene so that it appears as a mirage.

◁ *Layers of air of different temperatures spread light to produce this double image of an island. This sort of mirage is called a* fata morgana.

'hese may look like flying saucers, but in they are lenticular cloud formations 'ographed in Brazil in 1969. On crossing ntains, layers of air rise, then fall to create ies of waves. As water condenses around wave, layers of cloud are formed.

Flying colors

Falling raindrops can act like tiny lenses and will scatter white light into its spectrum of colors. So, if the Sun is shining on a rainy day, we may see a rainbow. Anyone searching for gold at the rainbow's end will have a hard task since, were it not for the horizon getting in the way, a rainbow would form a circle and have no end.

Sometimes a rainbow-like halo is visible around the Moon. This type of aura occurs when light is bent by ice crystals high in the atmosphere.

ining cats and dogs

asionally, air currents keep hailstones in freezing clouds for so long t they grow to be an inch or more across and cause considerable nage when they fall. There are also isolated cases of ice blocks eral feet wide hitting the Earth. Sometimes very strange things have n known to drop from the sky, including beans, fish, and frogs. The t explanation is that they were sucked up by tornadoes.

under and lightning

ring a thunderstorm, positive charges build up at the top of a storm ıd and negative charges collect at the base. Sometimes, the voltage is ıigh that the charge "jumps" in a bolt of electric lightning, either to next cloud or to the ground. The heat of the lightning causes the air xpand so rapidly that it lets out a huge crack of thunder. The force of ıtning can split trees, set fire to buildings, and kill people.

▽ Circles of flattened crops can seem mysterious, but many are hoaxes. Others may be caused by mini whirlwinds.

The Climate

Although the weather in a region may vary from day to day, and from season to season, there is almost always a cycle that is repeated each year. The average weather a location experiences, season by season, year by year, gives us a measure of its climate. Meteorologists take into account temperature, rainfall, air pressure, sunshine, humidity, and many other factors. Places around the world with similar climates can be grouped into nine distinct climate zones. These range from cold polar lands, to warm, wet equatorial regions, to hot, dry desert areas.

△ Tree rings can reveal much about the story of our climate. In a warm year, the rings that are laid down around the trunk are broad. Other years, when frosts are severe, there is less growth and the rings are thin.

The warming Sun

Climate is largely dependent upon the amount of the Sun's heat that reaches the Earth's surface. The Earth's rotational axis, running between the North and South Poles, is tilted toward the Sun and it is this that gives us the seasons. Depending on the angle of the Earth to the Sun, the areas closest to the poles receive different amounts of sunlight —so they have cold, dark winters and warm, light summers. The equator receives nearly the same amount of heat all year round, and as a result its temperature varies very little.

Ocean currents

The Earth's climate zones are also affected by the oceans. The sea absorbs much of the Sun's heat, and ocean currents spread this to other areas. This is why the winter climate of Britain, in the warm Gulf Stream, is milder than that of Newfoundland, Canada, even though they are on the same latitude. Away from the heat-storing oceans, the interiors of continents always have more extreme temperatures.

▽ Rock carvings found deep in the Sahara Desert suggest that 7,000 years ago this area had enough rainfall to support humans and animals.

Global greenhouse

Although a lot of the Sun's heat is absorbed by the land and sea, some of it is reflected back into space. But gases in the Earth's atmosphere act like the glass of a greenhouse and stop much of the heat from escaping. This greenhouse effect is responsible for fears about global warming, but it is also essential to life. Without it, most of the Earth would be about 5°F (–15°C). Ice would cover the planet and there would be no life.

◁ *Climate shapes our planet and determines the landscape, vegetation, and wildlife of each region.*

imate change

ernating periods of hot and cold reach back through the tory of our planet. Before the recent ice ages began 3.25 million rs ago, it was consistently warmer than today for 250 million rs. Prior to this long period there was a 100-million-year freeze. anging carbon dioxide levels, volcanic activity, or events beyond Earth are all possible causes for these changes in climate.

△ *The world can be divided into nine main climate zones. They are polar* (mauve), *subpolar* (light blue), *temperate* (light green), *subtropical* (orange), *desert* (yellow), *tropical* (dark green), *equatorial* (dark blue), *subpolar* (pink), *mediterranean* (red).

Sunspots

Sunspots, the dark patches on our star's surface, appear to have an effect on the Earth's climate. Between 1450 and 1800, sunspots were entirely absent. This coincided with a period that has been called the Little Ice Age, during which the Thames River in England froze over in winter and frost fairs were held on the ice.

△ *All three forms of water—ice, liquid, and vapor—are found on the Earth. Together, they help provide a climate that is just right for life.*

Climate Threat

△ *This image of Ferrybridge power station in England has been colored to highlight the sulfur dioxide in the smoke.*

Since 1958, scientists have been monitoring the amount of carbon dioxide in the atmosphere from an observatory high on a mountain in Hawaii. They have found that the concentration of the gas has been rising every year. It is now thought that this is primarily due to the burning of fossil fuels such as coal and oil. But extensive forest clearance also releases carbon dioxide and makes the problem worse by removing trees that would otherwise soak it up again. Overall, human activity is adding about 8 billion tons of carbon to the atmosphere each year, together with lesser amounts of other greenhouse gases such as methane, nitrogen oxides, and CFCs.

A global trend

Although temperatures vary from year to year, on average the Earth has been getting increasingly warmer for the past century. There is mounting evidence that this is due to the large quantities of greenhouse gases in the atmosphere. If greenhouse gas emissions continue at the current rate, temperatures will probably continue to rise, and the consequence could be a dramatic change in climate.

▽ *An aerial shot of the Brazilian rain forest reveals the extent of human damage. The forest shows up pink; areas cleared for agriculture are blue and green. The orange patch is a rainstorm washing away soil where the vegetation has been cleared.*

Predictions for the future

To find out what might happen to the climate in the future, meteorologists build models in supercomputers, rather like those used to forecast the weather. Most of their findings indicate that the world's overall temperature is likely to warm by four-and-a-half degrees during this century.

Climate change

The effects of such a temperature rise may be profound. Deserts would probably become drier and coastal regions would grow stormier. The warm Atlantic Gulf Stream that brings heat from the Caribbean to western Europe would probably be disrupted, too. Arctic water would not be cold enough to sink and return the flow south, like a conveyor belt. The circulation would stop and Europe would actually get colder.

△ *During an El Niño event* (top), *warm waters* (shown in purple) *reach the coast of South America* (right) *and prevent the cold, nutrient-rich waters* (shown in blue) *from rising. Normally* (bottom), *an upwelling of cold water occurs and the winds push the warm waters east, toward Australia* (left).

◁ *Greenhouse gases in the atmosphere insulate the Earth and prevent heat from escaping, thus raising the planet's surface temperature.*

Facing the consequences

The world's climate has, of course, changed in the past. The difference now is that human activity is probably responsible for the change, and humans—not dinosaurs—must face the consequences.

△ *When slash-and-burn farmers move into an area, they do just that—clearing forests, burning the timber, and releasing carbon dioxide into the atmosphere.*

Niño

ere is one ocean current that is already causing chaos with
world's weather. El Niño occurs when westerly winds reverse
ocean current in the South Pacific. This causes an accumulation
warm water off South America, and prevents the arrival of the cold,
trient-rich waters that are needed to sustain wildlife in the region.
a result of El Niño there are droughts and storms around the globe.

Water Power

△ *Acidic rainwater has eroded limestone by dissolving it, leaving these towering rock formations in China.*

The Earth is the only planet we know of where water exists in all three forms—ice, liquid, and vapor. And in each of these states, water holds a tremendous power, both creative and destructive. Water is responsible for circulating the Sun's heat around the planet. Solar energy lifts vast quantities of water from the oceans to the hills by vaporizing it, which causes it to rise. As it cools, the vapor condenses into the tiny droplets that make up clouds, and from there it falls to the ground as rain or snow. The rain becomes the rushing torrents of mountain streams and rivers. These are powerful forces, which sculpt the landscape into hills, valleys, and plains, and carry rock particles back into the sea.

The great leveler

A downpour of rain can wash away huge quantities of sand and stone in one go. And as the water races downhill, it will chisel away at the rock, so that over thousands of years, great V-shaped valleys will be carved out. Once clear of the hills, the river slows and drops its sediment, creating a new path for itself. Some sediment will be carried all the way to the sea, where it will settle to form a wide, fan-shaped delta.

Dissolving rocks

It is not just the physical force of water that cuts into rock. As it falls through the air, rain dissolves carbon dioxide to become weakly acidic. This particularly affects limestone rock, which is dissolved by this type of rain. Over many years, whole networks of caverns an passages can be carved out of hillsides. And as the wate flows, now saturated with dissolved calcium carbonate, it will deposit this to form stalactites and stalagmites.

▽ *Clusters of stalactites slowly grow when water, saturated with dissolved limestone, drips from the cave roof. These may eventually reach to the floor.*

▷ *As it leaves the mountain, the speed and cutting power of the river decreases and it deposits fertile soil across the plains, making rich lands in which to grow crops.*

ave power

awesome power of water flowing down toward sea is matched only by the power of the water in sea itself. Every few feet of an exposed coastline ives about 50 kilowatts of continuous power in the n of waves. Picking up stones, then dragging them k again, waves constantly erode coastlines. Although e power generators exist, none has been able to vive the destructive force of the sea. So far, no one managed to harness wave power economically.

▷ Water falls on high, cold mountains as snow. As it melts, it forms a raging torrent which races down the mountain, cutting out deep V-shaped valleys. Eventually, these mountains will vanish completely.

he Grand Canyon cut into the dry rocks of zona by the Colorado River. system of canyons stretches ver 185 miles (300 km) reaches a depth of 5,250 (1,600 m) in places. It slices ugh rock, some of which 0 million years old.

Floods and Droughts

Human life is dependent on water. We need it to drink and to irrigate our crops, and we harness its power to generate electricity. But if we lose control of our water supplies, if we find that we have either too much water or not enough, the effects can be devastating. The world's oceans contain over 240 million cubic miles (1 billion cubic km) of water. All the rivers, lakes, and clouds contain just 0.03 percent of that. Yet a flooded or dried-up river can mean the difference between life and death. Flood waters can come from any direction—from above in exceptional rainfall, from a bursting dam, or from the sea in a freak storm.

△ *Huge guns were once used to fire dust into clouds, in a failed attempt to trigger rain over parched areas of Australia.*

Upsetting nature

In the natural scheme of things, a river will meander across its broad floodplain, depositing fine sediment to make rich, fertile soil. But humans prefer a river that stays in one place and they build banks to constrain it. The mud gets deposited on the riverbed and the riverbanks have to be built higher. Before long, the river is raised up above the towns and farmland on its floodplain. If heavy rain occurs, the river may burst its banks, flooding hundreds of square miles.

△ *Dams hold water to supply homes and fields or to generate electricity. But a small crack in a dam can be catastrophic. The force of water behin it will turn a hairline crack into a gia hole in minutes. The result is a wall o water released onto the valley below.*

◁ *A Sudanese farmer looks in despair at his parched land. The failure of the rains means that his family could starve.*

Storm surge

On February 1, 1953, storm winds and high tides combined to drive a wedge of water down the North Sea onto the coasts of eastern England, Holland, and Belgium. Coastal communities were devastated Dutch dikes were breached, and the sea swept 37 m (60 km) inland. For Europe this was exceptional, bu in Bangladesh such flooding is a regular occurrence causing homelessness and disease on a massive scale

·ought damage

cessive rain in one place is often balanced by ›ught in another. Many semiarid countries rely on .y amounts of rainfall to sustain crops. Their lands ı only support a small population and are already ercrowded. When the rains fail entirely for a year more, the result can be famine.

ıture sea levels

global warming melts the ice caps and destabilizes western Antarctic ice shelf, the oceans could rise more than 33 feet (10 m). Even a 3-foot (1-m) e in sea level would threaten low-lying coral ınds such as the Maldives, as well as countries like ngladesh and Holland. A bigger rise in sea level ıld easily leave New York, Bombay, London, d Sydney underwater.

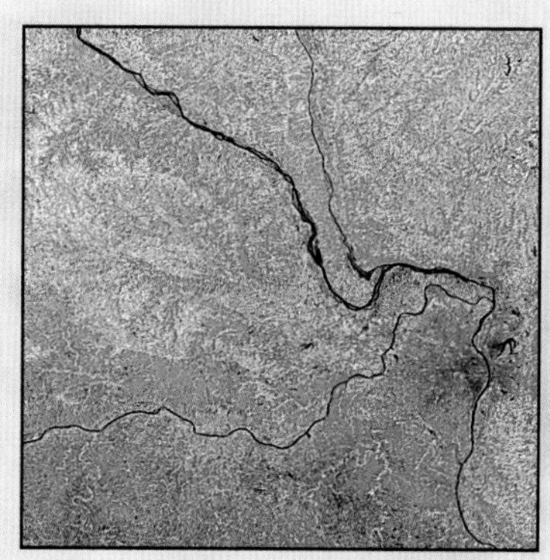

△ *Just north of St. Louis* (shown in pink and purple), *the Missouri and Illinois rivers flow into the great Mississippi.*

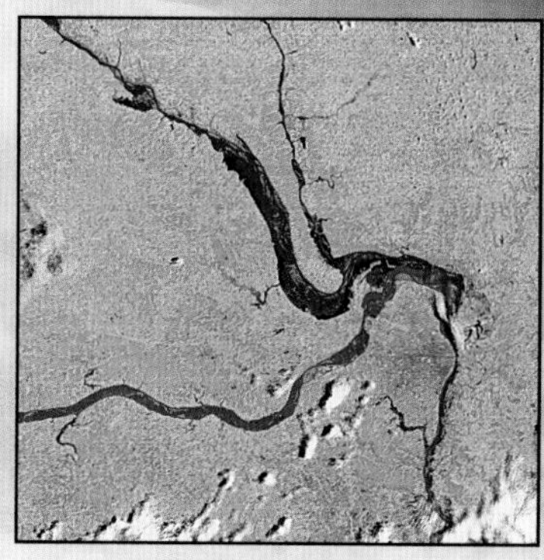

△ *In July 1993, the Mississippi River burst its banks* (shown in blue and black), *flooding an extensive part of the city.*

Lands of Ice

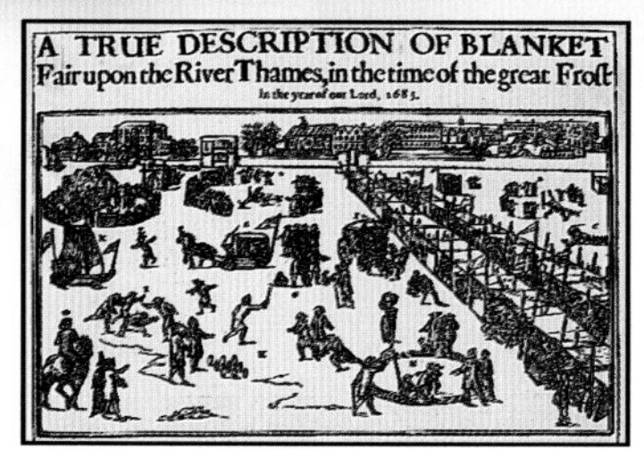

△ *Between 1645 and 1715, Europe experienced extreme winters during a "Little Ice Age." This engraving, from 1683, shows a frost fair held on the Thames River.*

One of the strangest features of the world that we inhabit is ice. No other substance has a solid form which is less dense than the liquid form. To put it another way, ice floats. So, when the temperature drops and the sea begins to freeze, the ice is on top of the sea, not underneath it. That is good news for life, since the ice creates an insulating layer which prevents the rest of the sea from freezing. In past ice ages, notably one about 700 million years ago, when sea ice stretched to the equator, life would have died out had the oceans frozen solid. The effects of ice on land are different. As water expands to become ice it can shatter a rocky landscape, and a large ice sheet can even push down a whole continent.

Waiting for an ice age?

Throughout the Earth's history, the temperature has fluctuated many times, perhaps due to changes in the Sun's activity or continental drift. The polar caps that exist today are a remnant of the last ice age, which began 3.25 million years ago. Since then, the northern ice sheet has advanced four times to cover large areas of North America and northern Europe. We may still be in an interglacial period today, waiting for the ice to advance once more.

△ *Where a glacier meets the sea, there is a constant battle between ice and water. Sometimes huge avalanches of ice break off and crash into the sea, as has happened with this Alaskan glacier.*

Secrets in the ice

The polar ice caps carry clues to the past. By drilling out cores of ice, scientists can reconstruct the Earth's history. The thickness of the layers gives clues to the snowfall. Dust and chemicals in the ice keep a record of recent pollution and ancient volcanic eruptions. Trapped within the ice are tiny bubbles of the ancient atmosphere.

Rivers of ice

Although solid, ice can slowly deform and flow. Vast areas of the Antarctic ice sheet are in motion, carrying thick slabs of ice from regions of high snowfall downhill toward the sea. Once there, they eventually melt and are washed by the tides until giant icebergs break off, some of them as big as a small country. In mountainous regions, the snow packs harder and harder into ice, forming glaciers which flow down valleys, gouging out the rock as they go.

△ *When a glacier finally retreats from the landscape, it leaves deep U-shaped valleys, some of them so deep that they are flooded by the sea, creating fjords like this one in Norway.*

ike a frozen river, a ier flows slowly through cky landscape shattered ce. Lines of rocky debris d up on its surface as it ges out a deep valley.

△ *Air and water can sculpt icebergs into complex shapes. But 90 percent of a berg is underwater, as ships such as the* Titanic *have found to their cost.*

Changing Times

If the mighty continents are only the scum on the surface of our vast planet, sedimentary rocks seem even less substantial. They are literally the dust of ages, accumulated on the ocean floor, then lifted up into mountain ranges. Yet these rocks represent the history book of the planet and within their pages, their layers, the story of life is told. The story is spelled out by fossils, but it is only in the last 100 years that we have started to understand the fossils, and so have been able to read the story. Before then, our ancestors must have wondered what these strange shapes were. Perhaps they had grown inside the rock? Many early Christians believed that they were the remains of creatures that died in the Biblical flood.

△ *What events had caused animals to either die out or alter dramatically? Had there been a great flood after all?*

The fossil hunters

In the nineteenth century, William Smith, a surveyor, realized that similar layers of rock containing similar fossils occurred in different places, and that the sequence of layers was always the same. Sir Charles Lyell, now seen as the father of geology, argued that, because rocks must have formed at the rate they do today, deep layers of sedimentary rock must be millions of years old.

Learning to read

As they looked closer, the early geologists noticed that some of the fossil forms seem to change subtly from layer to layer. If each layer was like a new page in the story of life, it seemed that the story was also divided into chapters. Between each chapter there were clearly great changes in the creatures that inhabited the Earth. At last, they were able to recognize each chapter heading—the geological periods. The question remained as to what caused these changes.

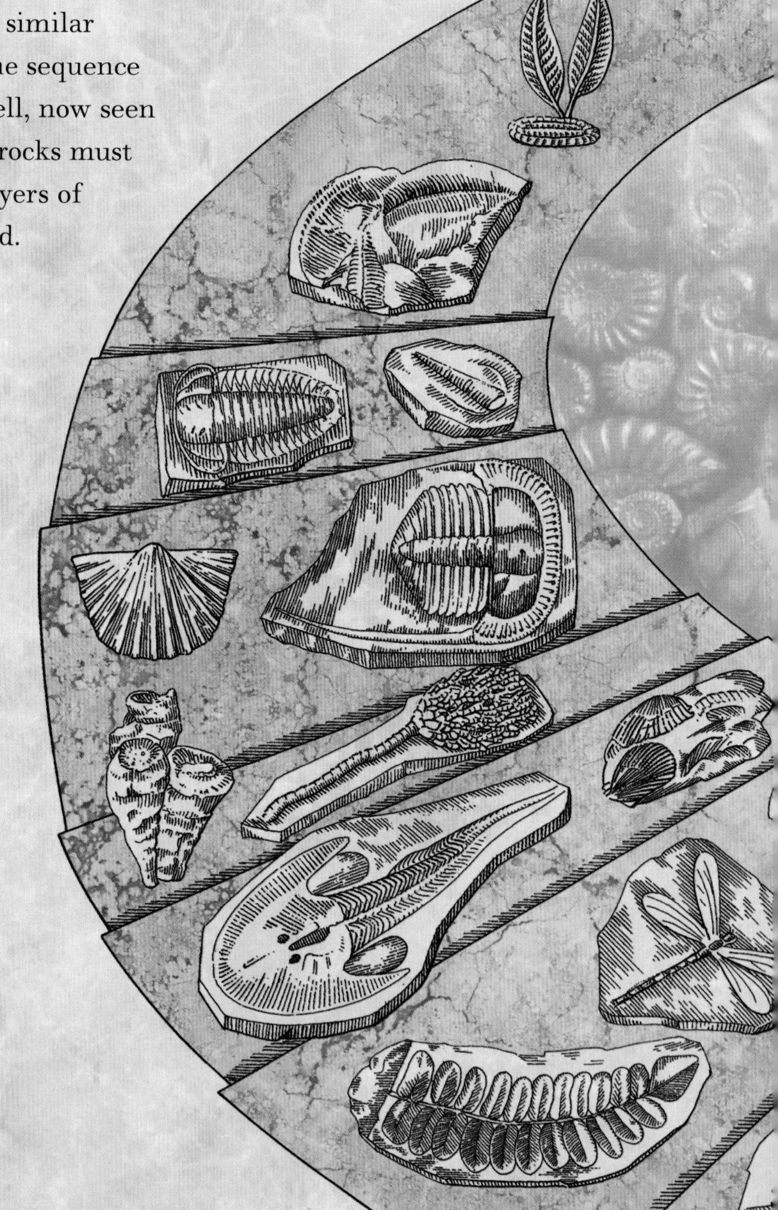

▽ *By the time creatures such as this fish were swimming in the Earth's oceans, the planet was around four billion years old. Yet the proliferation and diversification of life was only just beginning.*

umbering the pages

r many years, people have tried to estimate the e of the Earth. In 1650, an Irish bishop decided at the Creation occurred in 4004 B.C. By examining cks, Victorian geologists thought that it was 20 million ars old, a sensational suggestion at the time. Now, using lioactivity readings, we can put a much more accurate te on the rock layers of our 4.5-billion-year-old planet.

Ancient clues

For many years, geologists believed that fossils were animals that had been turned to stone. We now know that even if this is not true, quite often the original molecules of life can still be preserved in the rock. And though it is not yet possible to recreate these creatures in a real-life Jurassic park, they do give us invaluable clues to evolution.

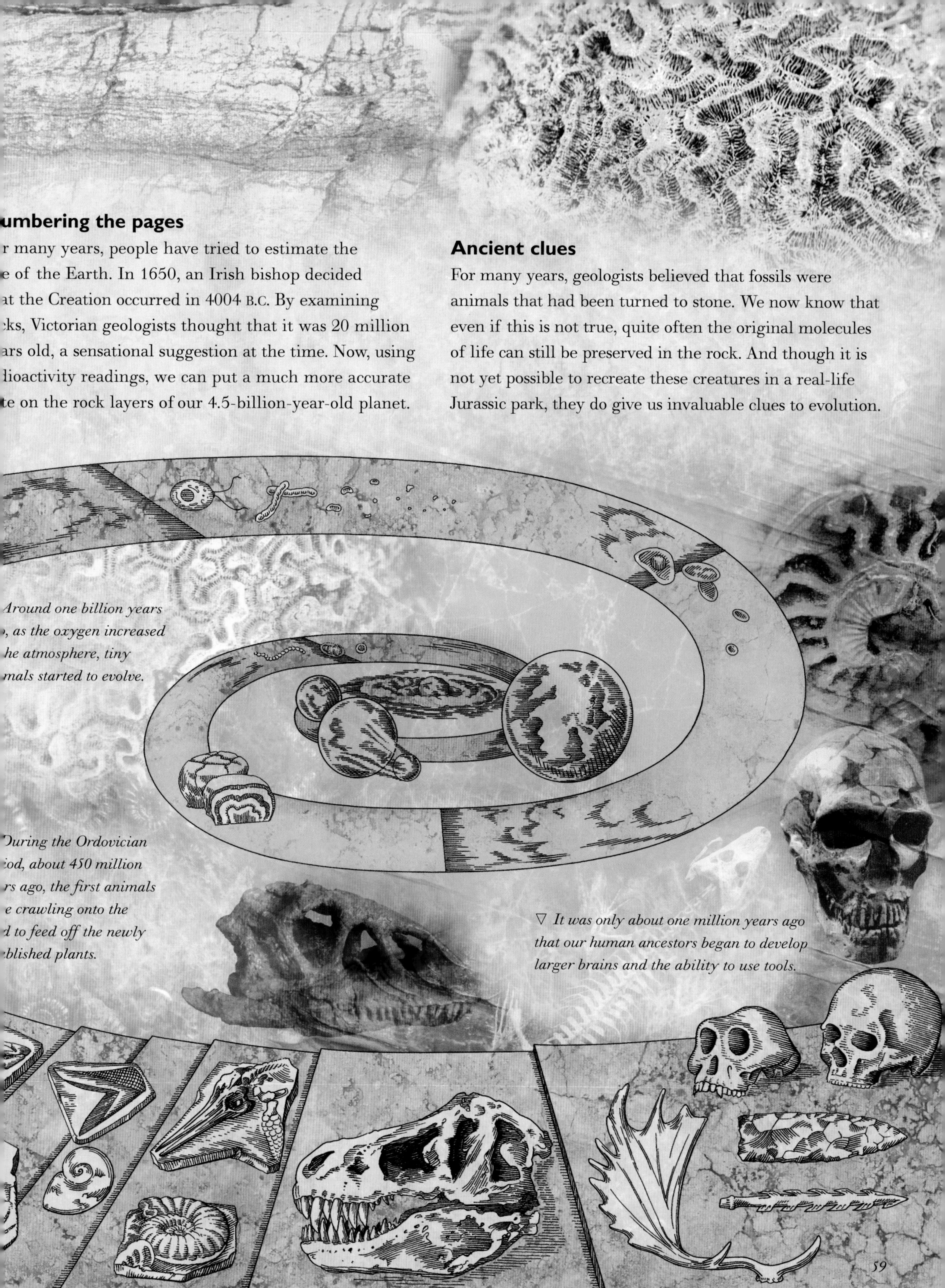

Around one billion years , as the oxygen increased he atmosphere, tiny mals started to evolve.

During the Ordovician iod, about 450 million rs ago, the first animals e crawling onto the d to feed off the newly blished plants.

▽ *It was only about one million years ago that our human ancestors began to develop larger brains and the ability to use tools.*

The Dawn of Life

No one knows how life on the Earth began. Present-day life forms seem far too complex and far too dependent on each other to have come into being spontaneously. But there are some new clues to suggest how and where life might have first arisen. Direct evidence in the fossil record is sparse, but research into chemical systems that can organize themselves, the discovery of new habitats where life can survive today, and studies of the genetic relationships of living organisms are all changing our understanding. In 1952, a chemist named Stanley Miller put methane, ammonia, and hydrogen gases—thought to be components of the Earth's early atmosphere—into a flask containing some water. Through them, he sparked an electric discharge to simulate lightning. By the next day, the flask contained amino acids, the building blocks of all life.

△ Charles Darwin's suggestion that humans had evolved from apes was greeted with a mixture of horror and ridicule.

▷ Darwin developed his theory of evolution as a result of observing finches on the Galapagos Islands. Their beaks had adapted to the type of food available on each island.

Building blocks

We now know that the early atmosphere was actually mostly made up of carbon dioxide and nitrogen, from which the chemicals of life form less easily. But they do form, and Stanley Miller's experiments began a whole new study into the chemical origins of life.

RNA world

There is a world of difference between a soup of organ chemicals and life itself. For life to get started, you nee chemicals that can store information, that can reprodu and can also mutate. Today, most life forms carry their information in genes made out of the chemical DNA. Although DNA would have had trouble reproducing or the young Earth, it may be possible for RNA, a simple version of DNA, to do so. Perhaps the start of life was an evolving chemical system based on RNA.

◁ *Stanley Miller used a flask to combine simple chemicals and electric discharges in order to investigate the complex chemical origins of life.*

The early years

It is extremely difficult to read the history of life in rocks from the Precambrian, by far the longest period in the Earth's history. Nevertheless, the microscopic traces of primitive bacteria and algae have been isolated. And, by the late Precambrian, there is evidence for much larger, multicellular organisms, which resemble jellyfish and worms.

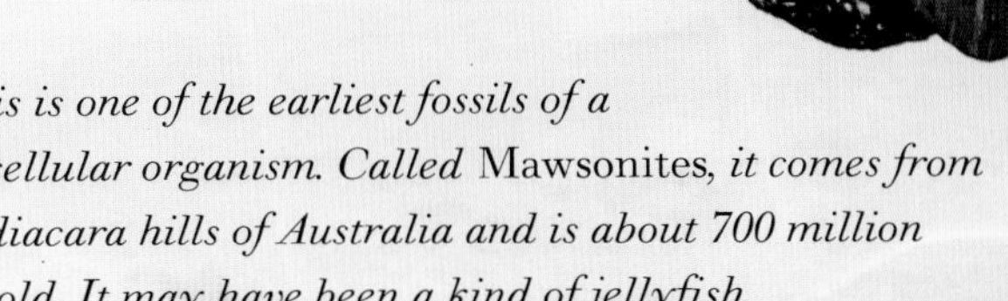

▷ *Some of the chemical building blocks of life may have been seeded on Earth in meteorites. This one is mostly made of iron, but others are rich in carbon—an essential component of all life.*

'e and ice

ır billion years ago, when life was beginning, the Sun s weak and the planet may have been icebound. If so, : may have begun around volcanic springs deep in the :an, or in pockets under the ice. In places, cometary pacts may have melted the ice. Warm pools may have :n life's birthplace, on a scaffolding of mineral grains.

ien invaders

the time that life was beginning, our planet was still der bombardment from space. So, life may have been stroyed and reborn many times. It is possible that life l not originate on the Earth at all, but came from ıce, wrapped up in comets and meteorites.

▽ *This is one of the earliest fossils of a multicellular organism. Called* Mawsonites, *it comes from the Ediacara hills of Australia and is about 700 million years old. It may have been a kind of jellyfish.*

Wonderful Life

▷ This small shellfish, a brachiopod called Lingula, *is one of life's success stories. It has managed to survive almost unchanged for more than 500 million years. A present-day specimen is almost identical to those found fossilized within Cambrian rocks.*

Well-preserved sedimentary rocks older than 600 million years are seldom found, so fossils prior to this date are exceptionally rare. Because of this, little is known about life on the Earth before that time. After this point, however, the fossil record reveals that something quite spectacular happened on the planet. From the start of the Cambrian period, there is evidence that the world was suddenly teeming with multicellular life forms. Most of the invertebrate groups in the world today also appear in fossils, alongside a wide variety of creatures that seem completely alien to us. This growth of new life was so rapid and diverse that it has been called the Cambrian explosion.

A moment in time

Each of the many layers of shale and sandstone that survive from the Cambrian period is like a page of a book, recording what happened on the sea floor. We might see the ripple marks produced by currents of water, disrupted here and there by the tracks of soft-bodied creatures that have long since disappeared. By examining these tracks, we can determine the behaviors and lifestyles of these ancient animals.

△ Trilobites were around for several hundred million years, swimming in shallow seas and burrowing in the mud. The trilobite's closest modern relative is the horseshoe crab.

This fossil creature from the Cambrian Burgess Shale ...ns so bizarre that it was named Hallucigenia.

...Around these pages are some of the extraordinary ...atures that inhabited the sea in the Cambrian period. ... left is Opabinia*; to its right,* Sanctocaris *and a ...fish. Small arthropods feed off a dead trilobite ...he left and along the bottom are sponges, corals, ... strange scaly creatures called* Wiwaxia. *Bottom ...t is the large crustacean* Canadaspis.

Meet the relatives

Much of our understanding of Cambrian life comes from the Burgess Shale in the Canadian Rockies. An amazing range of creatures has been found here, and it is possible to recognize the relatives of crabs, insects, corals, and worms that are in existence today. One creature, called *Pikaya*, looked like an animated anchovy fillet and could be our own ancestor.

Who's for dinner?

In one slab of rock, we can see the tracks of a trilobite, a predator that looked a bit like an oversized wood louse. The tracks lead up to the burrow of a small worm and you can still see where, one day 540 million years ago, the trilobite dug down into the burrow and had the unsuspecting worm for dinner.

Times of change

The fossil record shows that the course of evolution has been far from smooth and steady. Sometimes there were great bursts of diversification, with hundreds of new species appearing in a short period. At other times there were mass extinctions, probably caused by dramatic changes in the environment.

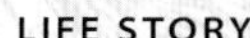

The Fossil Sky

For more than 500 million years, the Earth has been a generous host to life. But life has also changed the planet. Whether they are plants or animals, all living things are composed almost entirely of nutrients extracted from the Earth and carbon from the atmosphere. Plants begin the process using sunshine to convert carbon dioxide and water into living matter. In consuming carbon, these organisms help keep the planet at a constant temperature. And when they die, they are reabsorbed into the Earth to make new land and rock. Across the world, vast deposits of limestone and chalk are the end products of that process—they are, effectively, the ancient sky transformed into stone.

△ Diatoms are tiny, plantlike organisms that use carbon dioxide from the atmosphere for making food. The fossilized remains of these microscopic organisms form the rock diatomite

▷ Carbon is the basis for all organic compounds, including all living things and fossil fuels. Carbon is continuously recycled through the atmosphere, Earth, plants, and animals.

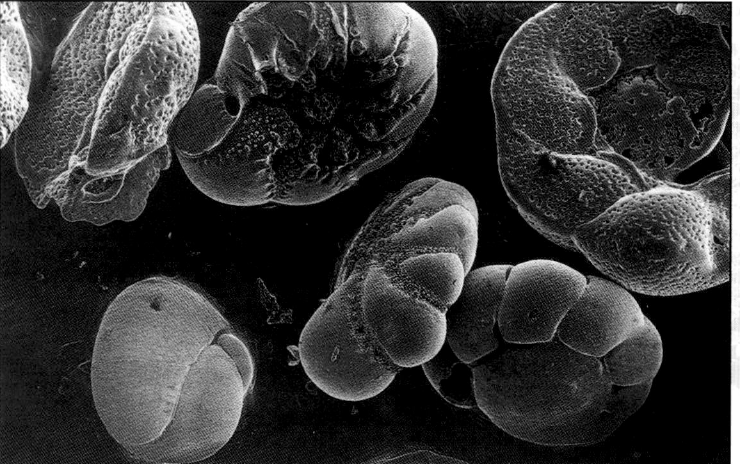

△ Deep-sea muds are often entirely formed from the tiny skeletons of microscopic organisms such as forams. They are also found in limestones and preserved in deep-water shales.

Limestone

Many fossils are found in limestone—a sedimentary rock made from calcium carbonate (carbon, calcium, and oxygen). There have been many periods in the world's history when thick deposits of limestone have formed. When there were no ice caps, higher sea level and temperatures caused limestone to amass around the edges of continents and on flooded basins of land.

Carbon body building

In these ancient shallow seas, the building materials of life were available in abundance. Vast quantities of calcium carbonate were used by microscopic organisms build their intricate skeletons. The chalky White Cliffs Dover, England are made of the fossils of these creatur

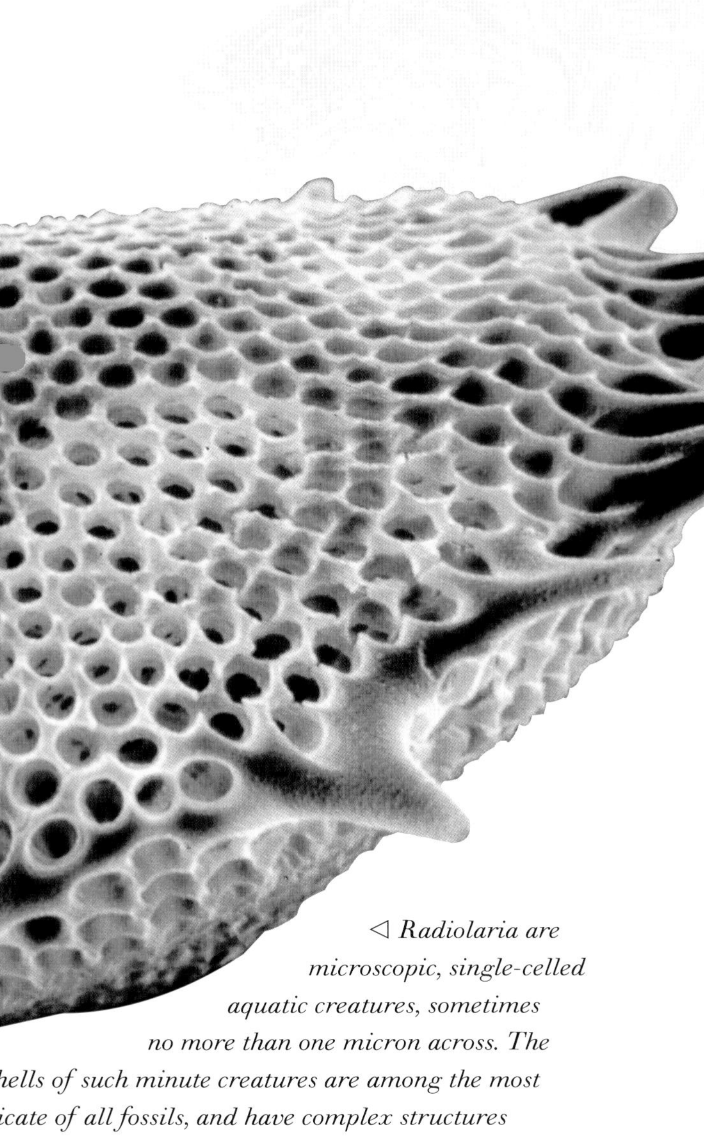

◁ *Radiolaria are microscopic, single-celled aquatic creatures, sometimes no more than one micron across. The hells of such minute creatures are among the most icate of all fossils, and have complex structures ɔikes, spindles, and crevices.*

nsumers of carbon

ger organisms, such as corals and shellfish, de use of calcium carbonate to build themselves tective shields. Tiny plants, which fed on carbon xide, were eaten by copepods. These tiny mals then excreted the carbon into the sea.

ssil formation

en an organism is buried in sediment, the parts start to decay, but the hard parts, like es and shells, are often preserved. Compressed ayers of rock, other minerals penetrate the :ks and crevices and harden. The calcium ɔonate structures that protected these creatures ife have helped them to survive as fossils.

△ *The shells of these fossil brachiopods are made of calcium carbonate, which originally derived from carbon in the atmosphere. Fossilization happens when an organism is buried and its bodily structures are slowly hardened by minerals such as silica and calcite.*

Climate control

If life did not consume carbon dioxide from the atmosphere, our climate might be more like that of Venus. There, a thick blanket of carbon dioxide traps the planet's heat and the surface temperature reaches 900°F (480°C). On the Earth, vast chalk cliffs and limestone mountains are reminders of just how much carbon has been turned into stone, ensuring that life has thrived.

▽ *In the past, people often identified fossils with mythical creatures. The curved shells of the oysterlike bivalve Gryphaea, found in many parts of Europe, were called "devil's toenails."*

Invasion of the Land

Until recently, there was little knowledge of life on land before about 400 million years ago. But we now know from fossil finds that more than 440 million years ago, plants, insects, and other animals all grew, crawled or walked on the land. Plants were first to invade the land from water. In water, they had no fear of drying out, and the water dispersed the plants' spores and brought them nutrients and provided them with physical support. The problem in water was that everything tried to eat you. Up above the waterline, a new, safe haven awaited plant colonization.

△ *Paleontologists thought* Coelacanth *had be extinct 65 million years ago, until living speci were caught off the coast of Madagascar.*

First land plants

During the Ordovician period, from 505 to 438 million years ago, plants took two steps toward a life on land. First, plants such as *Sporogonites* grew simple roots. Then, a plant called *Cooksonia* developed stiff, hollow tubes, through which water and food could reach its upper parts. Later, plants reproduced using seeds, and giant ferns and gymnosperms populated Earth's forests.

Giant wood lice and scorpions

Some of the first animals to follow the plants up on land were insects. Millipedes fed on rotting vegetat and predators such as centipedes sought them for lu With nothing much to hide from at first, some inse grew enormous. By 365 million years ago, 3-foot (1 long scorpions and a 7-foot (2-m)-long relative of th wood louse scuttled along the forest floors.

▽ *An army of* Ichthyostega *pulls itself ashore in this scene from the Devonian period 365 million years ago. These early amphibians had seven-toed back feet and tails like fish.*

Fish with lungs

Since the Ordovician period, the seas have been teeming with fish. Bony plates were grown early on for protection, although predatory fish, such as *Dunkleosteus*, had powerful jaws to crush th bony armor plating. For buoyancy, fish evolv internal gas-filled sacks called swim bladders. It is these tha may later have become lungs

\canthostega (top right) *already invaded the d, along with the lobe-ied fish,* Eusthenopteron, *giant wood louse,* hropleura, *a spider, ! a scorpion.*

These markings on the bark of giant club moss Lepidodendron *where leaves were once attached ie stem. Such fossils were mon in the swamps of the boniferous period.*

First legs and giant newts

By 380 million years ago, a newtlike creature called *Acanthostega* was walking around on the muddy shores of Greenland. It was soon followed by a much larger amphibian called *Ichthyostega*, which had stronger hips and shoulders and a hard, bony skull. A later, and even better adapted, land-living descendant was called *Eryops*.

LIFE STORY

The Real Jurassic Park

△ During the early 1800s, Mary Anning was frequently to be seen with her hammer along the Dorset cliffs near Lyme Regis, in England. She is said to have found her first ichthyosaur fossil at the age of 11.

By 205 million years ago, the great supercontinent of Pangaea had begun to break up. Between the continents of Laurasia to the north and Gondwanaland to the south, there was a new sea of warm shallow water, the Tethys. There were no polar ice caps and the global climate was warm. This was the start of one of the most successful geological periods for life, and a time when dinosaurs became dominant. It was a real Jurassic park.

Life in the sea

The Jurassic seas must have been thriving. A warm, tropical climate, plenty of nutrients, great blooms of plankton—all these provided rich pickings for larger life forms. Jurassic limestones and shales laid down in those seas are full of fossils—bivalves, gastropods, and ammonites—as well as rarer fish and reptile fossils.

△ *These fossil bones make up one of the pad[dles] or flippers, of an ichthyosaur. The top* (left) *i[s] made of fused limb bones, while the flexible part has evolved from the bones of the feet.*

Sea monsters

Ichthyosaurs must have been the dominant predators in the sea. Althoug[h] streamlined and similar to dolphins, th[ey] were not mammals, but reptiles. As we[re] long-necked plesiosaurs, with their pow[erful] paddles and sharp teeth. Could it be th[at the] legend of the Loch Ness monster is bas[ed] on sightings of a modern plesiosaur?

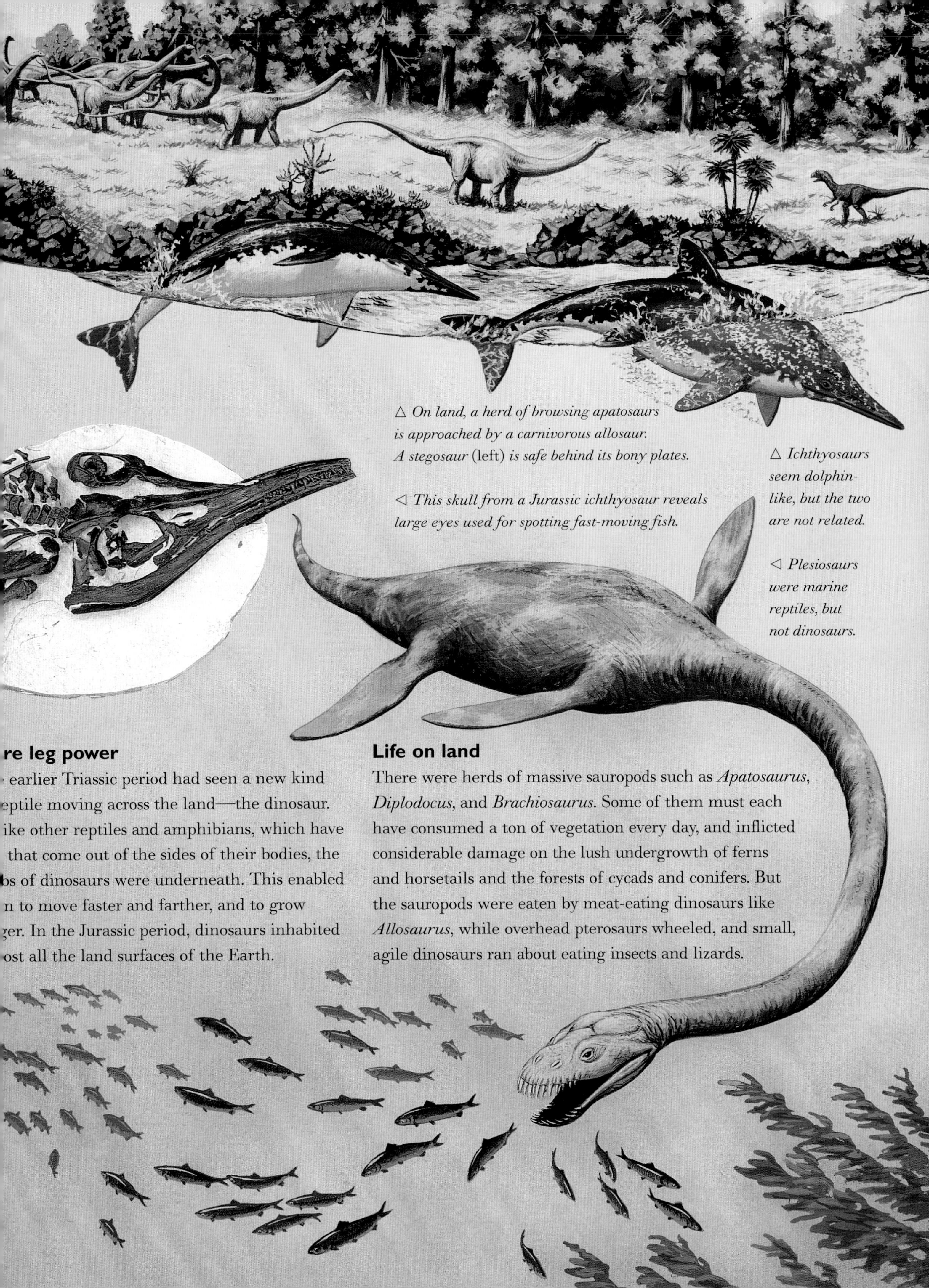

△ *On land, a herd of browsing apatosaurs is approached by a carnivorous allosaur. A stegosaur* (left) *is safe behind its bony plates.*

◁ *This skull from a Jurassic ichthyosaur reveals large eyes used for spotting fast-moving fish.*

△ *Ichthyosaurs seem dolphin-like, but the two are not related.*

◁ *Plesiosaurs were marine reptiles, but not dinosaurs.*

re leg power

earlier Triassic period had seen a new kind eptile moving across the land—the dinosaur. ike other reptiles and amphibians, which have that come out of the sides of their bodies, the bs of dinosaurs were underneath. This enabled n to move faster and farther, and to grow ger. In the Jurassic period, dinosaurs inhabited ost all the land surfaces of the Earth.

Life on land

There were herds of massive sauropods such as *Apatosaurus*, *Diplodocus*, and *Brachiosaurus*. Some of them must each have consumed a ton of vegetation every day, and inflicted considerable damage on the lush undergrowth of ferns and horsetails and the forests of cycads and conifers. But the sauropods were eaten by meat-eating dinosaurs like *Allosaurus*, while overhead pterosaurs wheeled, and small, agile dinosaurs ran about eating insects and lizards.

Kingdom of the Giants

During the Cretaceous period, dinosaurs ruled the Earth in greater numbers and with greater diversity than ever before. Growing big became a strategy for surviva While herds of huge *Apatosaurus* and *Triceratops* browsed in the vegetation, fearsome *Tyrannosaurus* and packs of agile *Velociraptor* preyed upon them. Overhead flew the biggest animals ever to take to the air, reptiles such as *Quetzalcoatlus*, with a wingspan the size of a small airc Flowering plants were replacing ferns and cycads, and small mammals scurried through the undergrowth.

△ *Dinosaurs are classified into two main groups. In bird-hipped dinosaurs, two bones point back toward the tail. In the lizard-hipped dinosaurs, one points forward.*

▽ *An* Edmontosaurus *has fallen victim to* Tyrannosaurus, *and a scavenger is already at work. An armored* Euoplocephalus (top left) *has less to fear.*

Dinosaur logjam

About 145 million years ago, a broad river flood-plain lay in an area that is now part of the Rocky Mountains on the Utah–Colorado border. When the river flooded, some dinosaurs drowned. Their bodies were washed onto a sandbar, creating a dinosuar logjan In 1908, more than 350 tons of fossil bones were taken from the site. Even so, the Dinosuar National Monume as it is now called, still holds over 2,000 bones.

◁ *These flies have preserved in amber 30 million years. G material has been o from insects twice t age, but it is poorly preserved.*

△ *In this scene from the film* Jurassic Park, *a baby dinosaur, supposedly reconstructed from fossilized genes, hatches from an egg.*

Warm-blooded?

One of the biggest arguments among dinosaur experts is whether dinosaurs were warm-blooded or not. Microscopic structures in some dinosaur bones are similar to those of warm-blooded birds and mammals today. This suggest that they could control their own body temperature. So perhaps some dinosaurs were not the cold-blooded monsters they are often portrayed to be.

Cretaceous Park

The film *Jurassic Park* implied that genetic ıaterial taken from blood-sucking insects reserved in amber could be used to reconstruct a living dinosaur. DNA has been recovered from Cretaceous insects found in amber, but it is likely to be damaged. Even with a limitless supply of perfect DNA from a living organism, mapping all its genes is a major task. For the time being, *Jurassic Park* remains fiction.

◁ *This claw bone from a* Baryonyx *dinsosaur was found in Surrey, England, in 1983. Its outer curve is 12 inches (31 cm) long. The claw would have enabled* Baryonyx *to hold onto prey such as fish.*

Extinction

The age of the dinosaurs came to an abrupt end 65 million years ago. Although individual species of dinosaur seldom survived more than a few million years, the group as a whole had persisted for 160 million years, showing a remarkable ability to specialize for many different ways of life. At the same time as the demise of the dinosaurs, 12 percent of all families of marine organisms became extinct, as did many land plants. Clearly, something dramatic must have happened to affect so many forms of life so severely.

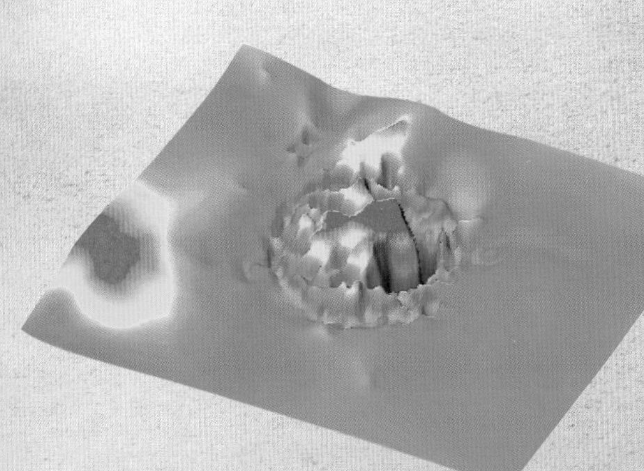

△ This magnetic map of the Chicxulub crater off the coast of Mexico displays the 75-mile (120-km)-wide structure left by a devastating meteorite impact 65 million years ago. Red, yellow, and blue magnetic peaks reveal where strongly magnetized rocks rose up to replace sediment vaporized by the blast.

A controversial theory

During the 1970s, Walter and Luis Alvarez were studying clay that dated back to the end of the Cretaceous period and found that it was rich in the rare metal iridium. The best-known source of iridium is outer space, leading them to suggest that a giant meteorite colliding with the Earth had caused the extinction of the dinosaurs.

▽ Radar on the space shuttle reveals this 11-mile (17-km)-wide crater beneath the sands of the Sahara Desert. It was formed several hundred million years ago and is one of many impact craters now identified.

Cosmic impact

The Alvarez theory had little to support it—until, in 1991, a giant crater was found under the sea off Mexico. To cause such a crater, a meteorite several miles across, traveling at great speed, must have hit our planet. The impact would have released more energy than one thousand nuclear weapons, causing tidal waves and global fires, and been followed by semidarkness for several years. It would have been a bad time to be a dinosaur.

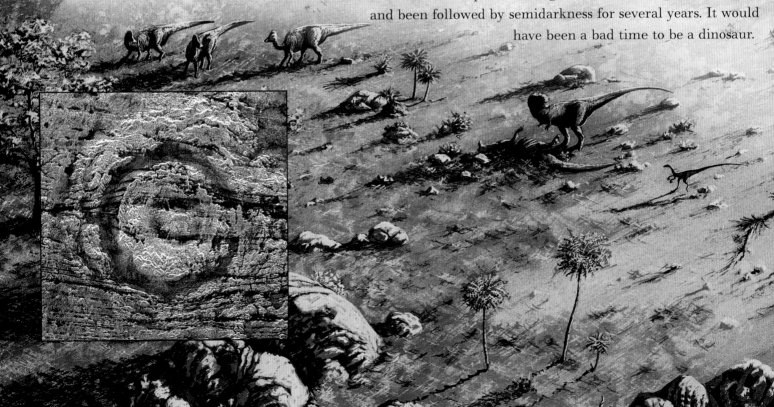

reats and opportunities

ny rival theories have attempted to explain mass extinctions—we never know which one is correct. What we do know for certain hat the extinction of one group of animals is the evolutionary ortunity for another. It seems that the largest and most cialized organisms suffer most, as was the case with the osaurs. And 65 million years ago, the small, adaptable nals that were waiting for their big chance were the nmals. Today, another mass extinction appears to be rogress, but this time it is caused by human activity. bal warming and the destruction of habitats are set to d thousands of modern species the way of the dinosaurs.

razing in what is now Mexico, herds of late aceous dinosaurs look on in bewilderment at the h of the giant meteorite. Their days are numbered estruction and extinction will soon follow.

◁ Rock samples from the Caribbean act as a record of the meteorite's collision with the Earth. At the moment of impact, thousands of tons of seawater and rock rose into the air. This fallout eventually dropped to the Earth to form a distinctive white layer in the rock.

The Birds and the Bees

In the late Jurassic period, 150 million years ago, in the part of southern Germany that now lies just north of Munich, there was a warm, salty lagoon. Fish swept in by storms perished in its stagnant waters and sank to the bottom. A horseshoe crab staggered around, leaving spiral tracks, before dying. Anything that entered the lagoon perished, and the remains were preserved in the fine layers of muddy limestone. The fossils that have been found there are not only of creatures that crawled or were washed into the lagoon. Some must have been blown in by the winds, or even flown there.

First flight

In 1860, a single feather was found preserved in the rocks of what had once been the lagoon. It was the same shape as the flight feather of a modern bird. A year later, the complete skeleton of a feathered creature was found. It was named *Archaeopteryx*, meaning ancient wing. It had teeth rather than a beak, but it was winged, with a feathered tail, and clearly could have flown.

▷ *Creatures of all sorts have taken to the air, including mammals, reptiles (pterosaurs), and birds (the only group to develop feathers). Here, a flock of* Archaeopteryx *looks down on a late Jurassic scene.*

Chinese flocks

A remarkable find in China in 1996 may shed some light on the evolution of *Archaeopteryx*. *Sinosauropteryx* was found in 120-million-year-old rocks. It was slightly smaller than a chicken and had distinct traces of downy filaments up to 1.6 inches (4cm) long all over its body. These proto-feathers may have originally evolved for insulation.

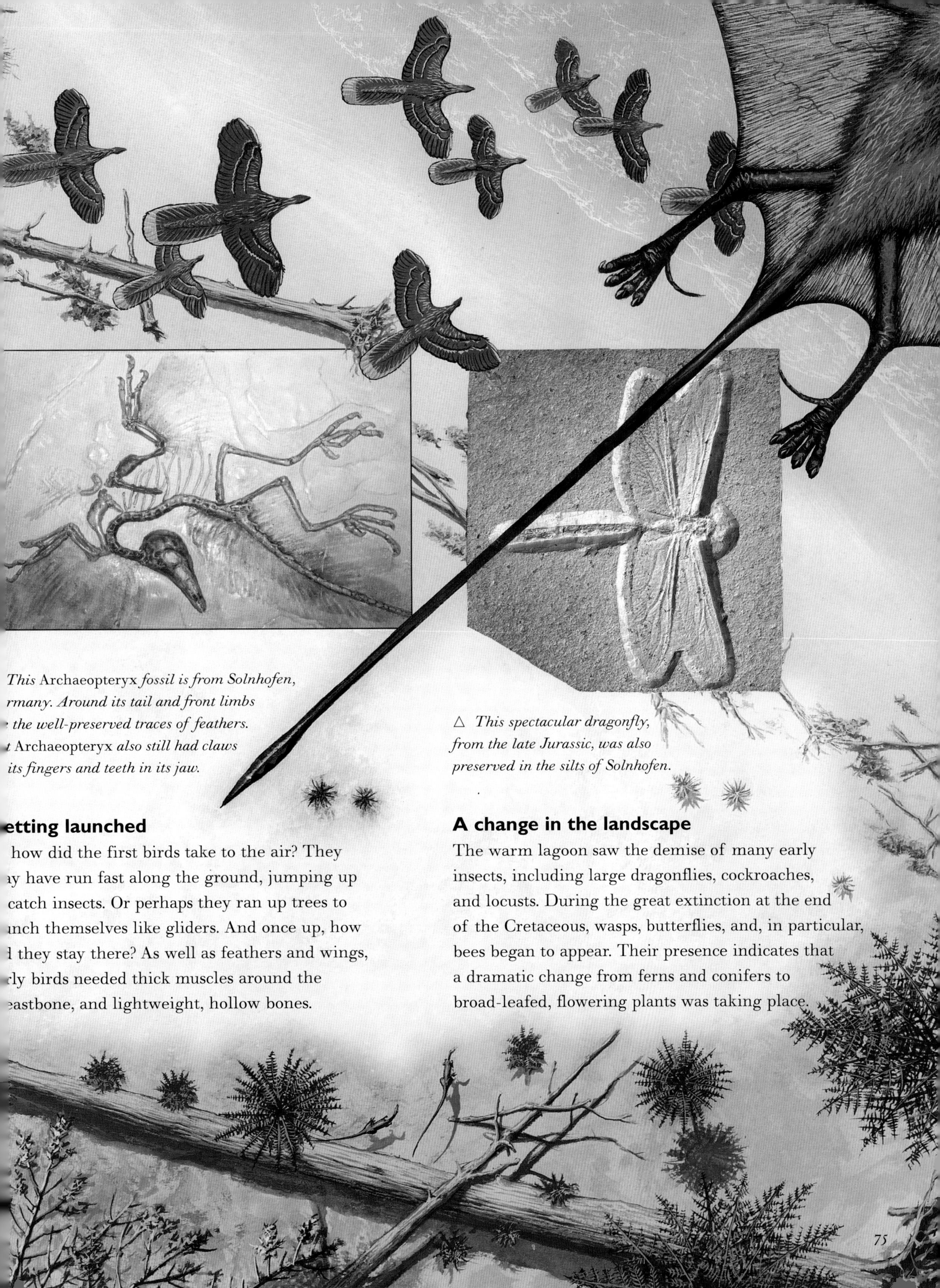

This Archaeopteryx *fossil is from Solnhofen,*
rmany. Around its tail and front limbs
the well-preserved traces of feathers.
t Archaeopteryx *also still had claws*
its fingers and teeth in its jaw.

△ *This spectacular dragonfly, from the late Jurassic, was also preserved in the silts of Solnhofen.*

etting launched

how did the first birds take to the air? They
ay have run fast along the ground, jumping up
catch insects. Or perhaps they ran up trees to
unch themselves like gliders. And once up, how
l they stay there? As well as feathers and wings,
rly birds needed thick muscles around the
eastbone, and lightweight, hollow bones.

A change in the landscape

The warm lagoon saw the demise of many early insects, including large dragonflies, cockroaches, and locusts. During the great extinction at the end of the Cretaceous, wasps, butterflies, and, in particular, bees began to appear. Their presence indicates that a dramatic change from ferns and conifers to broad-leafed, flowering plants was taking place.

Creatures of the Ice

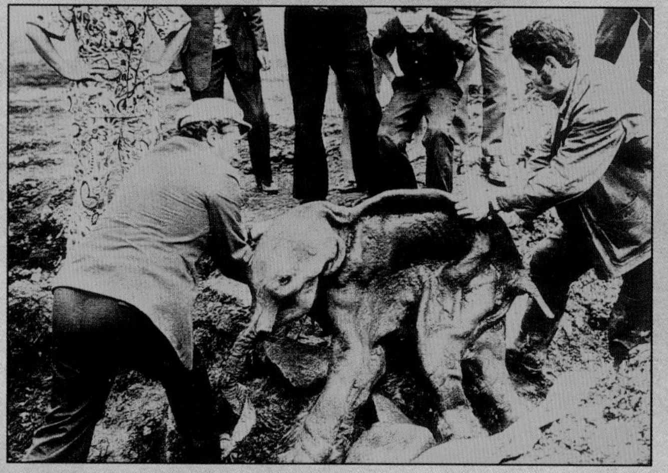

△ *This frozen baby mammoth was recovered in 1977 from the permafrost of Siberia. Though shrunken, its internal organs and reddish hair had been preserved for more than 9,000 years. Flesh like this is so well preserved that, in the past, such finds were fed to dogs. Today, they are kept for genetic analysis.*

Any creature that survived the cataclysmic events at the end of the Cretaceous lived in a time of great opportunity. All the large predators and herbivores had been wiped off the face of the Earth. The remaining reptiles—lizards, snakes, turtles, and small crocodiles—carried on much as they had before. However, small but adaptable creatures that had until then spent much of their lives in hiding were suddenly presented with the opportunity to inherit the Earth. This Tertiary era, the third age of life on the Earth, has been the age of the mammals and the birds.

Survival of the fittest

Whereas birds had developed insulating feathers from the hard scales of their dinosaur ancestors, mammals grew fur from soft, porous skin. This was just as well, because the world's climate grew progressively cooler over the next 50 million years. Mammalian evolution also saw experiments with size and ferocity. There were giant rhinos measuring 13 feet (4 m) at the shoulder and weighing 15 tons, and huge deer, such as the Irish elk. Saber-toothed tigers and their marsupial equivalents lived alongside a host of other mammalian monsters, such as the woolly mammoths of Europe and the mastodons of North America.

▽ *Woolly mammoths, woolly rhinoceroses, bears, and buffalo roamed over the ice-age tundra. These large creatures were well adapted for life at low temperatures, but they proved less adaptable than smaller mammals once the ice retreated.*

he great freeze

ɔllowing the breakup of the supercontinent Pangea, mammals volved differently on each landmass. Then, 15 million years ago, an e cap began to form on Antarctica and sea levels fell. This allowed imals to migrate between the different continents. It continued to t colder until, about 3.25 million years ago, variations in the Earth's bit were large enough to trigger the first in a series of ice ages.

dapt or die

s the polar regions froze, the ice reflected sunlight back into space d the Earth cooled further. When the higher latitudes cooled, uatorial regions became drier, forming the basis for the savannah asslands and deserts of today. Though some mammals developed ick layers of fat or fur to keep warm, the changing climate led the extinction of many species. But one group used its ingenuity to keep warm, clothing itself in the skins of others and lighting fires. These mammals were our own ancestors.

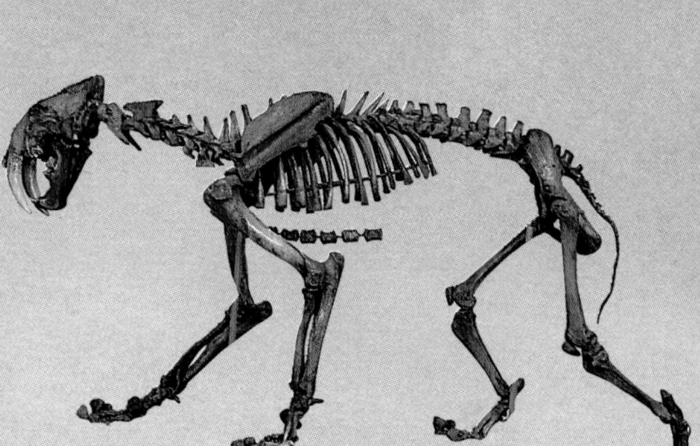

△ *The skeleton of* Smilodon, *a sabre-toothed tiger. This powerful cat had a large head, muscular shoulders, and a short tail. It was a ferocious killer, using its huge, serrated canine teeth to slash into the flesh of its prey—mostly large mammals such as mammoths and bison.*

◁ *Part of the skull and the spectacular tusks of an adult woolly mammoth that roamed the tundra of England during the last ice age. This one was found in what is now part of the suburbs of London, England.*

Our Ancestors

In 1974, a group of anthropologists found fragments of bone near Hadar, in Ethiopia. Before long they had built up much of the skeleton of a young hominid (human ancestor) called *Australopithecus*, meaning southern ape. Naming her Lucy, they established that she was about three million years old. She had an apelike skull and a small brain, but her arms were short and she could walk upright on her long legs. Since then, bones of a different *Australopithecus* have been found. These belong to a more apelike species which had a developed skull, but longer arms and short legs.

△ *These ancient handprints were found in an Argentinian cave, along with many paintings of animals.*

△ *Flint hand axes like this u… used by early … This one was f… Britain and is … 250,000 years …*

Footprints in the sand

One day, about 3.6 million years ago, on what is now the Laetoli Plain of northern Tanzania, a layer of fresh ash from a nearby volcano was softened by a shower of rain. Three creatures wandered across it, walking upright on two legs. Two may have been holding hands, the third, smaller and younger, walked behind. Were they our ancestors?

▷ *A group of* Homo erectus *about 1.5 million years ago plans a hunt across the African savanna. These intelligent early people walked upright, leaving their hands free to use tools.*

The toolmakers

In 1984, the bones of a 12-year-old boy were discovered near Lake Turkana in Kenya. They were nearly 1.5 million years old. He belonged to a species called *Homo erectus* (upright human), and was probably one of our ancestors. From about 1.8 million years ago, when *Homo erectus* evolved, the fossil sites are littered with the stone hand axes crafted by these early humans.

△ *These footprints, preserved in hardened volcanic ash, were left in Tanzania 3.6 million years ago, perhaps by a family of hominids. Whoever they were, they clearly walked upright. This ability may have resulted in a larger brain developing, as the hands became free to manipulate tools.*

The road to civilization

The first people to be called *Homo sapiens* (wise human) were a tall, big-brained group that appeared in Europe about 500,000 years ago. About 200,000 years ago, another intelligent group emerged in Germany, called the Neanderthals. The first modern humans, *Homo sapiens sapiens*, emerged 40,000 years ago.

▷ *A reconstruction of the skull of* Homo erectus pekinensis (1), *an early modern human* (2), Australopithecus africanus (3), *an Australopithecine skull from between 5 million and 1.2 million years ago* (4).

△ *Coal is usually mined by sinking shafts underground. Galleries are then cut along the lines of the coal seams. Since oil is liquid, an offshore oil production platform* (far right) *needs only narrow bore holes to pump it out.*

Fuel from the Earth

For more than one billion years, planet Earth has teemed with life. During that time, living organisms have trapped the Sun's energy and stored it in the chemicals of their bodies. Much of that chemical energy is now stored underground as fossil fuels—coal, gas, and oil. Today, we are releasing that trapped solar energy by burning the fuels, and putting the carbon they contain back into the atmosphere as carbon dioxide. The fuels provide us with energy to fire our power plants and generate electricity. They give us fuel for cars and airplanes, and they provide most of the raw materials for making plastics, artificial fibers, and a host of other chemicals.

△ *Oil is not always found where it is needed. The trans-Alaskan pipeline carries oil 798 miles (1,284 km) across the Arctic.*

▽ *This nuclear power plant at Sizewell in Suffolk, England is powered by uranium. Only a tiny quantity of fuel is needed, but the radioactive waste it produces is difficult and expensive to handle safely.*

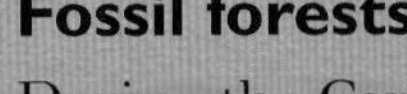

Fossil forests

During the Carboniferous period 300 million years ago, vast forests covered much of the Earth's land surface. Giant tree ferns and cycads grew, died, and decomposed. Where they fell in swampy ground, there was not enou oxygen for them to rot and they turned into thick layer of peat. Sometimes sea levels rose and covered the remains with layers of sand or shale. As it was buried deeper and deeper, the peat was compressed into coal.

Oil and gas

Many of the great multitude of creatures that live in the oceans are eaten or decomposed by bacteria. Howev some sink into oxygen-poor waters and get buried in th sediments. The abundant bacteria that live hundreds of feet beneath the sea floor survive off these organic remains and slowly convert them into oil and methane gas, which are cooked by the hot interior of the planet.

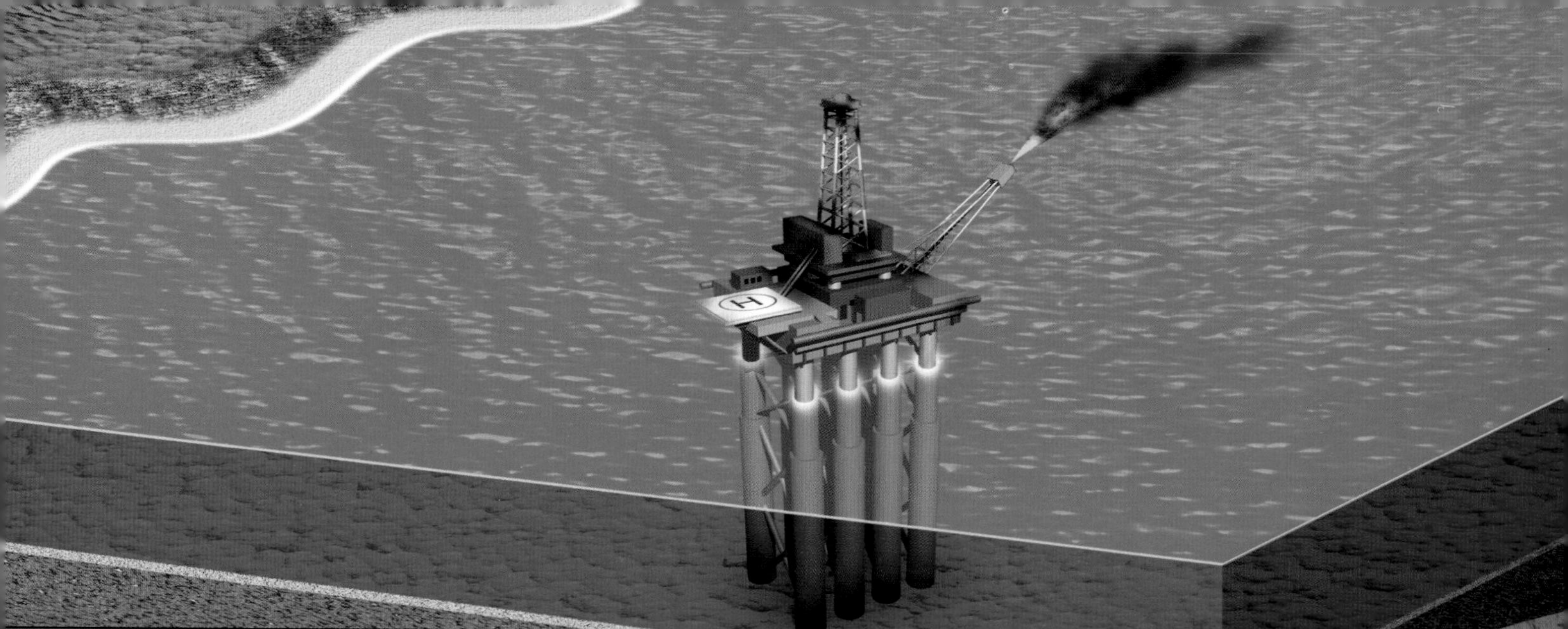

These wind turbines in California
vide an alternative source of energy to
l and oil. It has been estimated that by
'5, wind power could provide one quarter
he electricity needed by many countries.

ding oil fields

and gas are much less dense than rock. Once formed, y tend to rise up through porous rocks until they can go farther. Oil prospectors searching for the "black gold" gin by looking for the sort of geological formations that l trap it. The oil and gas themselves fill the tiny spaces hin rocks such as sandstone. Where rocks of the right are overlaid by domes of impervious rocks such as y or salt, huge reservoirs of oil and gas may collect.

strike!

e hundred years ago, shallow oil wells would often duce a gush of oil under natural pressure. Today, technology to extract oil has become complex and ensive. Pumping out the oil only extracts a fraction what is there. Seawater and chemical solvents help ract more. Even so, at the present rate, the oil will y last a few decades; the coal and gas a little longer.

△ Some time in the future, the coal and oil will run out, but the Sun will continue to shine. Banks of reflecting dishes such as these in Australia are already used to concentrate the Sun's energy and generate electric power.

Metals from the Earth

The Earth was formed from raw ingredients originally cooked up inside stars and spewed out into space. Processes inside the planet have concentrated the elements, such as metals, in quantities useful to humans. The minerals that contain these concentrated elements are called ores. Some minerals are carried along cracks and fissures in rock when molten igneous rocks rise through the crust. Other minerals are deposited in crystalline veins as heat drives off water containing dissolved minerals. Some of the richest mines of copper, lead, zinc, and gold are formed in this way.

△ When hot fluids containing dissolved minerals fill a cavity in a rock, they form a geode. First silica is deposited, then, as the cavity fills, larger quartz crystals grow, often colored by trace metals.

Extracting metals

Few metals occur in their pure form in nature. Gold is a notable exception. Most metallic minerals are chemical compounds with very different properties to the metals they contain. The process of smelting is used to extract the metal from the ore. Both heat and a reducing agent, such as carbon in the form of charcoal, are used to pull the metal's chemical companions away from it.

▽ Useful minerals are often deposited around hot, igneous rock. Water, saturat in dissolved minerals, is dri outward by the heat.

◁ Protected by heat-resistant clothes, a worker takes a sample of molten iron from a blast furnace. Inside the furnace, hot air fans the flames through a mixture of iron ore, coke, and limestone. Once the waste, or slag, is skimmed off, the molten iron is cast into ingots.

oles in the ground

ining techniques depend on the concentration of the e, its depth, and its value. Where ore lies in a thick vein derground, tunnels and shafts can be sunk. Sometimes there is a large body of less concentrated ore near the surface and it can be dug out from an opencast pit. Sometimes nature has already done the digging. Deposits of gold, for example, are concentrated in river gravels.

The other side

Despite the value of the metals they produce, mines have also left a legacy of pollution and damage. For every ton of ore extracted, there can be thousands of tons of waste rock spilled across the hillside. Sometimes the waste rocks contain poisons that kill the surrounding trees. Artificial dams burst, mines flood, and tanks leak, washing mud, debris, and toxic chemicals down rivers. In some cases the mines are located in environmentally sensitive areas or in populated territories.

Future prospects

As mines on the land become exhausted, we will need to look elsewhere. There are potentially rich sources in the ocean. Some areas of the ocean floor are littered with manganese nodules and other rare metals. However, they lie at great depths and are in international waters. One day, mining might happen in space. A single small asteroid, towed back to the Earth, could provide many of the valuable metals that the world needs for centuries.

▽ Once the rock cools, the minerals are left in cracks and fissures, forming metal-rich veins. Miners cut shafts and galleries underground to reach the veins.

▽ This great opencast mine in New Mexico is one of the largest artificial holes on the planet.

◁ *Lapis lazuli is a complex sodium aluminum silicate. This semiprecious stone is formed in igneous and metamorphic rocks that are rich in carbonate.*

Gems from the Deep

▽ *For centuries, the prospect of great wealth led alchemists to try to convert base materials into gold and gems. We know now that they could never have succeeded.*

Any stone or crystal worn as jewelry can be regarded as a gem. Some are organic in origin, such as amber (fossilized tree resin), jet (hard-black coal), opal (silicified wood), and pearl (shell). Many other semiprecious stones are silicate minerals such as quartz (rock crystal), amethyst, jade, garnet, and topaz. The most precious stones are also the rarest and the most durable—ruby, sapphire, emerald, and diamond. These mineral gems are formed under particular conditions of pressure and temperature, deep in the Earth's mantle. It is only later that they are thrown up to the surface.

△ *Natural diamond crystal is found embedded in volcan kimberlite rock. This type of rock is named after the area in which it is found—Kimberley, South Africa.*

▽ *Carbon is dragged down from the Earth's surface to the upper mantle, where the pressure transforms it into diamond.*

Humble beginnings

The tightly packed crystal structure of diamond makes it the hardest natural substance on the Earth. Yet it is made of carbon, the same element that makes pencil lead or soot. Where this carbon came from is uncertain Perhaps it was once limestone, coal, or even a carbon-ri meteorite (*see below, illustration* **1**) and was then pulle into the Earth's mantle on a slab of old ocean crust (**2**).

1

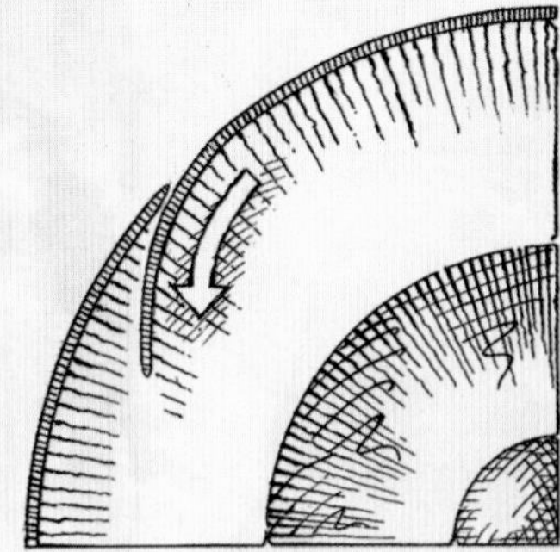

2

◁ *Quartz is a form of silica. This quartz crystal was photographed using colored light. Flaws in the quartz catch the light, making it shimmer.*

△ *Rutilated quartz contains needlelike crystals of rutile, an ore of titanium.*

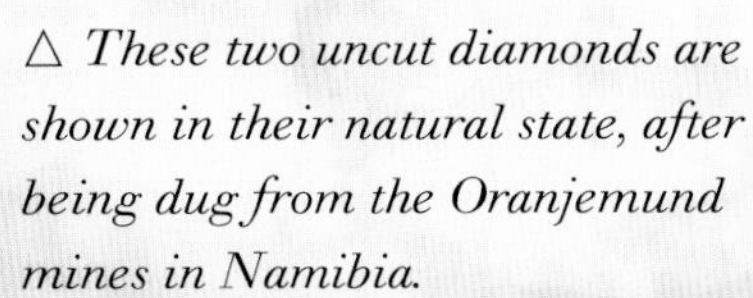

△ *These two uncut diamonds are shown in their natural state, after being dug from the Oranjemund mines in Namibia.*

△ *A cut, polished diamond may be worth several thousand dollars per carat. One carat is 0.01 ounces (0.2 g).*

e birth of a diamond

r millions of years and at about 375 miles (600 km) eath the Earth's surface, the carbon was slowly ısformed into a diamond. Its rise to the surface would e been much more rapid, however. This is because ıust have been ejected in the type of volcano, now rcifully extinct, which erupted at supersonic speeds (*3*).

ny facets

ough natural diamond has eight sides (*4*). To give it sparkle, the surface must be carefully cut so that it has ny facets (*5*). The best-known diamond cut is called rilliant and has 58 facets, making it especially sparkly. well as adorning jewelry, diamonds can also be used he blades of delicate saws or in drill bits.

Emerald alchemy

Emeralds usually form in hot granite when scaldingly hot fluids containing beryllium and chromium react with carborundum or aluminum oxide. Some of the most beautiful emeralds, however, are from Colombia and they seem to have formed when highly pressurized hot water dissolved salt and gypsum from sedimentary rocks, which then reacted with clay minerals in the surrounding shale.

3

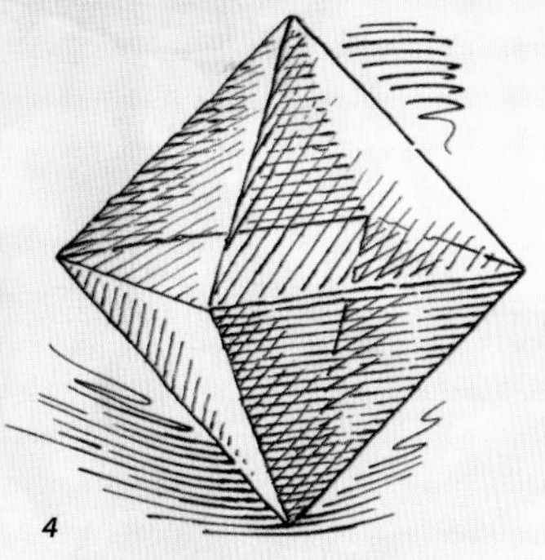

4

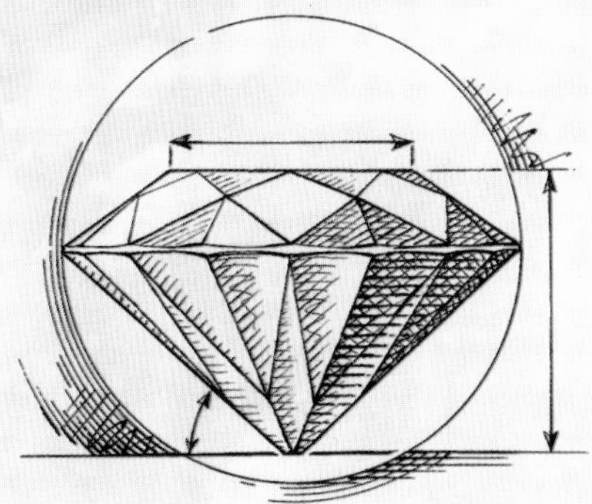

5

Human Creators

△ *Though now surrounded by jungle, the great Mayan pyramids of Tikal in Guatemala are impressive examples of human creativity.*

In the four billion years since the heavy bombardment of the Earth ceased, continents have split and collided, oceans have opened and vanished, mountain ranges have grown and then eroded away. But never has change been faster or more spectacular than over the past few thousand years. The recent transformation of the planet is mostly due to the activities of a single species, *Homo sapiens sapiens*—ourselves. It is hard to imagine what the world would be like without human beings. Since ancient times we have built and burrowed, chopped and changed—taming the landscape to suit our needs. The concrete jungles and cultivated landscapes are clear evidence that we have become the rulers of the surface of the Earth and all the species upon it. We are the creators and the destroyers of wonders.

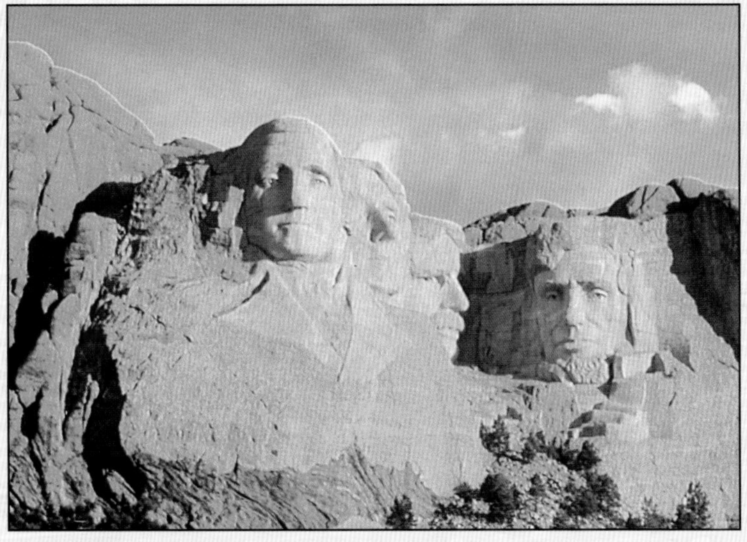

◁ *Powerful people of every era have tried to leave enduring monuments to their life and times. These giant faces of American presidents are carved out of the natural rock of Mount Rushmore in South Dakota.*

A new garden of Eden

Look down at the surface of the Earth from a plane, or even from space, and the patterns are striking. For hundreds of miles, parts of the Earth are a patchw of fields, outlined by the unnaturally straight lines of roads and fences. It is even possible to see political and economic boundaries, as different agricultural policies meet along lines that seem to be drawn with a ruler.

Protecting and preserving

Many regions of wilderness still remain on the planet, complete with a rich biodiversity of plants and animals. Work is in progress to preserve these areas and to prevent further pollution and destruction. We have also taken it upon ourselves to try to protect individual species, or at least the ones we have identified. Huge efforts are going into the preservation of rare animals such as the giant panda of China or the California condor.

The wonders of the world

Not all human industry is destructive—we have create some works of great beauty and benefit, too. Which on qualify as the wonders of our civilization is a matter of individual taste. Maybe they are the great buildings of our modern age. Perhaps they are products of science, such as space rockets and suspension bridges. They cou even be on a smaller scale—a painting, a piece of musi a book, or a garden in full bloom.

A web of knowledge

One of the greatest human achievements is the quest for knowledge and understanding. We have explored our planet's surface and journeyed into space. We are discovering the secrets of science and the mysteries of our own bodies. No one person can contain all this knowledge, but through our libraries and communications networks, we have spun a web of knowledge around the planet that people can access. It brings a potential far greater than that of any individual.

△ *Great buildings, ingenious structures, and powerful machines keep our economies thriving and our lives moving. But some human creations are designed to fulfill our spiritual needs, while others are simply for pleasure or amazement.*

Human Destroyers

△ *Untreated waste pours into the sea from an outflow pipe on the English coast. Untreated sewage can cause blooms of algae which use up oxygen from the water. Chemicals can poison life directly.*

◁ *Despite improved techniques for dealing with oil spills, it can take many years for an area to recover from a major spill.*

Life on the Earth may be facing an even greater crisis than the mass extinctions of the past. For the last 300 years, vertebrate species have been disappearing at an average of one per year, and today more than 3,500 animal species are under threat. Plants, fungi, and microorganisms are also vanishing. If the present trend continues, it has been estimated th at least one quarter of all living creatures will disappe before the human population levels out in about 50 years' time The reasons for current losses are hunting, competition from introduced species, and, in particular, loss of habitats.

Lost worlds

Humans have been changing the landscape since the ice ages. With the invention of the flint hand ax, the systematic felling of the forests of much of northern Europe began. In Australia, the telltale signs of charcoal show that the first human settlers arrived 40,000 to 50,000 ye ago, and this coincides with the extinction of large birds and marsupia there. Today, about one percent of the world's 7 million sq. miles (17 million sq. km) of tropical rain forest is cleared every year. This releases huge quantities of carbon dioxide into the atmosphere.

Polluted planet

Six billion people produce a lot of waste, much of which is dumped with little or no treatment. We live in an industrialized world that req the manufacture, use, and transport of concentrated chemicals and eve radioactive materials. It is often the case that laws are broken, not enfo or non-existent, and the land, rivers, and seas suffer as a result.

stricken oil tanker
s helplessly in the sea,
ecious cargo spilling
o clog beaches and
n wildlife.

nger for humankind

at about the idea of Gaia (named after the Earth goddess), that planet acts like a single organism to keep conditions favorable for Does that mean that we can leave nature to clean up the mess? essor James Lovelock, who introduced the concept of Gaia, does doubt that this theory is correct—but he has never claimed that ill operate in favor of one species, least of all humankind.

nds of hope

he sea of destruction, there are islands of hope. In the 1870s, the Industrial Revolution well underway, the world's first national was established—Yellowstone, in Wyoming. Today, there are more 3,000 national parks and wildlife reserves, covering more than 1.5 ion sq. miles (4 millions sq. km) of the world. Perhaps the invention pace flight has come just in time—not for us to evacuate, but to gnize the need to protect our planet. From space, polluted rivers, st fires, and deserts are clearly visible, national boundaries fade away.

△ *After the oil tanker* Sea Empress *ran aground off the coast of South Wales in 1996, trawlers towed floating booms to try to contain the oil slicks and prevent them from drifting onto beaches.*

◁ *During the Gulf War in 1991, many Kuwaiti oil wells were left blazing. The thick palls of smoke traveled hundreds of miles and were clearly visible from space.*

◁▽ *Several billion years into the future, and the Earth and Moon have been scorched to cinders. The Sun is expanding into a red giant and has boiled away the oceans and atmosphere. Planet Earth is no longer the blue and green jewel that we once called home.*

The End of the Earth

The Earth has been our home for about half a million years, and home to life in some form for most of its 4.5 billion years. But as we have discovered, the Earth is a dynamic and active planet. Volcanoes erupt, continents split in two, mountains rise up, even rock is not steady. One day, the radioactive heat sources that fuel such changes will decay, the molten outer core will freeze and the Earth will be nothing more than a dead ember floating in space. However, more immediately, our planet is under constant threat from outside and even from ourselves.

▷ *Whatever the cause, we c be sure that one day the Ea will not be as hospitable as it is now. If human life is to survive, we will have to find ourselves a new home elsewhere in the Universe.*

Heavy artillery

The Earth has been under more or less regular bombardment since its birth. The early impacts were huge, probably melting the entire surface. Though their size and frequency have lessened, they have not stopped. Comets and asteroids have caused mass extinctions in the past, and unless we can deflect them, they will almost certainly do so again. But even if there is a major impact, past evidence suggests that life will not only survive but make the most of a catastrophe.

Cosmic roasting

Space is a dangerous place for a small planet. Old massive stars, our Sun's neighbors, could explode as supernovas in a thermonucleur fireball. This would damage the Earth's ozone layer and affect life, but probably not destroy it altogether. Similarly, the gamma-ray burst released in a collision between two neutron stars would blast the Earth with radiation roasting it as it turns, like a chicken on a spit. But again, the damage would probably not be terminal.

e human threat

ld we destroy our planet by our own actions? h the powers that we have today, the answer is, ›ably not. For all the devastation they cause, nuclear pons are no match for explosive volcanoes and roid impacts. Maybe our activities will change the ıate, damage the ozone layer, or release dangerous organisms and chemicals into the environment. results would indeed be terrible, but life is resilient. ıehow the world would survive, with or without us.

e end of the Sun

en time does run out for the Earth, it will probably because the hydrogen at the heart of our Sun has n exhausted. As the Sun dies, it will begin to swell a bloated red giant. Then, over a few thousand years, ill engulf the Earth and scorch away the atmosphere, ans, and, eventually, all life. But there is no need to ry quite yet. It will be another four or five billion rs before this catastrophic event happens, and, by n, we should be well on our way to the stars.

△ *The last of a series of giant spacecraft pulls away from Earth orbit and leaves to colonize new worlds. Constructed out of an asteroid, the craft, named* Utopia, *carries a complete sample of life on the Earth—land, sea, plants, and animals, as well as the last 1,000 human descendants. Our planet is dead, but life goes on.*

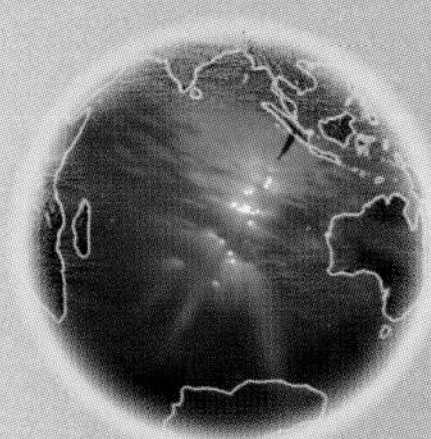

Planet Ocean

Oceans cover more than two-thirds of our planet's surface. A ship could sail around the world without touching land and, if it sank, would probably plunge more than 10,000 feet (3,000 m) before reaching the seabed.

These vast, hidden depths are home to millions of different plants and animals. Oceans also support life on dry land. All land plants and animals evolved in ancient seas. Even today, we could not survive without the oceans. They act like giant heaters, spreading the Sun's warmth around the globe. These vast reservoirs of water also recycle rain, preventing continents from turning to deserts. They supply us with seafood, and their colossal stores of oil, gas, and minerals help to fuel today's civilization.

Continents split the deep into four connected basins, containing the Pacific, Atlantic, Indian, and Arctic Oceans. The Pacific Ocean, the largest and deepest, could hold every continent, or the water of the other three oceans. The Arctic is the smallest, shallowest, and coldest ocean of all.

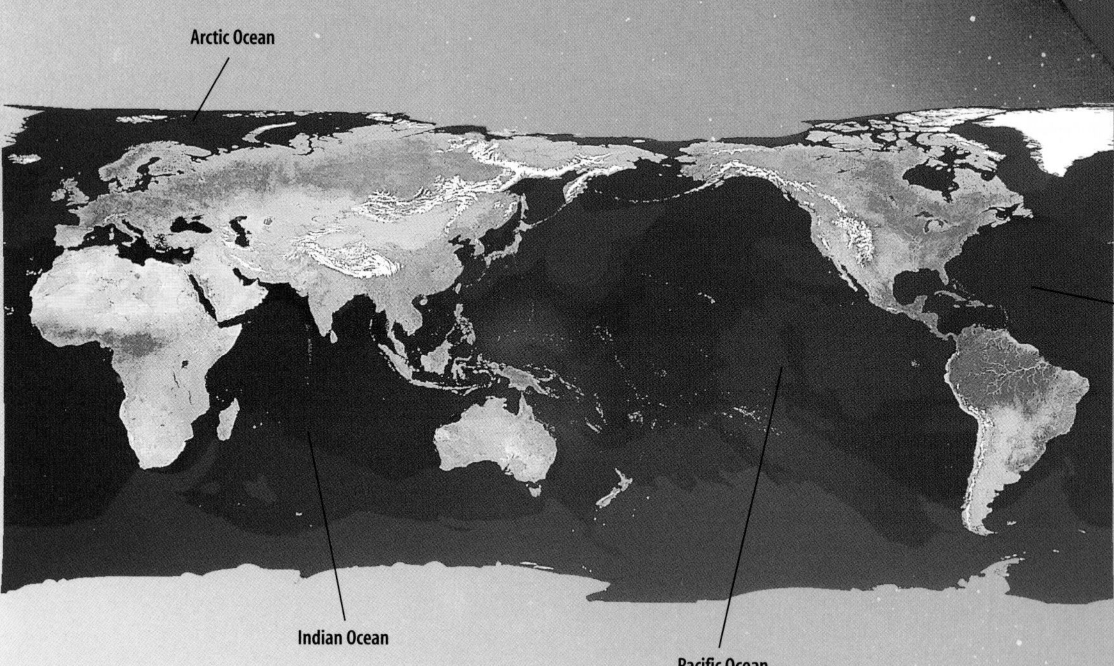

◁ *There are four main oceans—the Pacific, the Atlantic, the Arctic, and the Indian. Together they cover more than two-thirds of the Earth's surface.*

▽ *From above the Pacific, an astronaut's view of the Earth and Moon suggests our planet is almost all water. In fact, the Pacific Ocean covers just over one-third of the globe.*

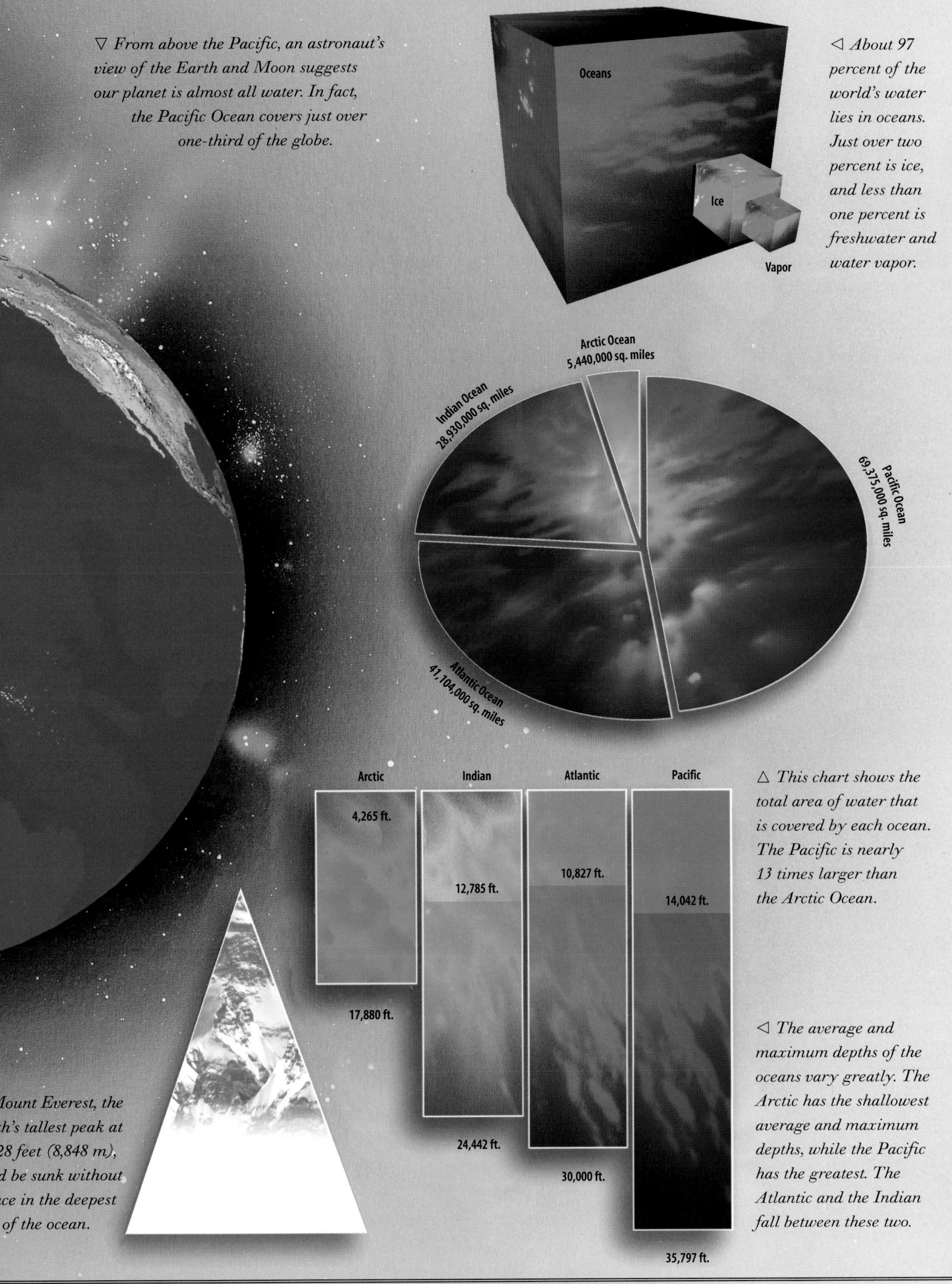

◁ *About 97 percent of the world's water lies in oceans. Just over two percent is ice, and less than one percent is freshwater and water vapor.*

△ *This chart shows the total area of water that is covered by each ocean. The Pacific is nearly 13 times larger than the Arctic Ocean.*

◁ *The average and maximum depths of the oceans vary greatly. The Arctic has the shallowest average and maximum depths, while the Pacific has the greatest. The Atlantic and the Indian fall between these two.*

Mount Everest, the ·th's tallest peak at ·)28 feet (8,848 m), ·ld be sunk without ·ace in the deepest ·t of the ocean.

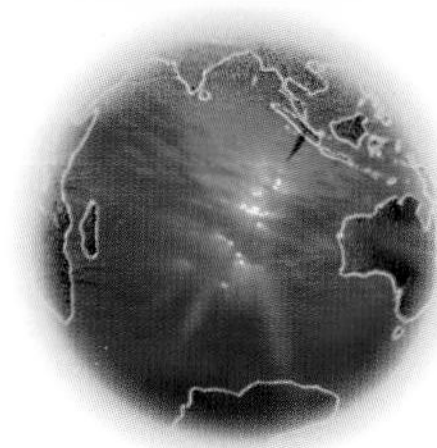

The Invisible Landscape

The seafloor, or ocean basin, is a landscape as mountainous as any on dry land. The rim of this basin, known as the continental shelf, is submerged up to 590 feet (180 m). From the shelf's outer edge, the continental slope slants down at least 10,000 feet (3,000 m) to form a colossal boundary wall. Deep canyons scar this slope. Sediment settling at the foot of the slope forms the continental rise. This gentle slope ends on the seafloor. Here the abyssal plains are found. These are coated with a smooth layer of sedimer Next come ridges of abyssal hills, occupying nea one-third of the seafloor. Beyond these rears a mid-ocean mountain range flanked by a central valley. Up to 6,560 feet (2,000 m) high, these ran run through all the oceans, creating Earth's grea mountain chain.

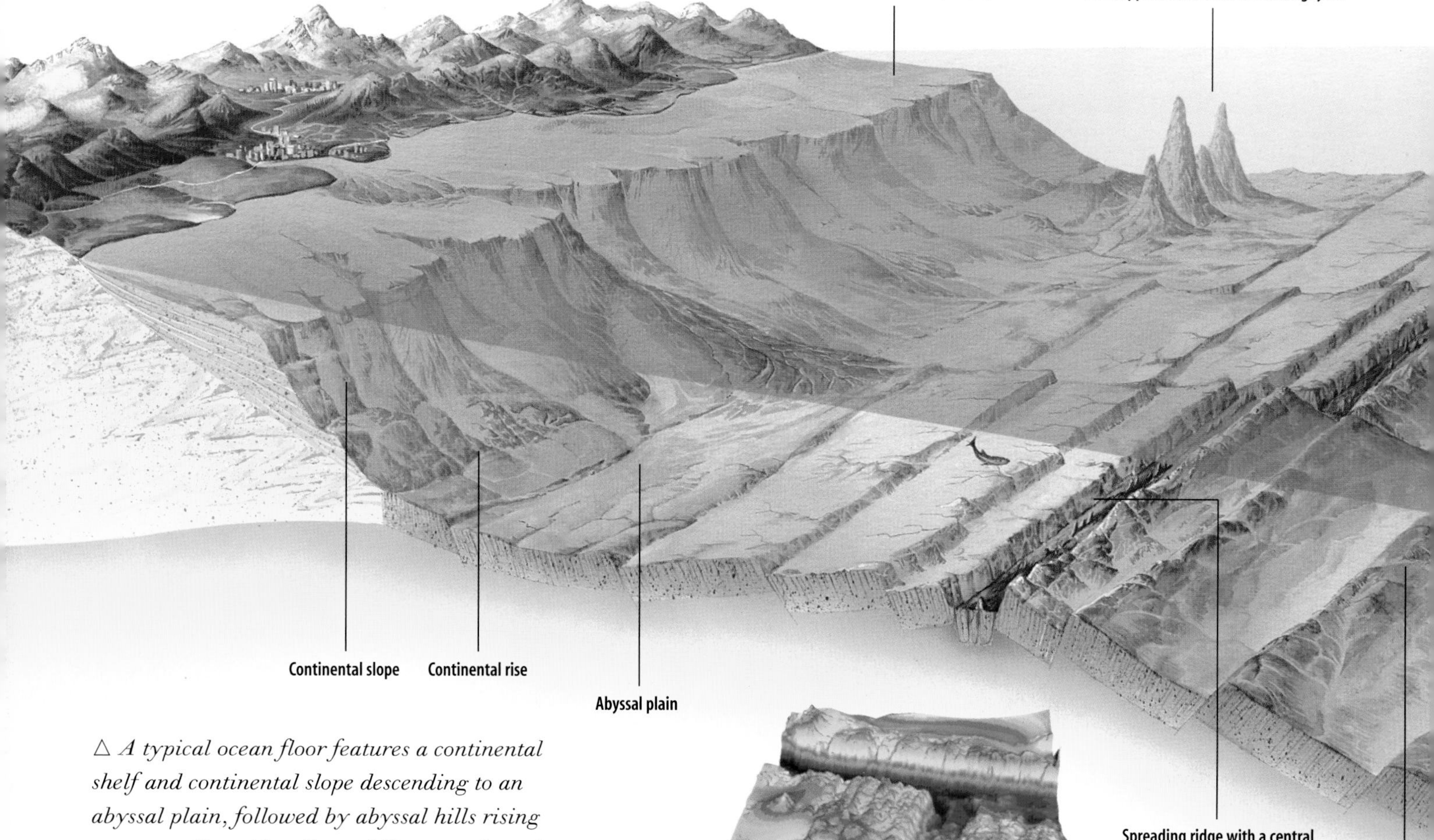

Continental shelf covered with sediment washed off the land

Seamounts (submarine volcanoes); Flat-topped seamounts are called guyots

Continental slope

Continental rise

Abyssal plain

Spreading ridge with a central rift valley flanked by steep-sided submarine mountains

Abyssal hills
parallel ridg
standing high
nearer they ar
spreading ri

△ *A typical ocean floor features a continental shelf and continental slope descending to an abyssal plain, followed by abyssal hills rising to a spreading ridge. Beyond lie more abyssal hills and a plunging ocean trench.*

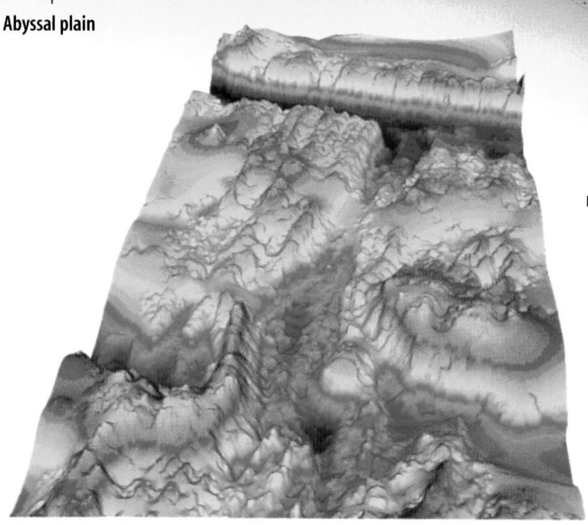

▷ *A computer-enhanced image reveals two transform faults cutting across the Mid-Atlantic Ridge. These cracks in the ocean floor break the long, curved, spreading ridges into shorter sections.*

)cean floor sediment 'udes mud and sand washed the land (terrigenous osits), dust from volcanoes l clay), chalky planktonic 'ls (calcareous ooze), and skeletons (radiolarian l diatom ooze).

Terrigenous deposits
Calcareous ooze
Red clay
Radiolarian ooze
Diatom ooze

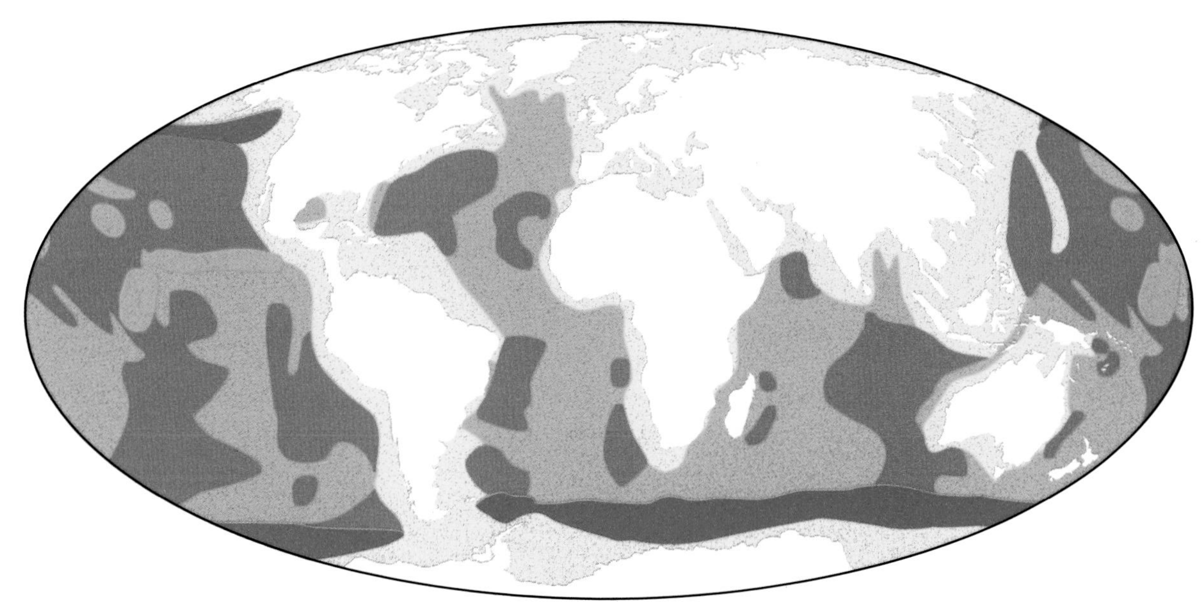

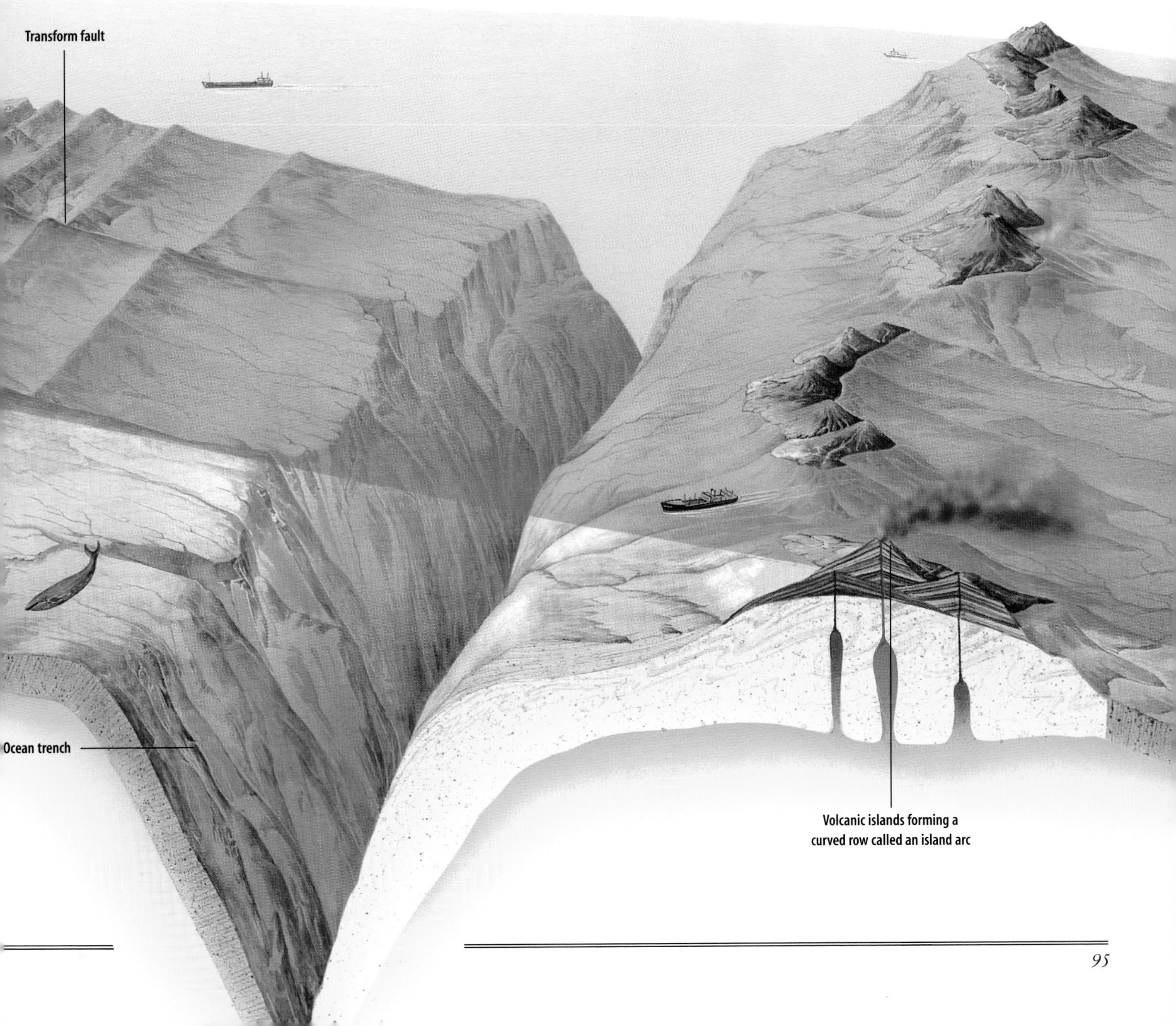

Transform fault

Ocean trench

Volcanic islands forming a curved row called an island arc

Tides

On most coasts, sea level rises and falls twice a day. The main cause of these tides is the pulling force of the Moon. Its gravitational attraction lifts the ocean surface on the side of the Earth facing the Moon. At the same time, the Earth's rotation tries to throw off water on the side of the Earth farthest from the Moon. These water bulges travel around the Earth at the same pace as the orbiting Moon, bringing high tides. In between are the troughs that cause low tides.

About twice a month, the combined pull of the Moon and the Sun creates the highest high tides and lowest low tides, called spring tides. In certain narrow bays these tides can rise higher than a house. Neap tides, with the smallest tidal range, occur between spring tides.

There are several factors that affect the behavior of tides. The Earth's rotation steers them to one side and slows them down, while coasts and seafloor ridges deflect or block them. Oceans are also divided into "tidal units." These units have a point at their center where there is no tide at all. The tidal range is greatest where waves move into shallow coastal water.

▷ Traditionally, fishermen in the Bay of Fundy, Nova Scotia, waited for low tide to collect fish that had been swept into staked nets by the high tide. The Bay of Fundy has the greatest tidal range on Earth.

△ Seawater pours through the barrage across the Rance Estuary, France. The rush of water spins turbine blades to generate electricity. Built in 1966, this was the world's first major tidal power plant.

▷ Spring tides (the highest high tides and lowest low tides) occur when the Moon and Sun line up, combining their gravitational pull. Weaker neap tides (the lowest high tides and the highest low tides) occur when the Moon and Sun pull at right angles. Spring tides happen at new and full moon. Neap tides coincide with the Moon's first and last quarters.

◁▽ *At low tide* (left), *a vast sandy beach links Mont St. Michel to mainland France. At high tide, the sea turns the rock into a small island.*

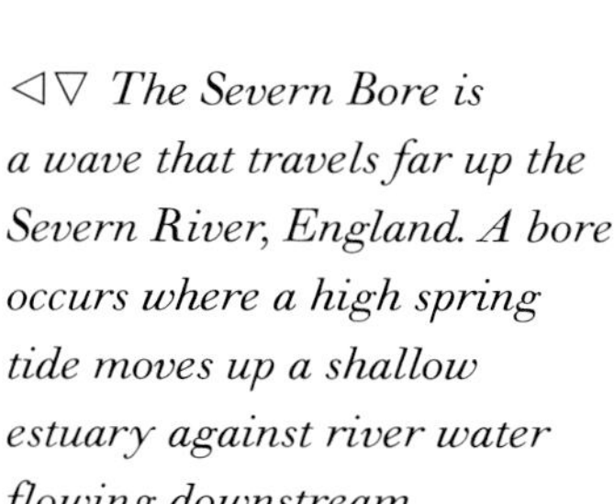

◁▽ *The Severn Bore is a wave that travels far up the Severn River, England. A bore occurs where a high spring tide moves up a shallow estuary against river water flowing downstream.*

Incoming tide

Tidal crest

River flow

Neap tides

Waves

Waves are raised by winds. A wave's size and speed depends on the win strength and its fetch—how far across the sea it blows. Strong, steady winds that blow across a great expanse of ocean can build huge smooth-topp waves called swells. The length between one crest and the next (the wavelength) can be over half a mile with speeds up to 35 mph (55 km/hr).

In 1933, during a North Pacific storm, a ship's officer measured a wave towering 112 feet (34.2 m) high. More than 60 years later this was still a wav height record for a storm wave. Its wavelength was nearly 1,310 feet (400 m)

Waves form rows of ridges and valleys moving through the water. Sometimes waves from two storms cross each other's path. If crest meets cres the waves increase in size. If crest meets trough (the bottom of the wave), th waves grow smaller. Waves meeting at right angles create a choppy sea.

The biggest waves to strike a shore are seismic sea waves, or tsunamis, set off by earthquakes, landslips, or volcanoes. Nearly 7,000 years ago, a tsunami wave 1,180 feet (360 m) high swamped the Shetland Islands.

△ *Floating objects in the open ocean often bob up and down on a passing wave without being carried along. Instead, the wave lifts the water particles that support the floating objects in a circular motion—up, forward, down, and back again.*

▷ *A huge ocean wave breaks inshore. As its crest rears up, the mass of water overbalances and starts to topple forward onto the shore.*

▷ *Fierce winds generate storm waves out at sea* (far right). *Hurricane-force winds can blow up to 105 mph (118 km/hr) and they may form waves more than 40 feet (13 m) high.*

A device installed on a
:indy coast is used to harness
:ve power. First, a wave
:ives air out of the chamber,
:inning the turbine blades
:at generate electricity. Then
:e wave recedes, letting in
:ore air for the next wave to
:ce out. This air trap system
:s been put to effective use
Ireland and Norway.

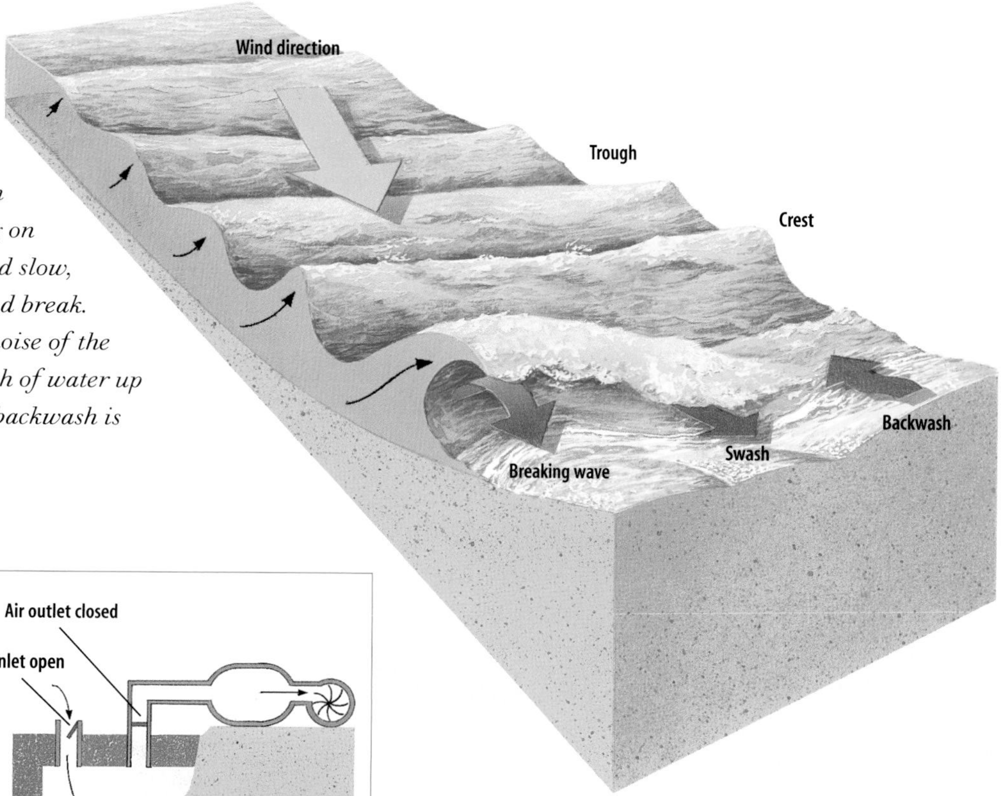

▷ *Wind-driven waves dragging on a shallow seabed slow, steepen, rise, and break. The swashing noise of the waves is the rush of water up the beach. The backwash is the return flow.*

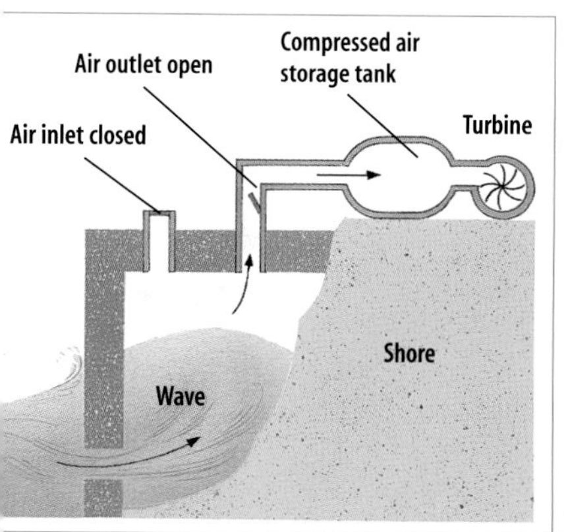

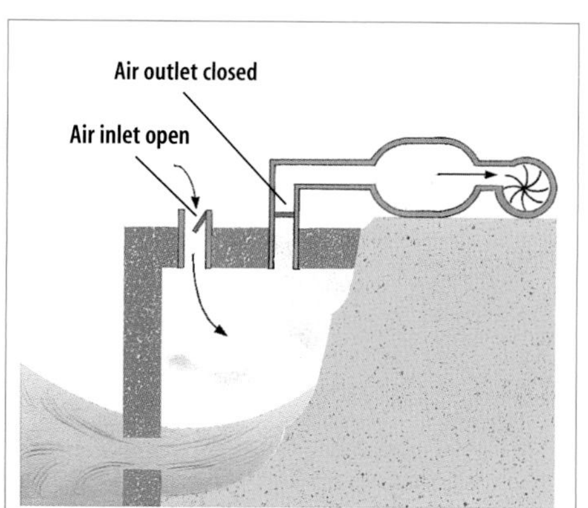

Fish

Sea fish are superbly adapted to life in the oceans. Their gills breathe oxygen dissolved in water. Most swim with powerful sweeps of the tail, steering and braking with fins. Nostrils, eyes, and vibration-sensitive cells on their flanks warn them of prey and predators.

Prey fish use various methods to avoid being eaten. Sardines swim in shoals for protection, their dark backs and pale bellies providing camouflage when viewed from above or below. If chased, flying fish leap from the sea and glide on winglike fins.

The great majority of the 20,000 different species of fish are bony fish. They have special bladders controlling the level at which they swim. Bony fish include tuna, sardines, flatfish such as flounder and sole, and sailfish—the world's fastest fish, which can reach speeds of up to 60 mph (100 km/hr).

The 600 cartilaginous, or gristly, kinds of fish include torpedo-shaped sharks and flat rays. Cartilaginous fish tend to sink unless they keep swimming.

△ The great white shark, the largest carnivorous fish, can weigh more than 1.5 tons. Some may grow to more than 20 feet (6 m) in length.

△ The distinctively-shaped ocean sunfish, or mola mola, appears to have more head than body. Weighing two tons or more, this weak swimmer is the heaviest of all bony fish.

△ A spiny "mane" gives the lionfish of the Indian and Pacific oceans its name. Its hollow spines are poisonous.

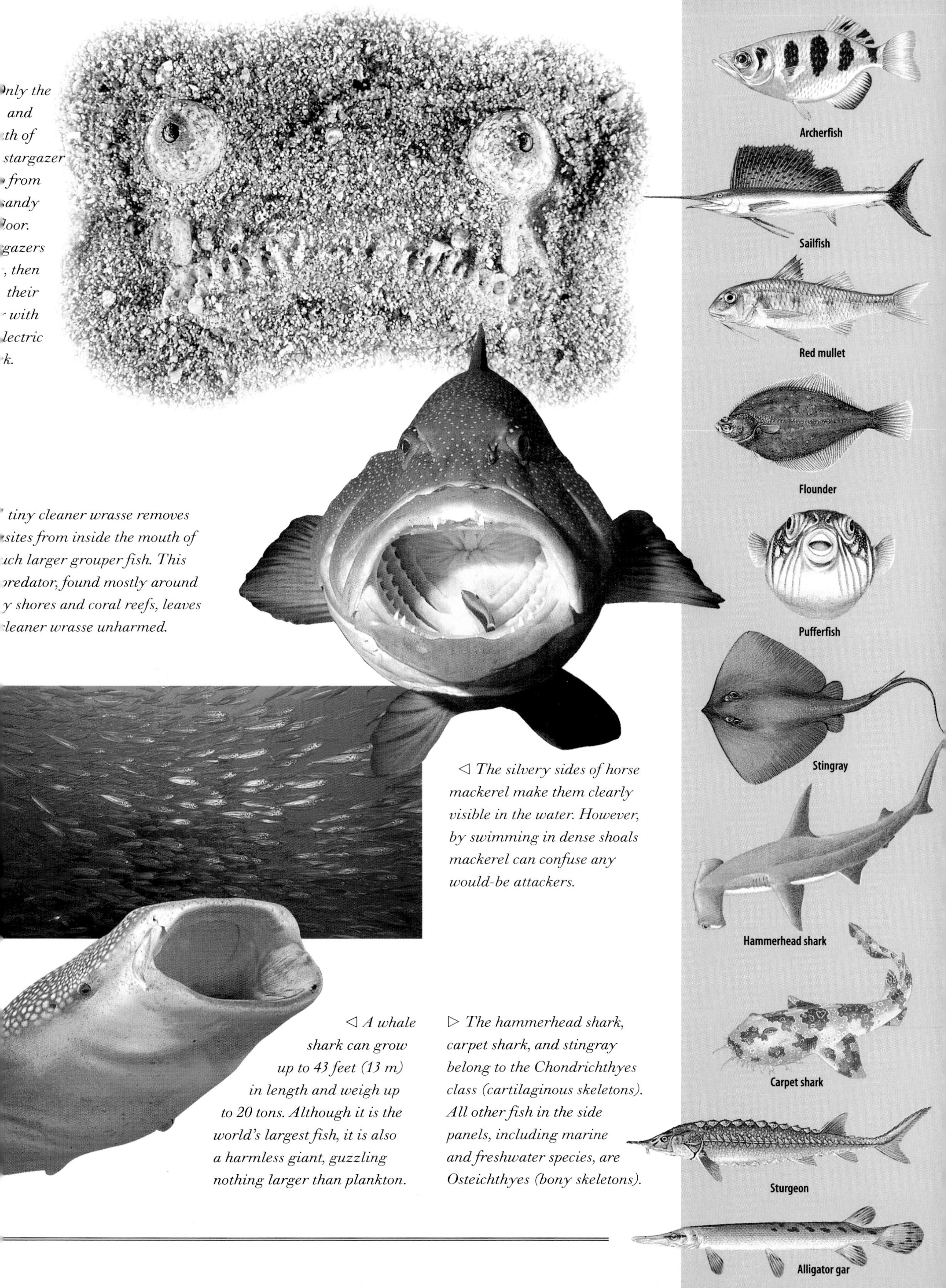

nly the and th of stargazer from andy loor. gazers , then their with lectric k.

tiny cleaner wrasse removes sites from inside the mouth of ich larger grouper fish. This redator, found mostly around y shores and coral reefs, leaves leaner wrasse unharmed.

◁ The silvery sides of horse mackerel make them clearly visible in the water. However, by swimming in dense shoals mackerel can confuse any would-be attackers.

◁ A whale shark can grow up to 43 feet (13 m) in length and weigh up to 20 tons. Although it is the world's largest fish, it is also a harmless giant, guzzling nothing larger than plankton.

▷ The hammerhead shark, carpet shark, and stingray belong to the Chondrichthyes class (cartilaginous skeletons). All other fish in the side panels, including marine and freshwater species, are Osteichthyes (bony skeletons).

Sea Mammals

Mammals are warm-blooded creatures that cannot breathe under water, yet millions of years ago some took to the sea to find food. Their descendants developed into expert swimmers, with flipper-shaped limbs and thick body fat to protect them against the deadly cold of the water.

Seals, sea lions, and walruses are graceful swimmers in water, but clumsy movers on land. Most come ashore only to breed or rest. Other sea mammals, such as sea cows and whales, cannot leave the sea at all, although their ancestors could. In 1994, scientists discovered the 50 million year old fossil of *Ambulocetus*, a small whale with hind legs.

Whales either have teeth or whalebone (baleen) plates. Toothed whales mainly hunt fish or squid, although killer whales seize penguins, seals, and even other whales. A baleen whale's plates trap tiny fish or plankton when it squirts out a mouthful of water. Baleens include the blue whale—the largest of all animals.

△ Male northern elephant seals fight for control of a beach. A victorious male mates with the females on the beach he controls.

▽ Manatees are distantly related to elephants. Their paddle-shaped forelimbs anc flat tails makes them powerf swimmers. Manatees never come ashore. They eat plant. growing in warm, shallow Atlantic waters and rivers.

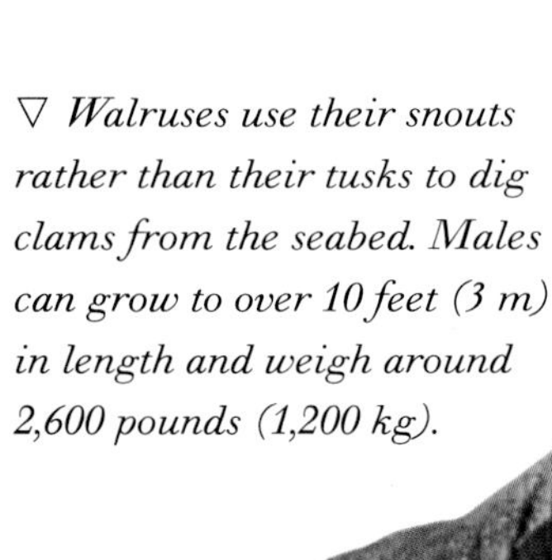

▽ Walruses use their snouts rather than their tusks to dig clams from the seabed. Males can grow to over 10 feet (3 m) in length and weigh around 2,600 pounds (1,200 kg).

△ *Sperm whales are toothed whales up to 65 feet (20 m) in length and weighing up to 70 tons. Males can dive 9,800 feet (3,000 m) to hunt squid on the seabed, and stay down for nearly two hours.*

△ *The largest creatures on Earth, blue whales can grow up to 110 feet (33 m) long and weigh more than 170 tons. Until their slaughter was banned, they were hunted almost to extinction.*

▽ *Sea otters eat and sleep on their backs. They swim off North Pacific coasts and feed on crabs, clams, fish, and mussels. A sea otter often uses its front paws to grasp a shellfish and smash it open against a rock balanced on its belly.*

3ottle-nosed dolphins are ɪll, fast, toothed whales with like fins and flippers. These ceful creatures hunt fish varm or tropical waters ɪund the world.

△ *The streamlined bodies of California sea lions make them very agile in the water. They hunt for fish among the kelp forests off the west coast of North America.*

Coral Reefs

Coral reefs are found in warm, shallow seas and oceans. A reef is made up from billions of little stony cups, most no bigger than a thumbnail. Each cup once hid a tiny coral polyp, a creature related to sea anemones and jellyfish. When the polyp dies, it leaves behind a hard, outer skeleton over which new polyps begin to grow. Colonies of living polyps create green, purple, orange, and yellow corals shaped like crusts, brains, branches, fans, or stags' horns.

Coral reefs support a huge variety of life. Sponges, sea anemones, lionfish, sea slugs, and predators such as sea snakes, groupers, and barracudas are just a few of the reef's many inhabitants. In fact, one-third of all fish species can be found on coral reefs.

The reef provides each creature with a plentiful food supply. Sponges suck in tiny organisms, and sea anemones paralyze and eat small fish. Butterflyfish probe coral heads for crustaceans and mollusks. Certain creatures, such as the crown-of-thorns starfish, feed on the coral itself.

▽ Coral reefs are found in clear, shallow water where the temperature is never less than 68°F (20°C). Coral polyps—the tiny creatures that build the reef —thrive in these light and warm conditions.

◁ Creatures of the coral reef include the sea turtle (1), the manta ray (2), and lionfish (3), which has deadly poisonous spines. The brilliant colors of the sea snail (4), nudibranch (5), and starfish (6) make them stand out against the other species. Top predators, such as the grouper (7) and sea snake (8), live among the sponges (9) and corals (10). The coral-

▽ A single coral colony can support hundreds of different animal and plant species. Although reef-forming coral grows only a few inches each year, many reefs started developing over 10,000 years ago. This long period has given reefdwellers

Life in the Depths

Most sea creatures depend on plantlike phytoplankton for their food supply, but not much of this can flourish in the dim light below 590 feet (180 m). Creatures of the twilight zone (490–3,280 feet/1,000 m deep) eat one another, or survive on dead animals and algae that rain down from above. Some swim up to feed at night, camouflaged by darkness. Down here, sharks find prey by scent or vibrations set off by their prey's bodies. Other inhabitants include swarms of squid, shrimp, prawns, and billions of deep-sea copepods.

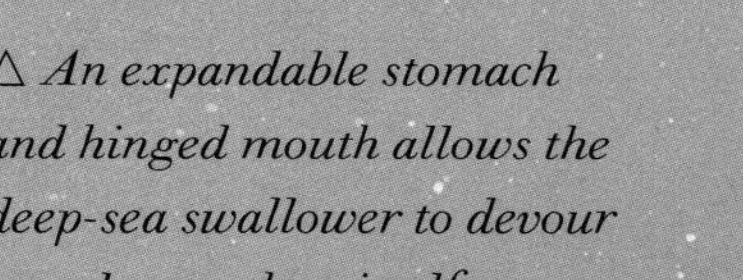

Black bodies conceal some fish from their enemies at these levels. Lanternfish and hatchet fish, however, glow with little lights or shine with silvery, reflective sides to confuse their predators.

No light penetrates below 3,280 feet (1,000 m). Small, flabby fish live here, such as viperfish and gulper eels with fanged jaws and elastic stomachs for the rare big meals that come their way. Few of these ferocious-looking deep-sea fish are more than 12 inches

△ *An expandable stomach and hinged mouth allows the deep-sea swallower to devour prey larger than itself.*

◁ *The razor-sharp fangs of the viperfish make it an effective predator. Like many deep-sea fish, the viperfish swims open-jawed, catching any prey between its sharp teeth before swallowing.*

▽ *The various species that survive in the depths of the ocean are rarely more than 12 inches (30 cm) long. Some live deeper than others, and several swim to the surface at night. Many have developed special adaptations to survive in this extreme environment. The viperfish (1) and lanternfish (2) have light organs on their bodies to confuse their enemies. Others such as the anglerfish (3) and stomiatoid (4) use luminous lures to attract prey. Male anglerfish sometimes attach themselves to the much larger female anglerfish (5) and live there permanently. The vicious teeth of the fangtooth (6) earn this hunter its name, while the pelicanlike mouth of the gulper eel (7) is almost a quarter the length of its body.*

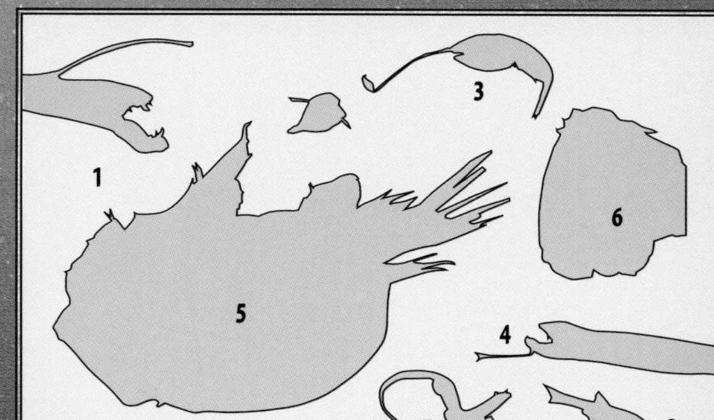

Rocky Shores

Where the sea meets the land, either might gain the upper hand. In some places the land thrusts out into the sea. Elsewhere the sea eats into the land. Storm waves can undermine a sloping coast until its top tumbles and it becomes a wave-washed boulder beach backed by a retreating sea cliff.

Rocky shores are battered by storm waves and drowned by high tides. They bake in the heat and almost freeze during cold spells. Organisms found on rocky shores have evolved to survive and make the most of the conditions.

Water buoys up the fronds of seaweed while their rootlike holdfasts prevent waves from wrenching them off the rocks. Sea squirts, sponges, sea anemones, acorn barnacles, and mussels also attach themselves to rocks. They eat scraps of food washed in with the tide. Limpets and top shells graze algae growing on the boulders, while dog whelks bore holes in fellow mollusks' shells and eat their flesh. At low tide, the shells of acorn barnacles and limpets keep them safe from predators and ensure their insides remain moist.

Tide pools hold water even at low tide. Crustaceans, such as shrimp and crabs, ferocious ragworms, starfish, and small fish all find food and hiding places here.

△ Some tide pools have sandy floors. Marine creatures such as this common shrimp can burrow into the sand to avoid predators.

◁ Over time, the endless pounding of waves has cut an arch through Gaada Stack in the Shetland Islands, north of Scotland's mainland. The sea is the main cause of coastal erosion.

△ Toppled boulders litter the shore around a rocky beach at Pondfield Cove in Dorset, England. Ti[...] pools, along with cracks and crevices in rocks and caves, provide a home for a large variety of creatures.

Pencil urchins have long, ...ad spines with sharp ends. ...ider tube feet with strong ...kers drag it along and hold ... place. The urchin's mouth ...elow the middle of its body.

◁ *The sea cucumber is related to starfish and sea urchins. It can grow up to 12 inches (30 cm) long. At low tide it can wedge itself into rock crevices. When a sea cucumber is threatened, it squirts out sticky threads to entangle an attacker.*

▽ *Rootlike holdfasts anchor this brown seaweed to a rock. The flexible fronds extending from the holdfasts prevent the seaweed from being ripped apart by the waves.*

▽ *A beadlet anemone's sticky base keeps it firmly attached to hard surfaces. Stinging cells in its tentacles stun small prey. At low tide, or when threatened, anemones withdraw their tentacles back into their bodies.*

◁ *Shells protect common limpets against enemies and drying out. At high tide they search for seaweed on rocks. After feeding, limpets always return to the same spot.*

Sand and Pebbles

Pebbly and sandy beaches often form gently shelving shores. Pebbles are stones that have broken off a rocky coast and been rubbed smooth against one another by waves. Most sand grains are specks of ground-down pebbles. Waves coming ashore at an angle drive pebbles and sand along a coast, sort them into sizes, and then drop them in sheltered waters where they accumulate and form beaches. Bay-head beaches develop between headlands (cliffs jutting out into the sea). Others include lowland beaches backed by dunes, bars (offshore beaches), and spits (beaches growing out into the sea).

Few organisms can survive the crushing force of stones rolled up and down a pebble beach by waves. A sandy beach also poses problems.

▷ *This gently sloping beach in California was built from eroded sea cliff ground down by the sea. Wind-driven waves have carried and piled up pebbles along the water's edge.*

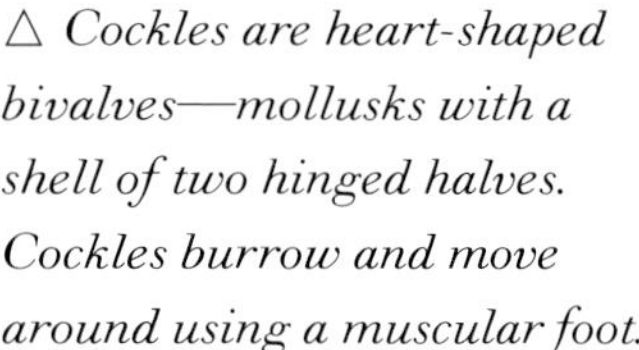

△ *Cockles are heart-shaped bivalves—mollusks with a shell of two hinged halves. Cockles burrow and move around using a muscular foot.*

▽ *Razor shells are long, narrow bivalves that bury themselves in the sand. At high tide their feeding tubes poke above the sand to suck in plankton carried in by the water.*

◁ *Winds have shifted sand and built up dunes behind t beach in Scotland. Marram grass, rooted in the loose sa helps to fix the dunes in pla*

The sand dries out in the sun, shifts in storms and lacks rocks for animals to grip or hide beneath. Even so, millions of burrowing creatures find safety a few inches underneath the surface of a sandy beach.

At low tide, tiny pits and bumps betray an invisible army of worms, mollusks, crabs, shrimp, echinoderms, such as heart urchins and sand stars. At high tide, some burrowers climb out and swim or crawl in search of food. Others stay put and suck in plankton through feeding tubes, or poke out tentacles to capture passing morsels. Lugworms remain buried, extracting nourishment from muddy sand.

Even burrowing does not always give protection to small inhabitants of sandy shores. At high tide, fish swim inshore to snap up the unwary. At low tide, wading birds with long, sensitive beaks pry molluscs from their crumbly caves.

◁ *Grunions lay their eggs on the beaches of southern California between February and September. These small fish wait until night, when very high tides sweep them up onto the sandy shores.*

▽ *A lugworm* (left) *sucks in sand containing scraps of food and squirts out waste in coils. At low tide, a hole betrays its burrow on the beach.*

When a masked crab rows in the sand, it draws ter through its long tube ennae. At high tide it wls out of the sand to feed.

Early Ocean Explorers

△ Brendan, *an ox-hide boat, was sailed from Ireland to Newfoundland by the British adventurer Tim Severin in 1976. Old Irish writings hint that an Irish monk reached North America in a boat made from animal skins in about A.D. 570. Severin's expedition proved it was possible to make this voyage in a similar boat.*

Tens of thousands of years ago, people were making sea crossings by canoe or raft to settle empty continents. The Old Stone Age ancestors of Australia's Aborigines arrived by sea from Southeast Asia at least 60,000 years ago.

From about 3000 B.C. Micronesian, Melanesian, and Polynesian seafarers began to discover the islands of the Sout Pacific. By A.D. 1000 the Polynesians, the greatest of these ear ocean explorers, had settled all the major islands lying in the area bounded by Hawaii, New Zealand, and Easter Island. Th islands form the tips of a vast triangle covering almost 8 million square mil (20 million sq km).

Farther west, Bronze Age traders and explorers were making daring voya in fragile sailing ships. Reed ships probably traded across the Arabian Sea 4, years ago. A thousand years later, wooden cargo ships sailed the Mediterran carrying precious goods such as gold, ostrich eggs, and ivory.

Experts disagree about which navigator first reached North America. Vikings had sailed to Newfoundland from Greenland by A.D. 1000. However, it is also possible that Chinese sailors, ancient Egyptians, or an Irish monk m have set foot in Nort America much earlie

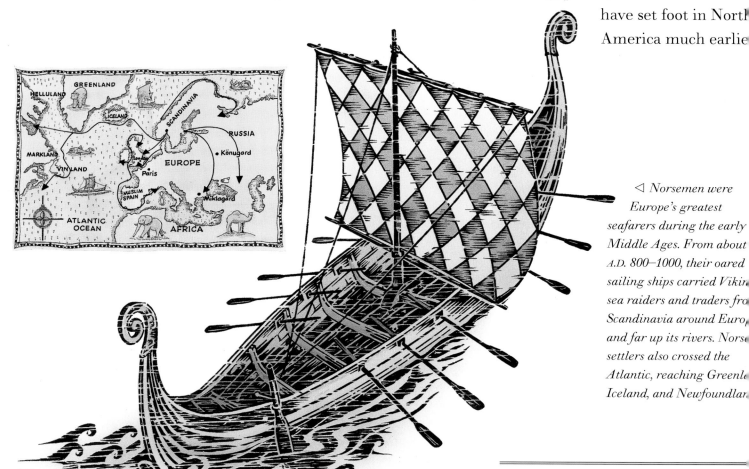

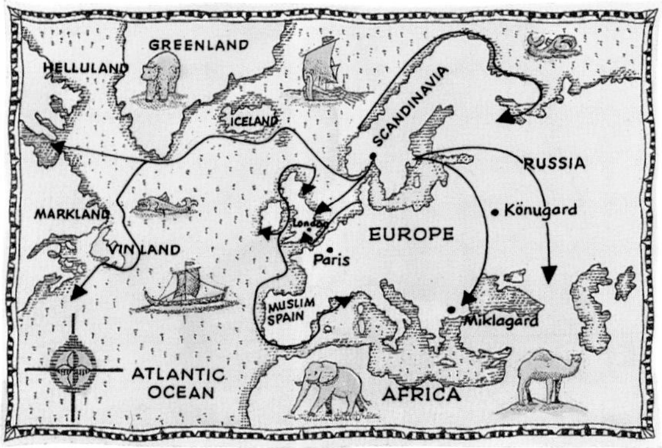

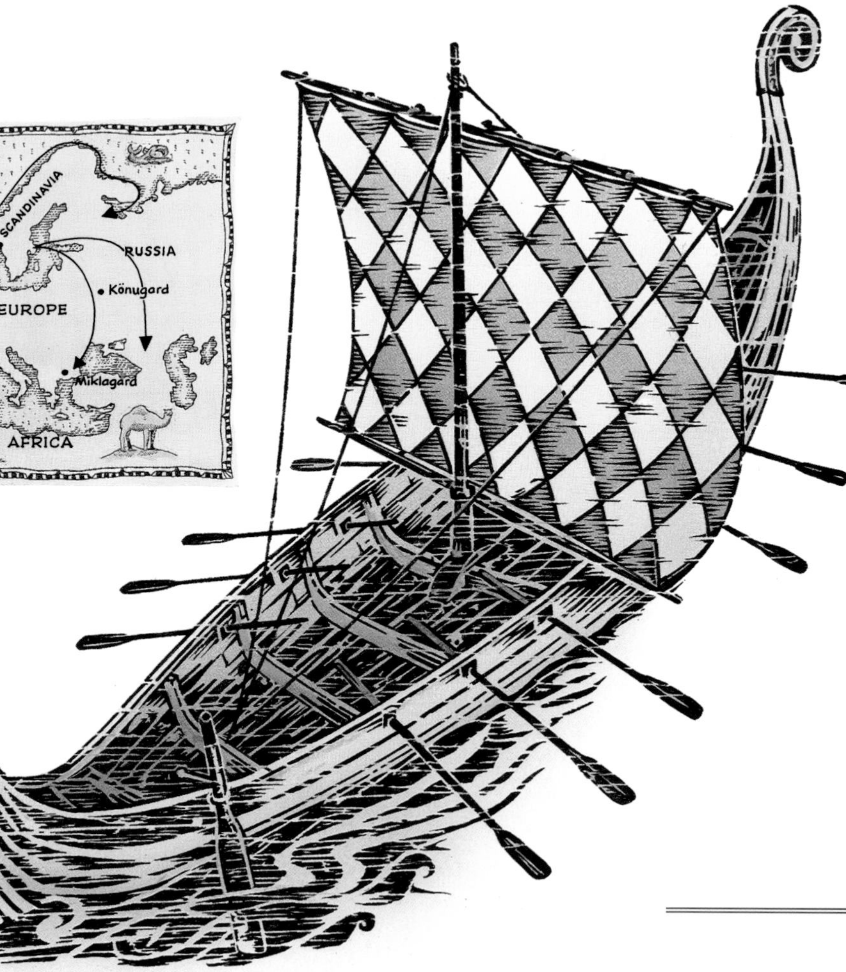

◁ *Norsemen were Europe's greatest seafarers during the early Middle Ages. From about A.D. 800–1000, their oared sailing ships carried Viki sea raiders and traders fro Scandinavia around Euro and far up its rivers. Nors settlers also crossed the Atlantic, reaching Greenl Iceland, and Newfoundla*

The Pacific islands lying in vast Polynesian triangle ned by Hawaii, New land, and Easter Island e settled by voyagers n about 1500 B.C. They l two canoes, fixed ther with a platform, arry passengers, nals, and plants.

n 1970, Norwegian lorer Thor Heyerdahl ed from Morocco to Caribbean in a reed t. He believed that this rney showed that ancient yptians from North Africa d similar boats to reach Americas thousands ears ago.

△ *Thor Heyerdahl holding a model reed boat. His 1947 voyage in the raft* Kon-Tiki *showed that ancient seafarers from South America may have reached the Polynesian islands before settlers from the west.*

The Age of Exploration

▽ *These modern replicas of Christopher Columbus's ships* Santa Maria, Niña, *and* Pinta *set sail from Spain in 1992. Five hundred years earlier, Columbus's fleet of three ships, sponsored by Queen Isabella of Spain, crossed the Atlantic and reached the Bahamas.*

Five centuries ago, sailors from Europe began crisscrossing the oceans and exploring the world. In the 1400s, improved navigation aids and new sailing ships, called caravels and carracks, gave European navigators the confidence to sail beyond the sight of land. First, Portugal sent caravels do the west coast of Africa to bypass hostile Mediterranea powers and find a new sea route to the spice-rich lanc of India and Southeast Asia. By 1488, Bartholomew Dias had rounded the tip of southern Afric and by 1499, Vasco da Gama had sailed to India and back.

△ *Henry the Navig (1394–1460) played major part in starti off the great age of ocean exploration b European seafarers. This Portugese prin organized and sent 50 naval expedition Many explored the coast of Africa as fa south as Sierra Leo*

Soon Spain was competing with Portugal for Asian trade. 1492, Christopher Columbus sailed west to seek a transatlantic ıte to Asia on behalf of the Spanish crown. Instead he found e islands of the Caribbean, marking the start of Spain's nquest of the Americas. In 1519, Ferdinand Magellan led a ree-year Spanish expedition which became the first to cumnavigate the world and prove that it was round. But war, ease, and shipwreck took its toll—of the five ships and 241 en who set out, only the *Victoria* and 19 men returned.

Little by little such journeys helped cartographers to map the ges of the oceans. Major discoveries were still being made in e 1700s. Between 1768 and 1779, Captain James Cook led three itish voyages of exploration probing the Pacific and visiting ıstralia, New Zealand, and Hawaii.

△ *The* Victoria *was the only surviving ship from a fleet of five that set out to circle the globe in 1519. Its return to Spain three years later proved to Europeans that the world was round.*

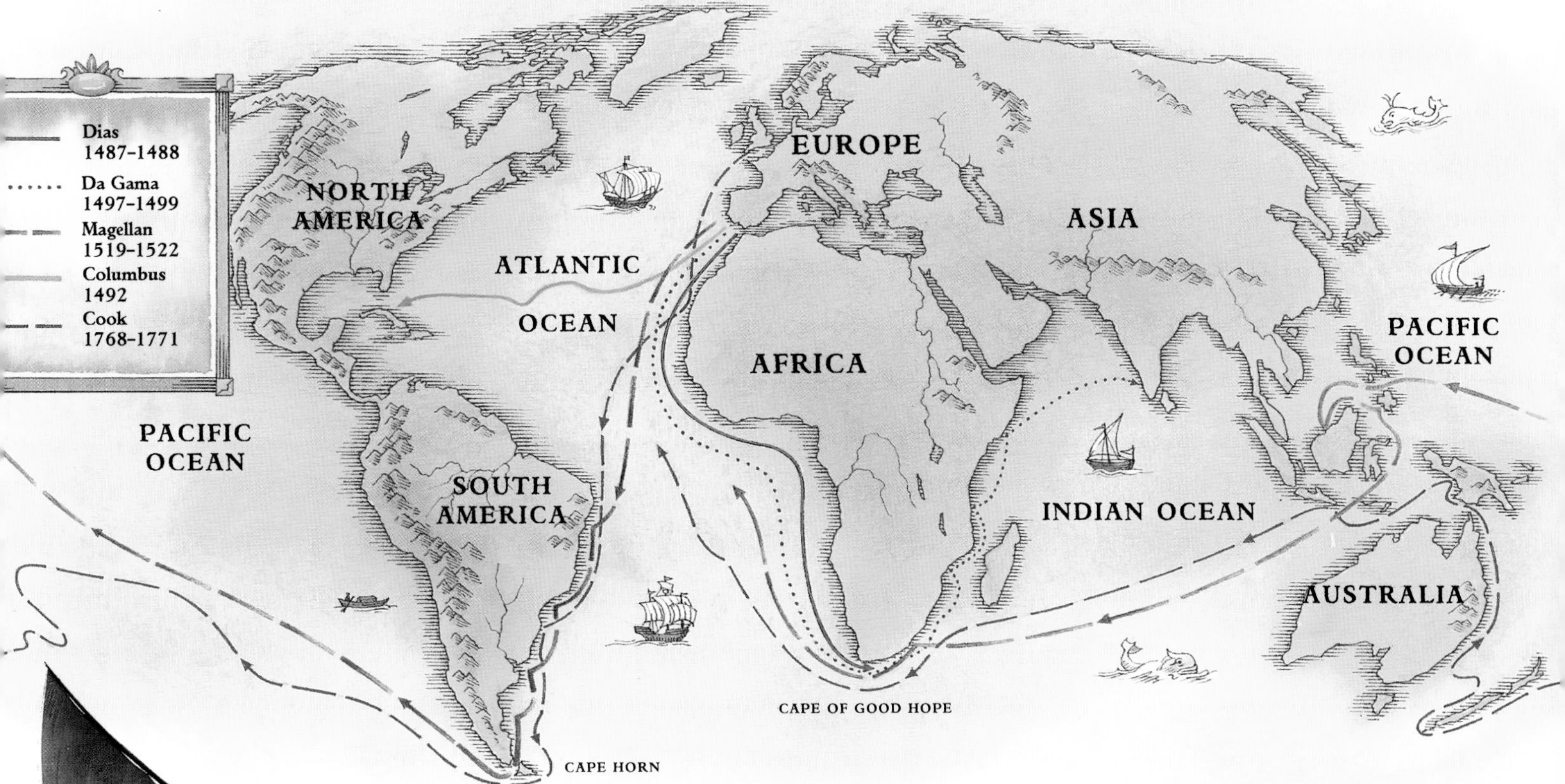

◁ *An Arab* dhow*—a type of boat in use for over 1,300 years—moves against the wind by angling its lateen, or triangular, sail. Spanish and Portugese ship designers in the 1400s copied this type of sail to make their vessels faster and more maneuverable.*

△ *Five great voyages of exploration helped to open up the world. Bartholomew Dias rounded the Cape of Good Hope and discovered a sea route to the East. Vasco da Gama was the first European to reach India by sea. Christopher Columbus crossed the Atlantic, reaching the Americas. Ferdinand Magellan's expedition circled the world, and James Cook's voyages charted the coasts and islands of the Pacific.*

Advances in Navigation

Without navigation equipment it is easy to become lost in the open ocean. Most early sailors kept within sight of land, but bolder mariners steered by steady winds or currents, or by following migrating birds. Even so, many lost their way before more accurate navigation aids were invented.

By 1200, the magnetic compass was being used by European sailors to plot direction. Later, the astrola and cross staff enabled them to find their latitude (north–south position) by measuring the Sun's midday height or the North Star's height at nigh

By the 1500s, latitude could be measured wit some accuracy. Longitude (east–west position) remained a problem for another two centuries. Measuring longitude, which relied on precise tim keeping, was finally made possible in the 1760s wit the development of accurate clocks called chronomet

The twentieth century saw many advances in navigation. Gyroscopic compasses, which are unaffected b magnetic forces, always give exact readings. Loran (long-rang navigation) allows a ship to determine its position using radio signals beamed from a pair of transmitters. Radar helps a navigator locate obstructions, while ships' computers receivin signals from satellites can plot positions to within 100 feet (30

△ *In the 1500s, navigators used the astrolabe to calculate latitude by observing the Sun at midday.*

△ *At night, a navigator held a cross staff to his eye and slid the cross piece to line up with the horizon and a star. A scale along the cross staff's arm gave the star's height, enabling the ship's latitude to be measured.*

▽ *In the late 1500s, the maps of Gerardus Mercator introduced a new way of showing the globe on a flat piece of paper. His system, which used lines of latitude and longitude, helped navigators plot more accurate routes.*

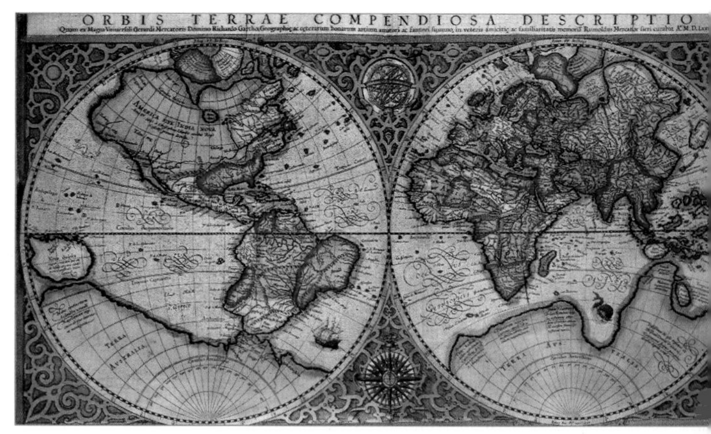

◁ *The English naturalist Charles Darwin used this sextant on his voyage around the world betwen 1831 and 1836. Sextants are still used today to determine latitude.*

n this Micronesian stick , curved sticks stand for n swells and the shells esent islands. Micronesian arers used such maps to t parts of the Pacific.

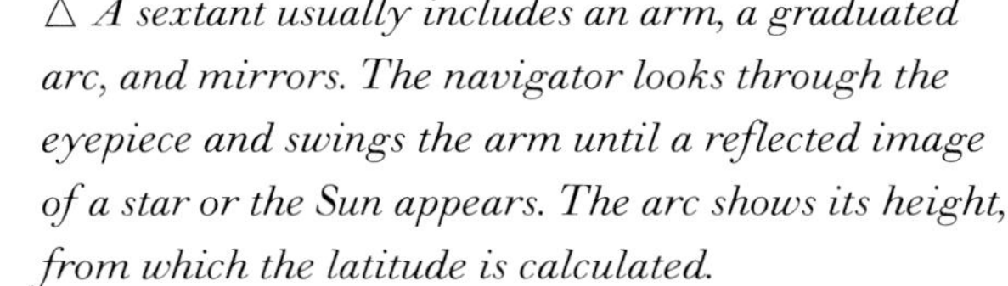

△ *A sextant usually includes an arm, a graduated arc, and mirrors. The navigator looks through the eyepiece and swings the arm until a reflected image of a star or the Sun appears. The arc shows its height, from which the latitude is calculated.*

l radar screen helps a igator to plot a course. lar bounces radio signals a target. The returning als indicate the position bstructions and other els even in thick fog.

▷ *Harrison's chronometer of 1760 allowed longitude to be measured by comparing the time in London with the local midday time. This enabled navigators to calculate their east–west position accurately.*

The Sea and the Arts

Over the last 250 years the sea has inspired many composers, writers, and painters. But the sea has not always been a subject in its own right. In paintings of the 1400s and 1500s, for example, it was used as a background for gods and goddesses, or historical events.

From the late 1700s, however, the sea began to loom large in poems, paintings, and music. Some artists saw it as a world of terror and mystery, others as a place of gently changing moods or as a setting for pleasure.

Artists such as William Hodges and J. M. W. Turner painted the sea to show nature at its most powerful. Their pictures show the helplessness of people in the face of an overwhelming sea storm or waterspout. The terrifying dangers of the open sea are brilliantly caught in the shipwreck paintings of Winslow Homer. Mystery and terror also feature in works of literature and music, such as Herman Melville's novel *Moby Dick* and Richard Wagner's opera *The Flying Dutchman.*

△ *Winds that blow across the sea are given human form in this detail from* Birth of Venus (see bottom right).

The sea's changing moods fascinated French impressionist painters of the late 1800s, as well as composers from Felix Mendelssohn to Benjamin Britten. The opera *Peter Grimes,* written by Britten in 1945, shows the sea raging in a storm, glinting in the sun, and sulking in the fog.

△ *A whale snatches up a boat in a poster for a movie based on* Moby Dick, *the novel by the American writer Herman Melville (1819–1891). This adventure tells the story of Captain Ahab's fanatical hunt to catch a fierce white whale that eventually kills him.*

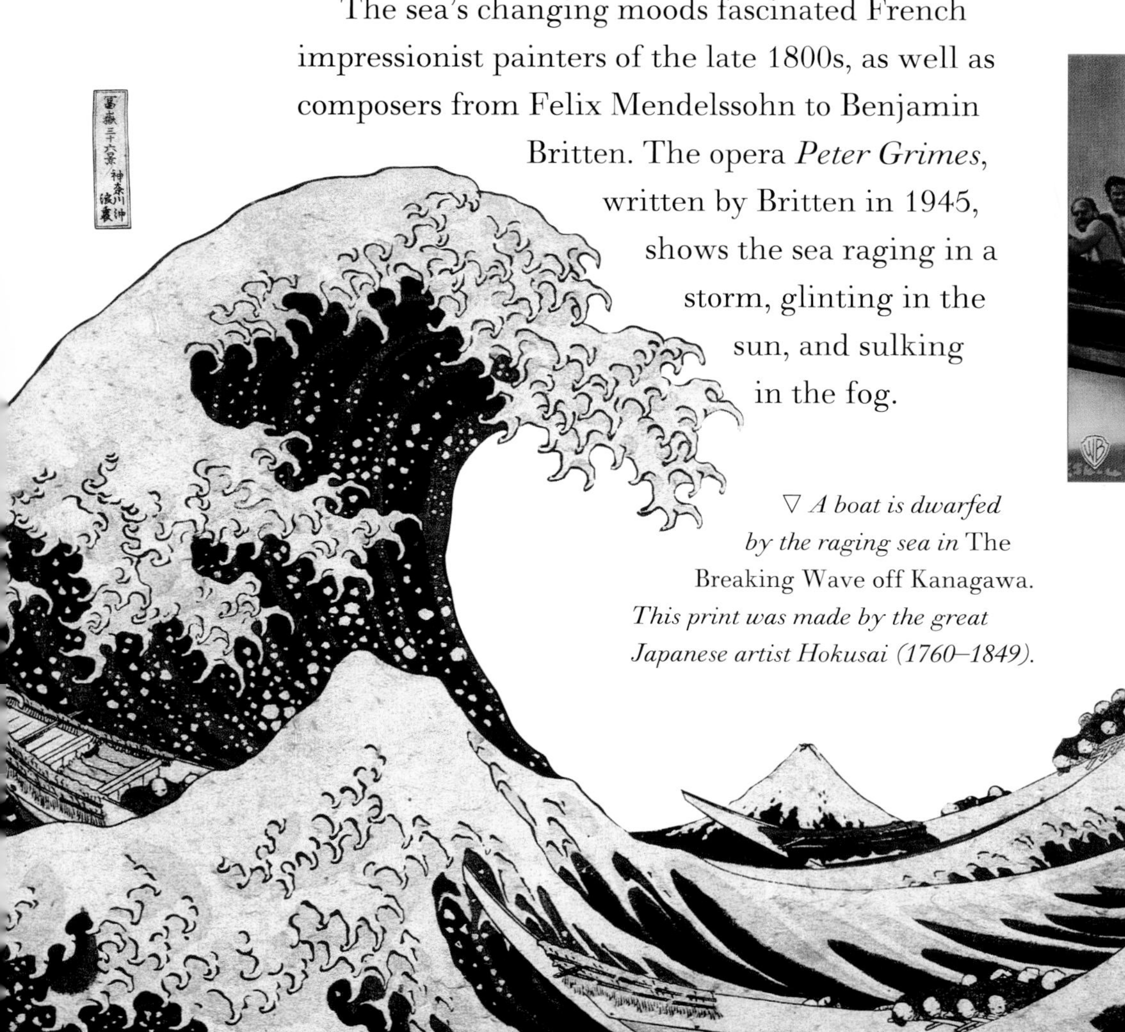

▽ *A boat is dwarfed by the raging sea in* The Breaking Wave off Kanagawa. *This print was made by the great Japanese artist Hokusai (1760–1849).*

◁ *A lone man drifts helplessly on a battered boat circled by sharks.* The Gulf Stream, *by the American artist Winslow Homer (1836–1910), captures human powerlessness when faced by one of the ocean's many dangers.*

△ *A visit to the Scottish island of Staffa inspired the German composer Felix Mendelssohn (1809–1847) to compose* The Hebrides (Fingal's Cave).

A sandy beach crowded with hers features in The Beach ront of the Casino Café, *by American artist Martha lter (1875–1976). By the mid-1800s railroads had put coasts within easy reach of city-dwellers. Artists began to paint the seaside as a popular playground for vacationers.*

▷ *The sea provided little more than a background for Renaissance paintings, such as* Birth of Venus. *This picture by the Italian artist Sandro Botticelli (1445–1510) is based on a Greek myth. It tells the story of how Venus—the goddess of love—was born in the sea and blown ashore in a seashell.*

Food from the Sea

△ *A wood and wire cage, filled with lobsters caught off the coast of Brazil, is raised from the sea. Lobster pots, or traps, are baited with fish or fish offal and lowered to the seabed.*

Fish provide much of the world's protein food supply. Every year, about 75 million tons of fish are caught. The richest fishing grounds lie where seawater contains plenty of nutrients for the plankton on which fish depend. Mackerel, pollack, herring and tuna are important pelagic, or surface-living, fish. Popular demersal, or bottom-living, fish include cod, flounder, plaice, haddock, and shellfish such as crabs, lobsters, and shrimp.

Inshore, nets are thrown and traps set by hand to catch fish, crabs, and octopuses. Out at sea, sonar devices help fishing boats track down large shoals, and special nets or hooks catch fish living at different depths. Trawlers hunt demersal species by dragging trawl nets over the seabed. Purse seine nets are pulled shut to trap mid-water species. Pelagic fish are either snared on long curtainlike drift net hung from buoys, or caught on baited hooks attached to long lines.

Small craft may supply one big factory ship, where fish are gutted, frozen, and stored for several weeks. A factory trawler may catch and process up to 600 tons a day. However, intensive fishing can also threaten ocean resources. Overfishing has dramatically reduced the stocks of some species.

▷ *The plaice is a species of bottom-dwelling flatfish. It is of great commercial value for the European fishing industry. Trawlers catch plaice in nets dragged along the seabed.*

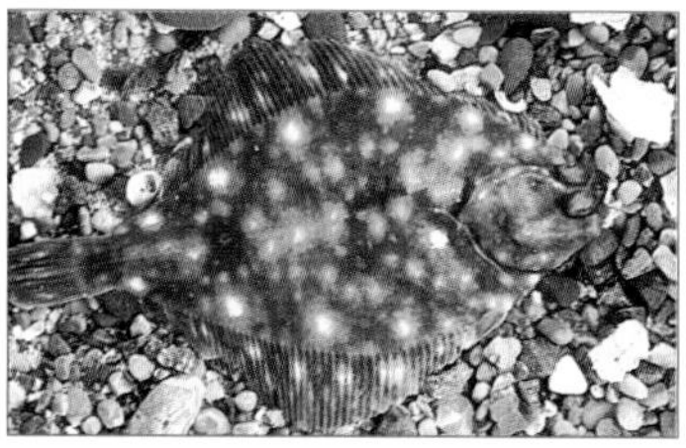

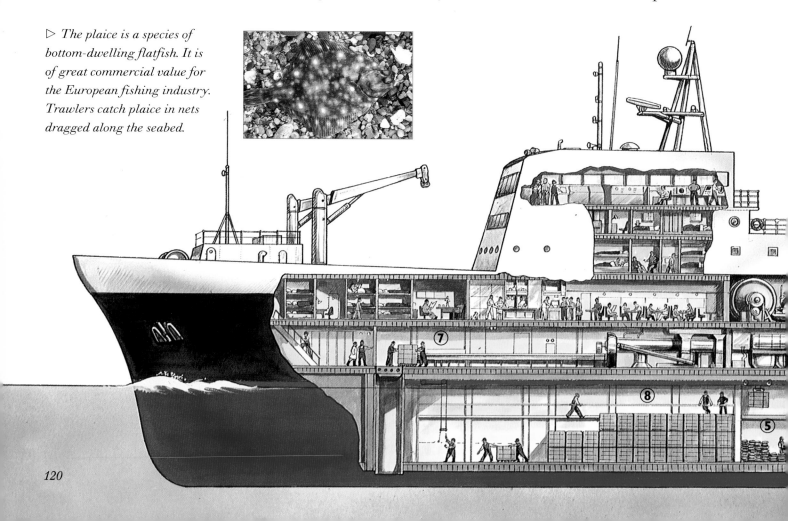

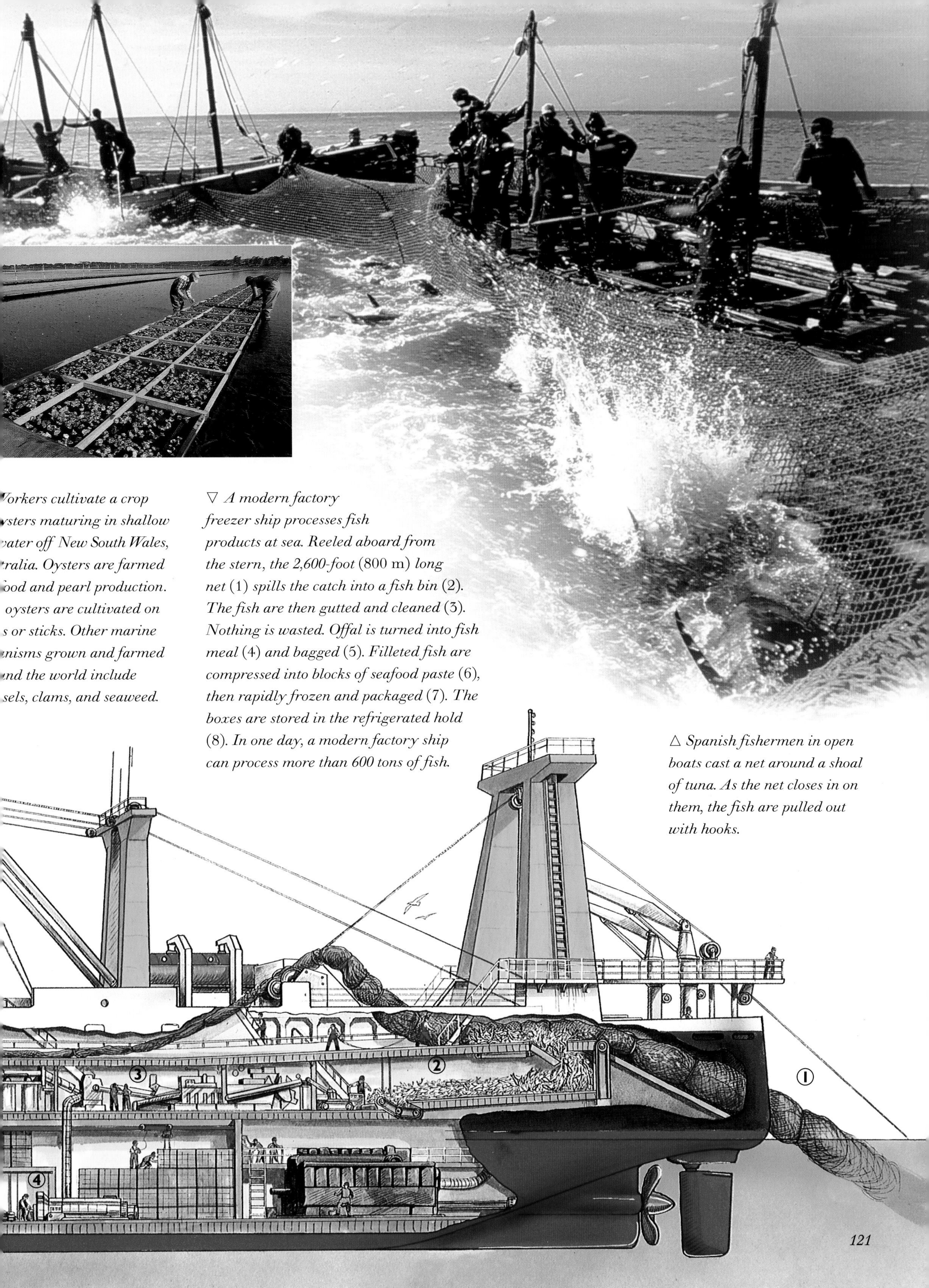

Vorkers cultivate a crop
ysters maturing in shallow
vater off New South Wales,
tralia. Oysters are farmed
food and pearl production.
oysters are cultivated on
s or sticks. Other marine
anisms grown and farmed
und the world include
ssels, clams, and seaweed.

▽ *A modern factory freezer ship processes fish products at sea. Reeled aboard from the stern, the 2,600-foot* (800 m) *long net* (1) *spills the catch into a fish bin* (2). *The fish are then gutted and cleaned* (3). *Nothing is wasted. Offal is turned into fish meal* (4) *and bagged* (5). *Filleted fish are compressed into blocks of seafood paste* (6), *then rapidly frozen and packaged* (7). *The boxes are stored in the refrigerated hold* (8). *In one day, a modern factory ship can process more than 600 tons of fish.*

△ *Spanish fishermen in open boats cast a net around a shoal of tuna. As the net closes in on them, the fish are pulled out with hooks.*

Hidden Dangers

△ *Even in clear weather, icebergs can be a danger to ships that sail too close— 88 percent of a castle iceberg lurks invisibly under the sea.*

▽ *An aerial photograph shows salvage work on the wrecked and still smoking* Piper Alpha *oil platform. The explosion, in 1988, sparked off by a gas leak, caused the North Sea's worst-ever oil rig disaster.*

Ships face many dangers at sea. Icebergs that have drifted from polar regions into shipping lanes are one of the most feared of all naturally-occurring hazards. In 1912, just over 1,500 people drowned when the liner *Titanic* hit an iceberg. After this disaster, ice patrols began to keep watch for dangerous, drifting icebergs in the North Atlantic.

Underwater rocks and reefs have also been a risk since ships first put to sea. Shifting sandbanks are another invisible menace. Since 1500, more than 5,000 ships have foundered on the Goodwin Sands off southeast England. In recent years, several supertankers have run aground off Alaska, France, and England.

Disasters have also been caused by human errors such as faulty ship design, overloading, navigational mistakes, and even the failure to close a car ferry's sea doors. Poor maintenance killed 167 people in 1988 when a fire at sea gutted the *Piper Alpha* platform, a North Sea oil rig. However, the greatest of all sea catastrophes occured during World War II when a Soviet submarine sank the German liner *Wilhelm Gustloff* and 7,700 passengers lost their lives.

◁ *In 1912, newspaper headlines around the world reported the sinking of the ocean liner* Titanic. *On her maiden voyage from England to New York City, the world's largest ship struck an iceberg in the freezing waters of the North Atlantic. Believed to be unsinkable, the double-hulled liner sank in about two and a half hours with the loss of over 1,500 lives.*

In 1993, the tanker ıaer *leaked oil and sank* er *grounding on rocks off* *Shetland Islands. Even* rse *oil spills have occurred* en *supertankers have* ıgged *on hidden reefs.*

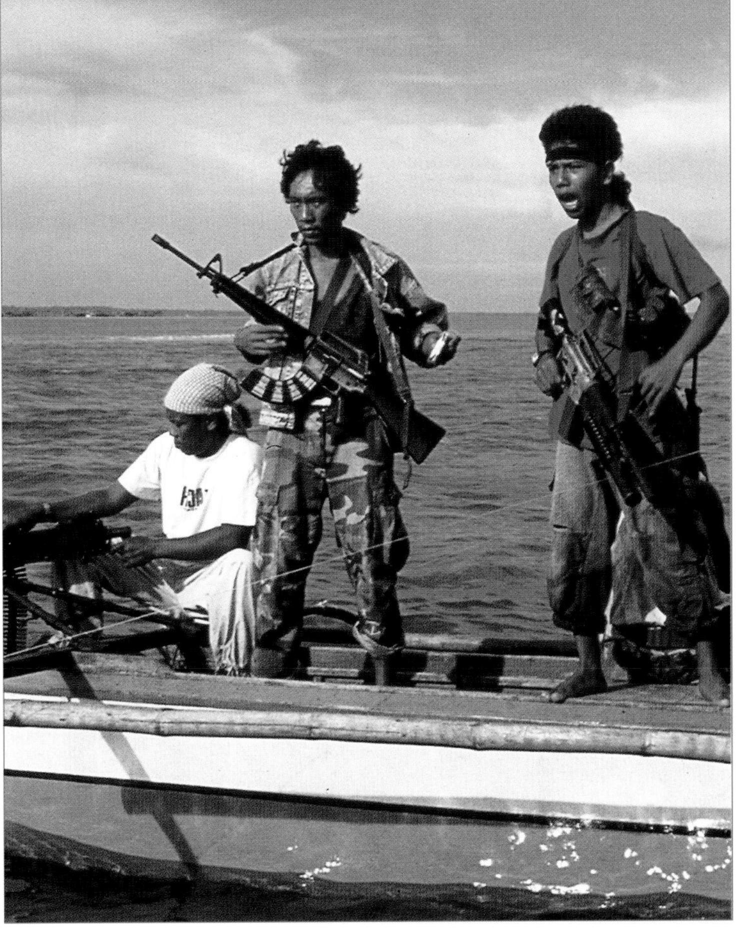

▷ *Modern-day pirates in fast, small boats pose a major threat to cargo ships sailing off Indonesia. Crews fend them off with barbed wire fencing and jets of water squirted from hoses.*

Future Prospects

△ *Billions of manganese nodules litter the seabed. These metallic lumps are rich in manganese, iron, copper, nickel, and cobalt. However, until less expensive ways are found to mine them, manganese nodules remain a vast, untapped resource.*

People will always depend on the sea's many resources. As wild fish stocks decline, more people are turning to fish farming. The billions of shrimplike crustaceans called krill also offer a potential food supply, and small-scale harvesting has already begun.

The seabed holds vast mineral deposits. Deep-sea trawling for manganese nodules, the extraction of methane gas and the mining of spreading ridges for copper and zinc will become increasingly important as resources on land dwindle. However, high costs make deep-sea mining unlikely until well into the twenty-first century.

Scientists are learning more about the crucial part that oceans play in the Earth's climate. If global warming continues, people will have to cope with melting ice sheets that raise ocean levels worldwide, drowning atolls and low-lying coasts. Planting mangroves could protect tropical deltas better than building high seawalls, but large tracts of low coast would have to be abandoned. Climatic change could also "switch off" the North Atlantic Drift that warms western Europe. If that happens, London might become as cold as the icy Labrador coast in the North Atlantic.

One way or another, the future of the Earth and its inhabitants is closely bound up with the oceans.

▽ *The oceans would rise some 200 feet (60 m) and drown cities if the ice caps suddenly melted. Some scientists believe that an increase of about 12 inches (30 cm) by the year 2050 is more likely, as a result of global warming. Even so, this would cause severe flooding in low-lying areas.*

△ *Billions of krill live in the oceans and provide the main source of food for baleen whales. Harvesting krill for human consumption has already begun. As well as being rich in protein, they contain chitin, a substance of great value for the medical industry.*

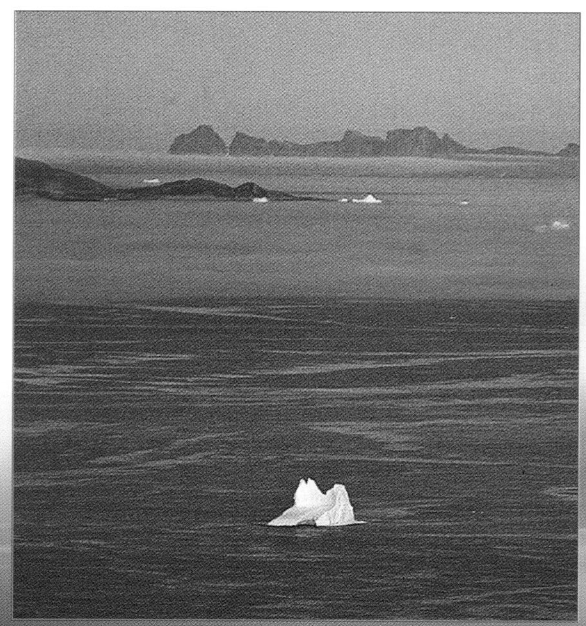

▷ *If certain ocean currents are disrupted by changes in climate, London could one day have winters as cold and icy as this one in Labrador, Canada. Although on the same latitude as Labrador, the British Isles are kept warm by the North Atlantic Drift.*

A Place in the Cosmos

Our ancestors once believed that the Earth must be the center of the Universe. Every morning they watched the Sun rise in the east and move across the sky. At night, the Moon, stars, and planets filled the darkness, and all appeared to revolve around the Earth. For almost a thousand years, the Church encouraged this view because it placed humans, God's special creation, at the center. By the 1500s, some astronomers began to argue that the Earth went around the Sun and, in the end, their evidence was overwhelming. Since then we have discovered that the Universe has no real center. We inhabit one of nine planets orbiting a medium-sized star in a galaxy containing billions of other stars. This galaxy itself is just one among billions of other galaxies. The search for our place in the Universe must be played out on an altogether bigger stage than ever imagined by our ancestors. And that search is the story of this book.

△ *Great stone calendars such as Stonehenge, built over 4,000 years ago, helped people keep track of the Sun's daily and yearly movements.*

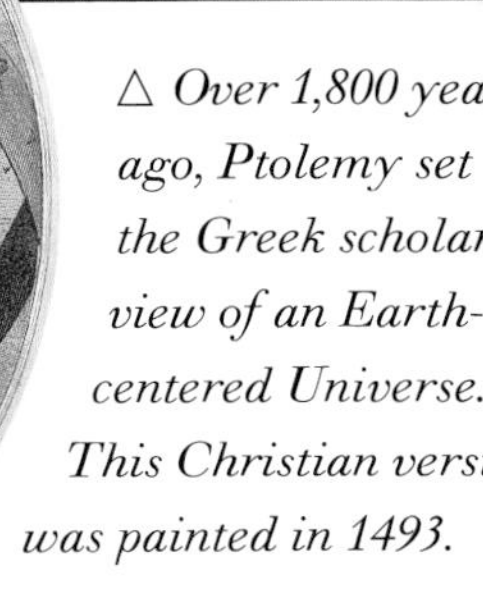

△ *Over 1,800 yea ago, Ptolemy set the Greek scholar view of an Earth-centered Universe. This Christian versi was painted in 1493.*

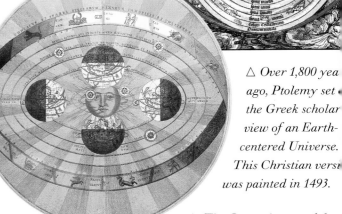

△ *The Copernican model of the Universe has the Sun at its center. Copernicus first published his ideas in 1543.*

The view from Greece

In 270 B.C., a Greek philosopher called Anaxagoras suggested that the Earth went around the Sun. His ideas seemed so ridiculous to the people of Athens that he was thrown out of the city! Aristotle's theory, developed by Ptolemy in about A.D. 120, put the Earth at the center of the Universe with the planets revolving around it in simple circles.

Heavenly revolutions

Nicolaus Copernicus and Galileo Galilei suggested that calculations explaining the motions of planets only made sense if the Earth went around the Sun. Aristotl model of a Sun-centered Universe was finally overturned in 1610 when Galileo, using his newly invented telescope, discovered that Jupiter had moons orbiting it.

ɪe scale of the Universe

· galaxy *(right)*, lies in a tiny corner of the .verse. The Sun, around which we orbit at an rage distance of 93 million miles (150 million), is only a dot in one of the galaxy's spiral ıs. Light takes 100,000 years to reach the th from the other side of the galaxy and billion years from the farthest galaxies.

▽ Albert Einstein provided the framework for our modern understanding of the Universe. In 1915, he proved that space and time cannot be clearly separated, and space itself is curved.

:dwin Hubble was the person to prove that e are galaxies other ı our own. In the late)s, he showed that the ıxies are rushing apart ı each other and that Universe is expanding.

Looking Up

△ *Galileo's detailed sketches of the Moon were made using the telescope he constructed in 1609.*

In 1609, news reached Italy that a Dutch instrumentmaker had used two curved pieces of glass in a tube to magnify a distant object. The first lens focused the object into an image, and the second magnified it. The Italian astronomer Galileo realized that this "telescope" could be used to observe the sky, and the heavens became open to serious astronomical study. With this new scientific instrument, Galileo revealed four moons orbiting Jupiter, evidence for the idea that the planets might in turn orbit the Sun. The first telescopes used lenses. Reflecting telescopes invented in the 1660s, have a concave mirror inste a lens to focus and catch starlight. The mirror neec be curved on only one side, so it can be made bigge and can detect fainter objects in greater detail.

▽ *William Herschel's telescope, completed in was used to study and calculate the distribu of thousands of stars throughout space.*

▷ The 100-inch Hooker Telescope *on Mount Wilson, California, remained the biggest and most powerful telescope in the world until 1948.*

◁ *The* Very Large Array *is a series of 27 radio telescopes in the New Mexico desert. Together they have the resolution of an instrument 17 miles (27 km) across, and provide detailed maps of distant galaxies.*

◁ *The 14-foot (4.2-m)* William Herschel Telescope *is built on a high, dry mountain peak on La Palma in the Canary Islands. The lines in the sky are the trails of stars.*

rror power

eflecting telescope's power depends on the size of mirror. The latest generation of telescopes have rrors over 26 feet (8 m) in diameter. Computers keep mirrors in alignment. When it is completed in 2002, *Very Large Telescope* in Chile will have the power spot a firefly 6,214 miles (10,000 km) away.

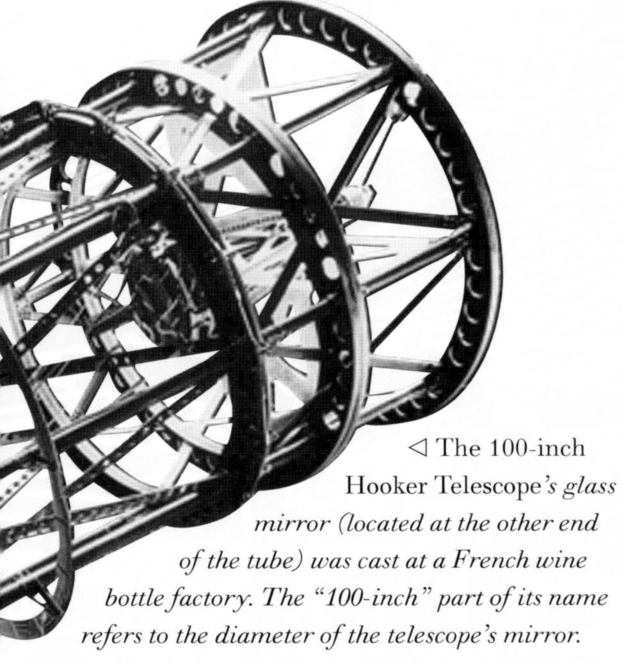

◁ The 100-inch Hooker Telescope*'s glass mirror (located at the other end of the tube) was cast at a French wine bottle factory. The "100-inch" part of its name refers to the diameter of the telescope's mirror.*

ight is only one octave on the great keyboard of the tromagnetic spectrum. Only visible light and part of the io spectrum penetrate far through the Earth's atmosphere.

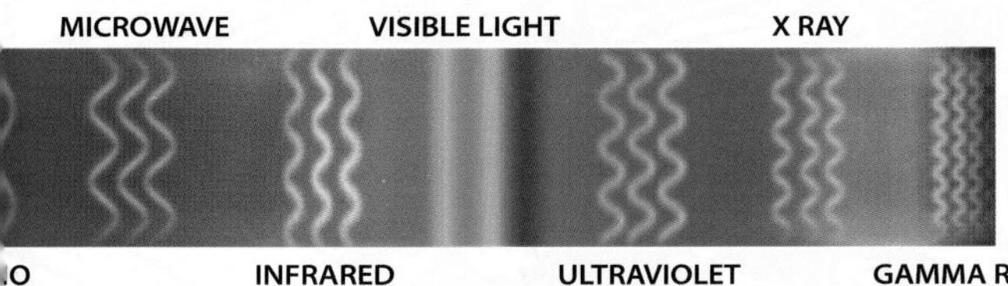

High and dry

Even on a clear night, the Earth is not a perfect place to put a telescope. Water vapor and turbulence in the atmosphere blur the images and make the stars seem to dance around. In order to avoid this, optical telescopes are usually built on mountains. But even there, the window of the Universe is not fully open—visible light is just one part of a whole spectrum of different wavelengths.

Radio waves

Besides light, only radio waves can penetrate the Earth's atmosphere. Radio waves are longer than light waves, so radio telescope mirrors do not have to be so finely polished. Today, individual radio telescopes on different continents can be linked by computer to give the equivalent of a single dish thousands of miles wide.

△ *High, dry mountain peaks provide the best location for observing the sky. This radio telescope* (left) *and optical telescope* (right) *are found at Cerro La Silla in the Andes Mountains of Chile.*

△ *The* Hubble Space Telescope, *launched from the space shuttle in 1990, has been a phenomenal success. Although its 8-foot (2.4-m) curved mirror was polished to the wrong shape, correcting lenses were fitted in 1993. The* Hubble Space Telescope *can also "see" in the ultraviolet and infrared wavelengths.*

Looking Out

▽ *The* Infrared Space Observatory *detected heated radiation with a curved mirror. Liquid helium kept the sensors cool.*

△ *Images from the* Hubble Space Telescope, *such as this one of a dying star, are radioed back to Earth.*

A journey just a few miles up above the atmosphere opens up a whole new window to the Universe. There is no reflected glare of city lights to dazzle an observer, and there is nothing to blur the stars or make them twinkle. As a result, it is possible to see objects in far greater detail than from the ground. The *Hubble Space Telescope* is the first big optical telescope to be put into orbit. It has allowed astronomers to peer into the hearts of galaxies and out to the farthest reaches of the Universe. As well as visible light, there is also a full rainbow of radiation to explore, from microwaves and infrared, to ultraviolet, x rays, and gamma rays. The only drawback is that you have to launch your telescope into space!

-aunched from the space shuttle Atlantis, the Compton Gamma · Observatory is named after Arthur Holly Compton, an erican scientist who pioneered the study of gamma rays.

Ultraviolet

Ultraviolet light comes from hot gas and stars. It carries the fingerprints of the atoms that emitted it and the gas clouds through which it has traveled. The *International Ultraviolet Explorer (IUE)* is one of the most successful astronomy satellites to date. Launched in 1978 with a planned life of three years, *IUE* focused the light with a 1.6-foot (0.5-m) mirror and, instead of taking a picture, spread the light out into the spectrum of wavelengths, revealing these atomic fingerprints. It was finally switched off in 1997 after nearly 19 years in service.

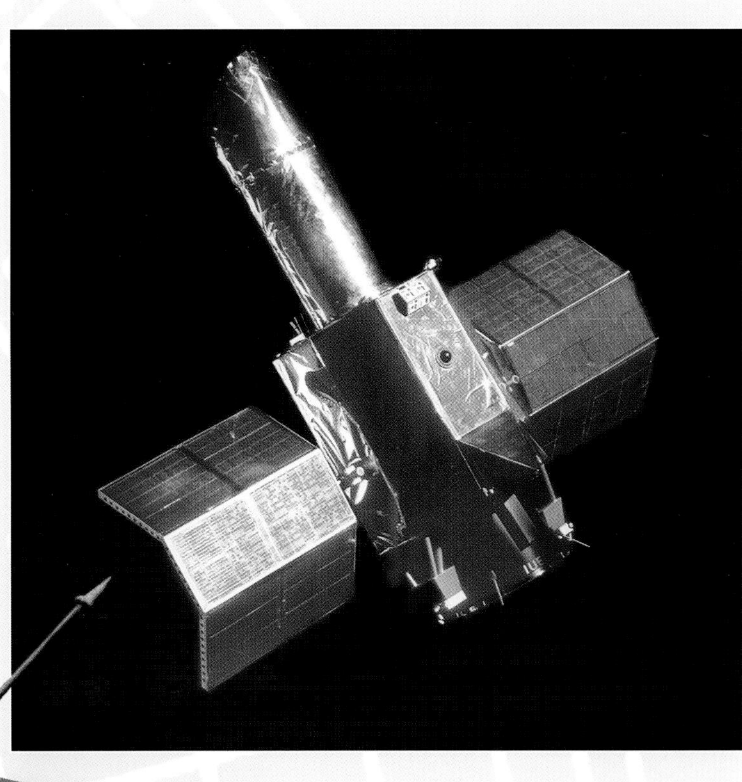

△ *The* International Ultraviolet Explorer *was the only ultraviolet observatory in space until the launch of the* Hubble Space Telescope *in 1990.*

:at detection

rared, or heat radiation, comes from warm objects t are not as hot as the stars we see. These include nets and comets, regions where new stars are ning, and distant galaxies ablaze with young stars. hough telescopes located on high mountains can see ie infrared radiation, the first comprehensive study ie with the *Infrared Astronomy Satellite (IRAS)* in 3. In 1995, Europe's *Infrared Space Observatory O)* was launched to look in even greater detail.

.mma rays

mma rays are released by the most energetic cesses in the Universe. These processes lude matter falling into a black hole, tter and antimatter annihilating h other, and explosions in the es of galaxies. Launched in 1991, *Compton Gamma Ray servatory* is an orbiting oratory that has detected den bursts of gamma rays ning from every direction.

:xosat *was designed to study ıy sources. Between 1983 and 5, it made and sent back ırts of over 2,000 ·rvations.*

Rise of the Rocket

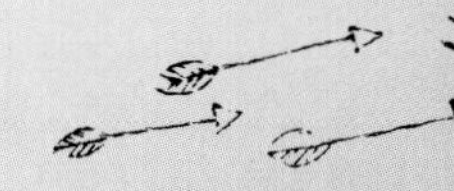

Gravity keeps us earthbound. To escape its pull and leave our planet far behind, we need to travel at an incredible 7 miles (11 km) per second (about 24,900 miles [40,000 km] per hour). To reach such speeds calls for the power of a rocket. The first rockets were more like fireworks and followed China's invention of gunpowder in the 1000s. They used rocket-propelled flaming arrows, launched from a basket, against their enemies (*see picture above left*). Warfare continued to be the driving force in developing rocketry. During World War II, the V2 rockets of Nazi Germany terrorized British cities. Captured V2s were sent to the United States, and their successors, the intercontinental ballistic missiles, helped to launch the space age.

△ *Robert Goddard designed the first successful liquid-fuel rocket. Its maiden flight in March 1926 lasted 2.5 seconds.*

△ *After World Wa II, captured Germ V2 rockets, togethe with their inventor Wernher von Brau played a key role in the U.S. space program.*

The pioneers

After the end of World War II, the pace of rocket research accelerated, with Wernher von Braun in the United States and Sergei Korolev in Russia leading the way. A race soon developed between the two superpowers—if a rocket could send a payload into Earth orbit, it could also deliver a bomb to the other side of the world.

Winners and losers

On October 4, 1957, the Soviet Union demonstrated they had the edge when they put *Sputnik 1*, a 23-inch (58-cm) aluminum sphere with a radio transmitter, into orbit. Meanwhile, the U.S. Navy *Vanguard* rocket blew up on the launchpad. Wernher von Braun was called in with his army team and on January 31, 1958, his *Jupiter-C* rocket put *Explorer 1*, the U.S.'s first satellite, into orbit.

◁ *The mighty* Saturn V *rocket lifts off from Cape Canaveral, Florida, on July 16, 1969 to put the first men on the Moon.*

◁ *Rockets often have several stages, ea carrying its own oxygen with which to burn the fuel. The first stage of* Saturr *had five great engines, burning 15 tons kerosene and liquid oxygen every seco It produced a thrust of 3,500 tons and lasted for less than three minutes before falling back to Earth.*

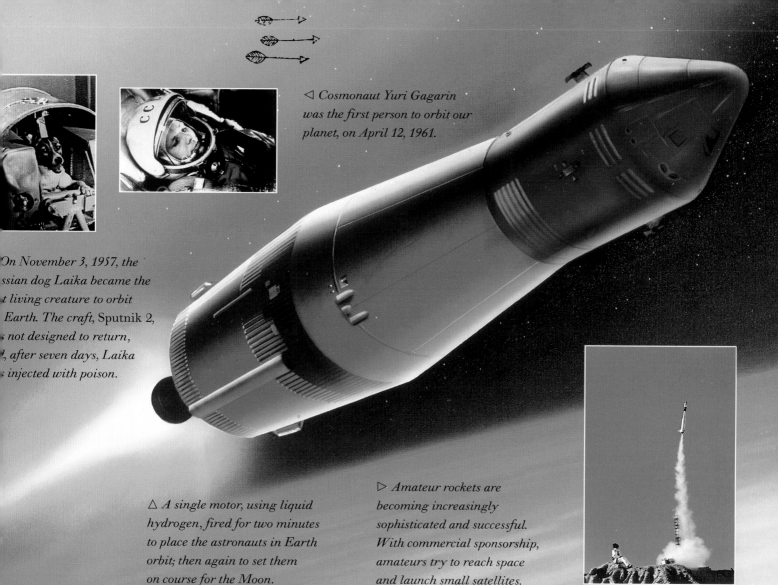

◁ *Cosmonaut Yuri Gagarin was the first person to orbit our planet, on April 12, 1961.*

On November 3, 1957, the ssian dog Laika became the t living creature to orbit Earth. The craft, Sputnik 2, *s not designed to return, l, after seven days, Laika s injected with poison.*

△ *A single motor, using liquid hydrogen, fired for two minutes to place the astronauts in Earth orbit; then again to set them on course for the Moon.*

▷ *Amateur rockets are becoming increasingly sophisticated and successful. With commercial sponsorship, amateurs try to reach space and launch small satellites.*

acemen

e first man in space followed shortly after the first ellite. Again, Russia won the race, launching Yuri Gagarin into a single Earth orbit on April 12, 1961. Three weeks later, Alan Shepard became the first American to be blasted into space, though not into orbit, landing 15 minutes later in the Atlantic. Finally, on February 20, 1962, the American John Glenn made three Earth orbits.

Two seconds after the first stage broke away, the rocket motors on the second stage fired, burning id hydrogen and liquid oxygen. This stage lasted six minutes, during which time the escape tower use in a launchpad emergency) was jettisoned.

Popular destination

Since the late 1950s, thousands of rockets have been launched and hundreds of people have visited space. But it has never become routine. The dangers are such that each mission involves thousands of people on the ground, checking and rechecking the complex systems of spaceflight.

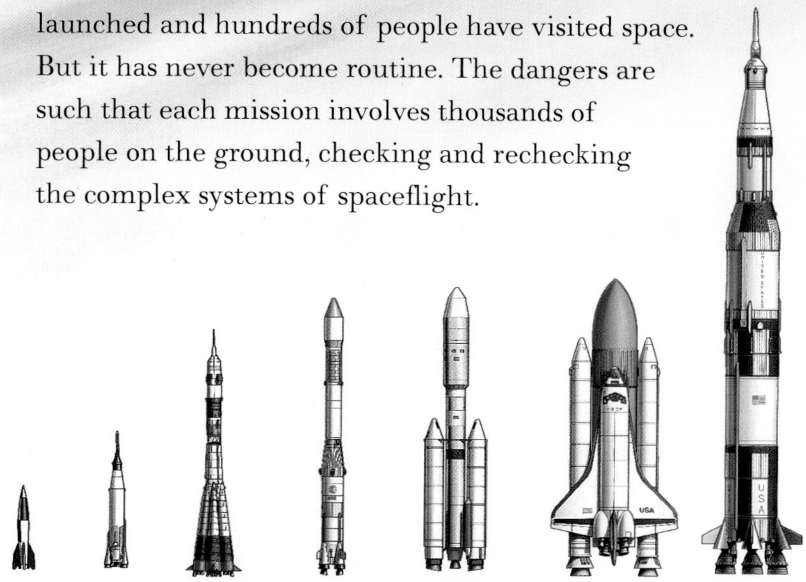

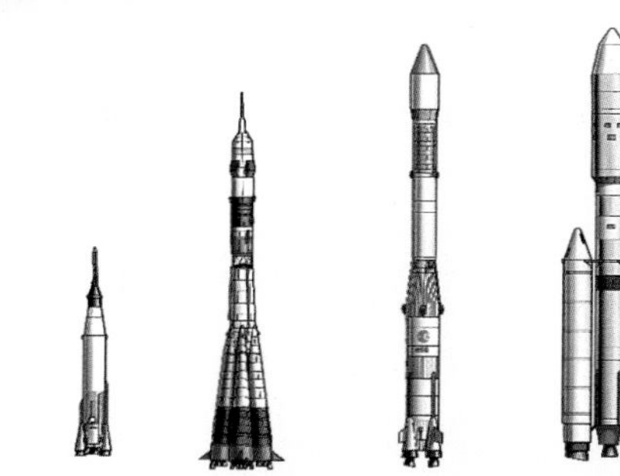

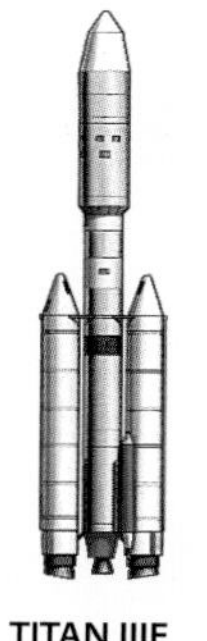

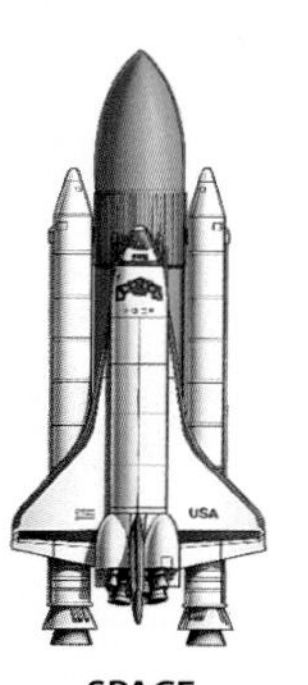

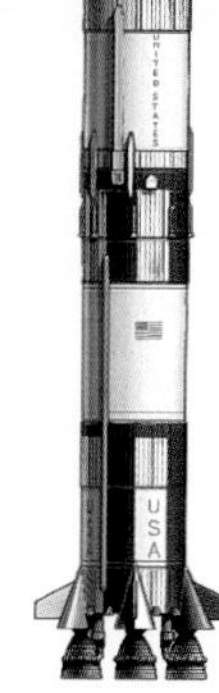

△ *At 360 feet (110 m) high,* Saturn V *towers over other rockets. These include the German* V2, *first used in 1944, and* Atlas *and* Soyuz, *which took astronauts into space. The* Titan *and* Ariane *launch satellites.*

Race to the Moon

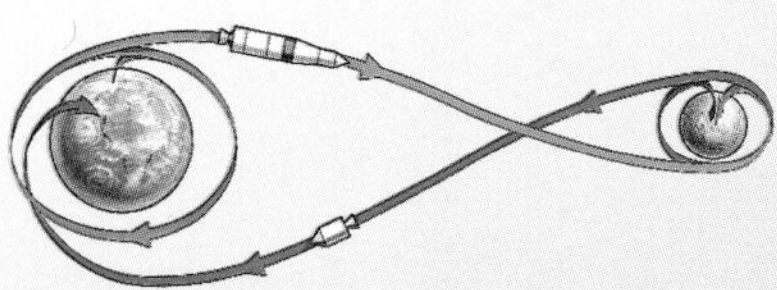

△ *From its Earth orbit, the final stage of the* Saturn V *rocket boosts the Command and Service Module (CSM) on its 250,000-mile (400,000-km) journey to the Moon. The CSM stays in orbit around the Moon while the lunar lander visits the surface. The lander rejoins the CSM for the journey home.*

As soon as rockets could break away from the Earth's gravity, the next goal became the Moon. It was a whole new world waiting to be explored—and claimed! The Russians again took the lead, landing the first craft on the Moon and photographing the dark, or far, side in 1959. Meanwhile, the United States launched 11 unmanned Moon missions, without one completing its objective. Then, on May 25, 1961, President Kennedy committed the country to putting a person on the Moon by 1970. The Apollo program began, and on July 20, 1969, *Apollo 11* landed the first astronauts on the Moon.

▷ *Their mission completed, the lunar lander blasts off from the Moon, leaving the bottom half of the lander and a remote camera behind.*

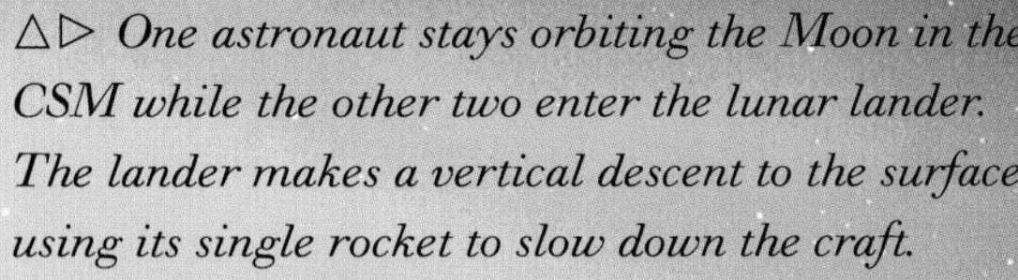

△▷ *One astronaut stays orbiting the Moon in the CSM while the other two enter the lunar lander. The lander makes a vertical descent to the surface, using its single rocket to slow down the craft.*

△ *James Irwin salutes the U.S. flag in front of* Apollo 15*'s lander, after returning with a collection of rocks on the lunar rover* (right).

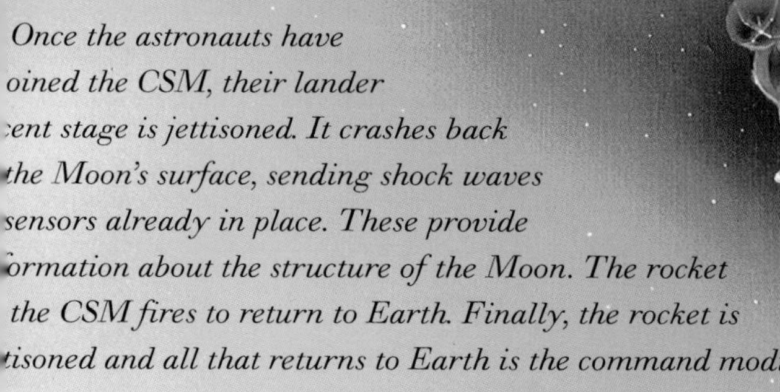

Once the astronauts have oined the CSM, their lander :ent stage is jettisoned. It crashes back the Moon's surface, sending shock waves sensors already in place. These provide ormation about the structure of the Moon. The rocket the CSM fires to return to Earth. Finally, the rocket is tisoned and all that returns to Earth is the command module.

ilure rate

om 1959 to 1976, there were 48 Russian d 31 American unmanned Moon missions. these, about half failed, but the pressure to t to the Moon was great, and both sides kept trying. Reliability improved, but there were sualties: three U.S. astronauts died in the *ollo 1* when fire broke out on the launchpad, d four Russian cosmonauts died returning m the *Salyut* space station.

△ *Parachutes slow the command module before splashdown into the sea. Airbags inflate to keep it upright as the astronauts disembark.*

change of direction

land people on the Moon and return them Earth required a very powerful and reliable ket. While the U.S. *Saturn V* fitted the bill, Russian *N1* rocket suffered four failures. 1974, Russia canceled its program and ncentrated on establishing a permanent esence above the Earth with its space stations.

Houston, we have a problem

On April 13, 1970, *Apollo 13* was 56 hours into its flight when command module pilot Jack Swigert reported, "We have a problem." An oxygen tank had exploded, and the crew had to conserve power, air, and water for four tense days before they could return to Earth.

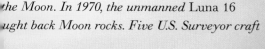

LUNA 2

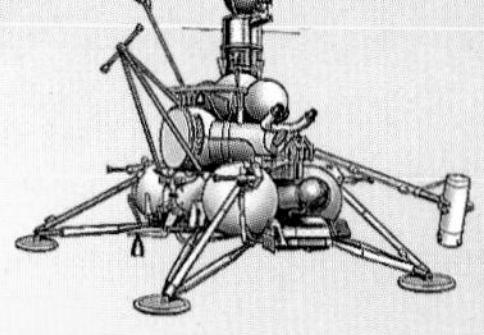

LUNA 16

SURVEYOR

LUNOKHOD 1

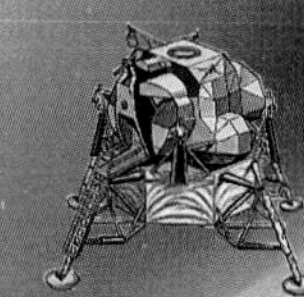

APOLLO

In 1959, Russia's Luna 2 *was the first space probe the Moon. In 1970, the unmanned* Luna 16 *ught back Moon rocks. Five U.S. Surveyor craft landed in the 1960s. Russia's* Lunokhod 1 *traveled 6.5 miles (10.5 km) on the surface. Six Apollo spacecraft landed on the Moon.*

△ *As the command module meets the Earth's atmosphere, friction makes it glow red-hot.*

The Space Shuttle

△ *Using a Manned Maneuvering Unit (MMU) like a sort of jet-propelled armchair, an astronaut can fly freely from the shuttle's cargo bay. The MMU is used to help retrieve faulty satellites, take photographs, or just to admire the view.*

After Apollo, the United States set out to create a cheaper alternative to maintain its presence in space. The space program wanted a craft that could go into orbit and return to the Earth again and again. The space shuttle was designed to do this, but it was not a simple task. A single-stage craft could not carry enough fuel to reach orbit. Instead, two solid-fuel rocket boosters and a giant, external fuel tank filled with liquid oxygen and hydrogen, power the shuttle almost into orbit. The shuttle orbiter is covered with 32,000 heat-resistant tiles, each shaped and attached by hand, which protect it on reentry into the atmosphere. *Columbia*, the first operational orbiter, made its maiden flight in April 1981.

Life in orbit

Life aboard a space shuttle is much more comfortable than that inside the cramped quarters of the Apollo modules. There is a wash room and bunk beds. The food is better, and there is plenty to do, with fantastic views of the Earth through the windows. After takeoff, the crew (of up to eight people) wears comfortable clothes. There are racks of experiments in the living quarters. In the cargo bay, satellites can be carried for launch, or retrieved for repair. Astronauts put on space suits and go out through an air lock to work outside the orbiter.

△ *Once in space, the shuttle orb can open its 60-foot (18-m)-long cargo-bay doors to deploy satell. perform experiments, or point instruments at the Earth or into space.*

▽ *A space shuttle blasts off from the Kennedy Space Center in Florida. The brilliant jet from the two solid-fuel rocket boosters (one of which is in the foreground) provides five times more thrust than the shuttle's three main engines* (on the right).

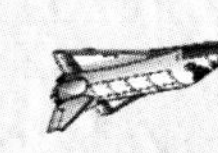

△ *At blastoff, the shuttle's main engines (using fuel from the external tank) and rocket boosters provide thrust equivalent to 140 jumbo jets. Two minutes later the boosters break away. Then the external tank falls away and it is MECO (Main Engine Cut-Off). After the mission is complete, the main engines slow the orbiter and it begins to fall, glowing red from friction, on reentry. It lands like a glider on a runway.*

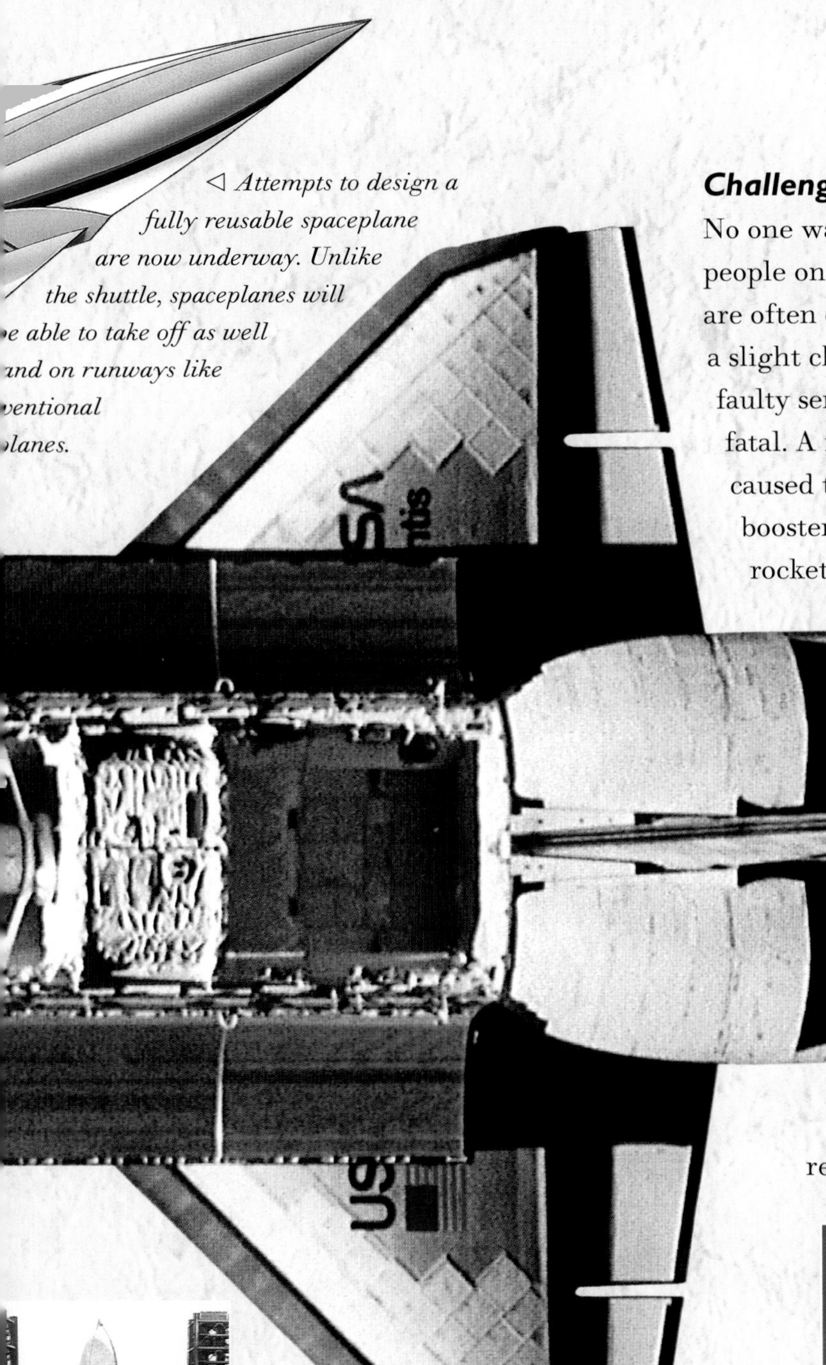

◁ *Attempts to design a fully reusable spaceplane are now underway. Unlike the shuttle, spaceplanes will ›e able to take off as well ınd on runways like ›entional ›lanes.*

Challenger disaster

No one wants a space mission to fail, but when there are people on board, safety is the most important issue. Launches are often delayed or called off at the last moment because of a slight change in the weather, a minor computer glitch, or a faulty sensor. On January 28, 1986, however, one fault proved fatal. A frosty night before the launch of shuttle *Challenger* caused the rubber "O" rings sealing the sections of its rocket boosters to become brittle. After takeoff, a flame from the rockets broke through a seal, sending a jet of fire onto the huge external fuel tank. Little more than a minute into the flight, the tank exploded and the seven astronauts were killed.

Satellite triumphs

After the *Challenger* disaster, shuttle missions were suspended for two and a half years. Since then, among the shuttle's biggest triumphs have been the refurbishment and repair of satellites. For example, after its launch in 1990, the *Hubble Space Telescope* was found to be faulty. In 1993, shuttle astronauts retrieved the telescope and repaired it in space.

▽ *One of the two solid-fuel rocket boosters veers away from the exploding wreckage of the* Challenger *shuttle just 73 seconds after liftoff.*

The Soviet space shuttle ›an was much like the . shuttle but had no ines itself, rising on the ›rgia rocket. It flew in ›e only once, in 1988, ın unmanned test.

Unmanned competition

Although the shuttle is the most versatile manned spacecraft, the unmanned satellite launch market is very competitive. The U.S.'s leading competitor is the European Ariane rocket, with over 100 successful launches. Russia, China, Japan, and India also have rocket programs.

△ *The* Ariane 5 *rocket sits on its launchpad in French Guiana in June 1996. The first flight was a disaster (a computer fault caused it to veer off course), but the second succeeded. Unlike its rivals,* Ariane 5 *can launch up to four satellites at once.*

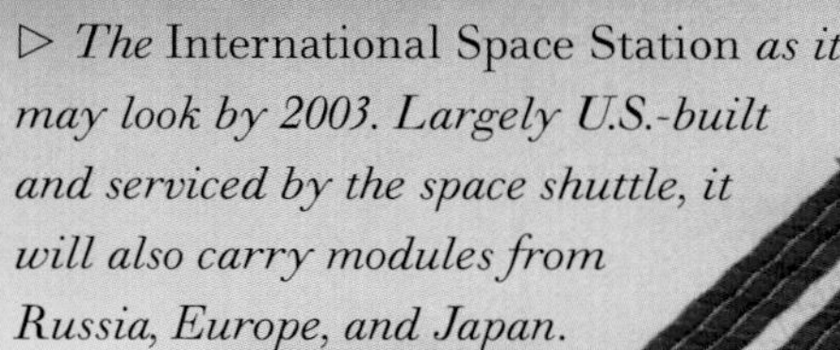

▷ *The* International Space Station *as it may look by 2003. Largely U.S.-built and serviced by the space shuttle, it will also carry modules from Russia, Europe, and Japan.*

△ *Spacelab is a pressurized module that flies in the cargo bay of the space shuttle. On this mission, in 1993, there were around 90 experiments, including ones on the effects of weightlessness on astronauts.*

▽ *Astronauts train underwater* (inset) *to simulate the effects of weightlessness in space and to practice repairing satellites. In space itself, an astronaut uses the shuttle's robot arm like a cherrypicker to control his or her movements above the open cargo bay.*

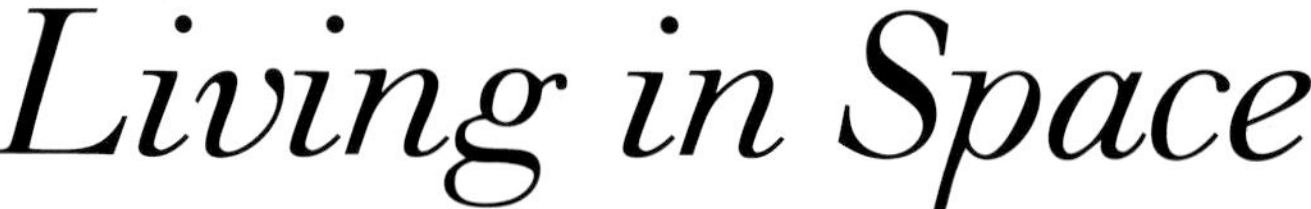

Living in Space

On May 27, 1973, the space station *Skylab* was launched. Made of modified *Saturn V* and Apollo units, it offered the first long-stay, orbiting laboratory for microgravity research and studying the Sun and the Earth. It also provided an opportunity to practice space repairs when the crew had to replace damaged shielding. Its last crew set a space endurance record when they spent 84 days living in *Skylab*. In 1977, the Russians launched *Salyut 6*, the first space station to have two air locks, allowing one crew to arrive before the other departed. This was replaced in 1982 by *Salyut 7* and then, in 1986, by *Mir*, in which the endurance record has been broken over and over again.

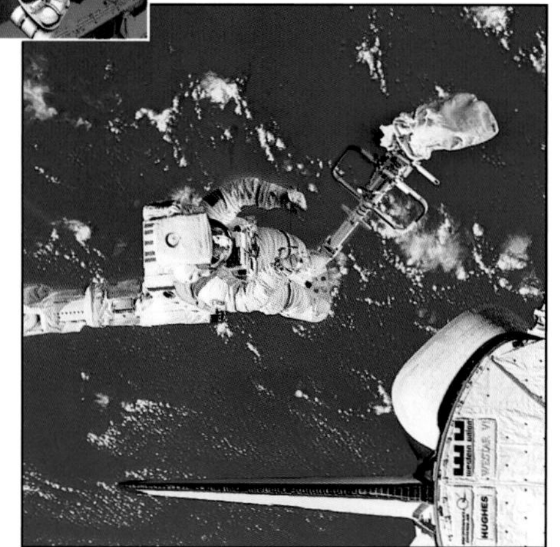

Working in space

In space, some of the most difficult tasks are Extra-Vehicular Activities (EVAs). A space suit must be worn as protection from the vacuum, radiation, and temperature extremes. Large objects, though weightless, still have mass and, once in motion, can wreak havoc. Even turning a screwdriver can cause problems. Unless an astronaut is well anchored, the screw stays in place while the astronaut rotates!

△ *In June 1995, the U.S. shu* Atlantis *docked with* Mir *an both crews posed for camera. was the start of a collaborat that provided much-needed for Russia's space program and hardware for the U.S.*

◁ *Huge arrays of solar cells, assembled in space, provide the electrical power for the space station.*

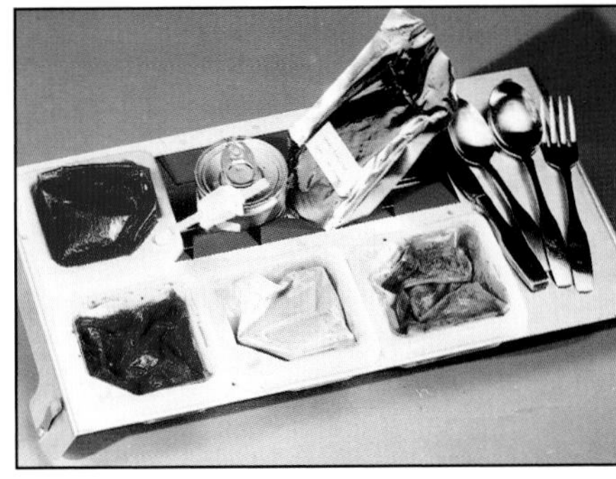

△ *The meals served on board the space shuttle are a great improvement on the dried and concentrated capsules given to Apollo astronauts.*

◁ *This unisex toilet is designed for the* International Space Station. *It comes with foot and thigh restraints. Air flow removes the waste, which is then dried and compressed.*

Space stations of the future

The *International Space Station* is due for launch in the late 1990s. It is a laboratory for microgravity research and provides a testing-ground for future plans. Space stations could serve as assembly points for interplanetary craft and manned missions to Mars. They could be used as astronomical observatories or factories for manufacturing new materials. A rotating space station with artificial gravity might even one day become a hotel for tourists.

during *Mir*

e core module of the Russian space station *Mir* was nched in 1986 with a planned life of five years. Ten rs later, surrounded by add-on modules, it started to w signs of aging. First, waste water pumps and air ditioning malfunctioned.

e oxygen generators failed t, followed by a potentially ous fire which was caused an oxygen-releasing candle. en, in June 1997, an unmanned ply craft crashed into one *Mir*'s modules, cutting forty cent of the power. Only ssian determination and . money kept *Mir* going.

◁ *This close-up of* Mir, *taken from the Progress M35 supply craft in July 1997, shows damage to a solar array* (right) *and a thermal radiator* (left). *The damage was caused by another unmanned* Progress *supply craft that crashed into* Mir*'s* Specktr *module six weeks earlier.*

◁ *The Russian space station* Mir *was launched in 1986. Since then, several new modules have been added, increasing its mass from 21 tons to over 100 tons. Astronauts live and work in the largest module, which is 43 feet (13 m) long. The other modules are used for experiments and storing equipment. Handrails on* Mir*'s exterior aid astronauts as they work outside.*

Using Space

Rocket launches are very expensive and not always reliable, yet governments and businesses are lining up for slots on board launch craft. Space is potentially so useful that it is well worth the risk and expense. Some satellites look at the Earth, following its weather patterns, monitoring the environment, searching for oil and minerals, or even spying on countries. Others are used by astronomers to look out at the stars. The most popular use of space, however, is for communication. In 1945, the writer Arthur C. Clarke predicted that we would communicate via space. This was before the silicon chip was invented, and Clarke imagined vast space stations with teams of engineers to service the unreliable, bulky equipment.

△ *In 1962,* Telstar *relayed the first live transatlantic TV transmission, which lasted for 20 minutes.*

△ *The Global Positioning System (GPS) uses the signals from at least three satellites to calculate any position on land or at sea.*

Staying in touch

One of the most popular satellite orbits is called geostationary orbit, 22,400 miles (36,000 km) above the equator. Here, satellites orbit at the same speed as the Earth rotates, and so always appear to be overhead. But the distance is so great that either a big dish is needed to receive a satellite's signal, or the signal must be concentrated in a single, powerful beam. Now, networks of satellites are launched into low orbits, so there is always one in range of the hand-held receiver of a mobile phone.

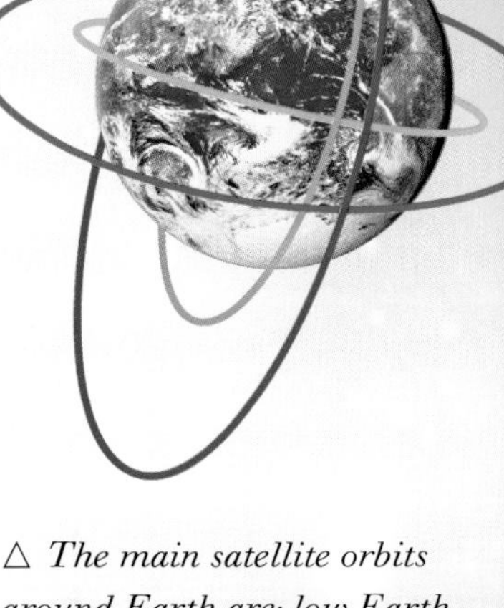

△ *The main satellite orbits around Earth are: low Earth orbit* (orange), *polar orbit* (blue), *elliptical or Molniya orbit* (green) *and geostationary orbit* (red).

▽ *The giant radio dish at Goonhilly Downs, Cornwall was used to pick up the first transatlantic satellite links.*

△ *In 1997, Tony Bullimore spent five days beneath the hull of his capsized yacht. He was saved when satellites located his radio distress signal.*

Space junk

As more and more rockets and satellites are launched, unwanted junk accumulates in spac[e]. Space junk ranges from dropped wrenches and chips of paint to spent rocket motors and defunct satellites. The U.S. Air Force is tracki[ng] over 8,500 large objects, but even small pieces can be dangerous—a space shuttle window was once chipped, probably by a flake of paint. Operat[ors] are encouraged to relocate old satellites in unused orbits, or force them to burn up in the atmospher[e].

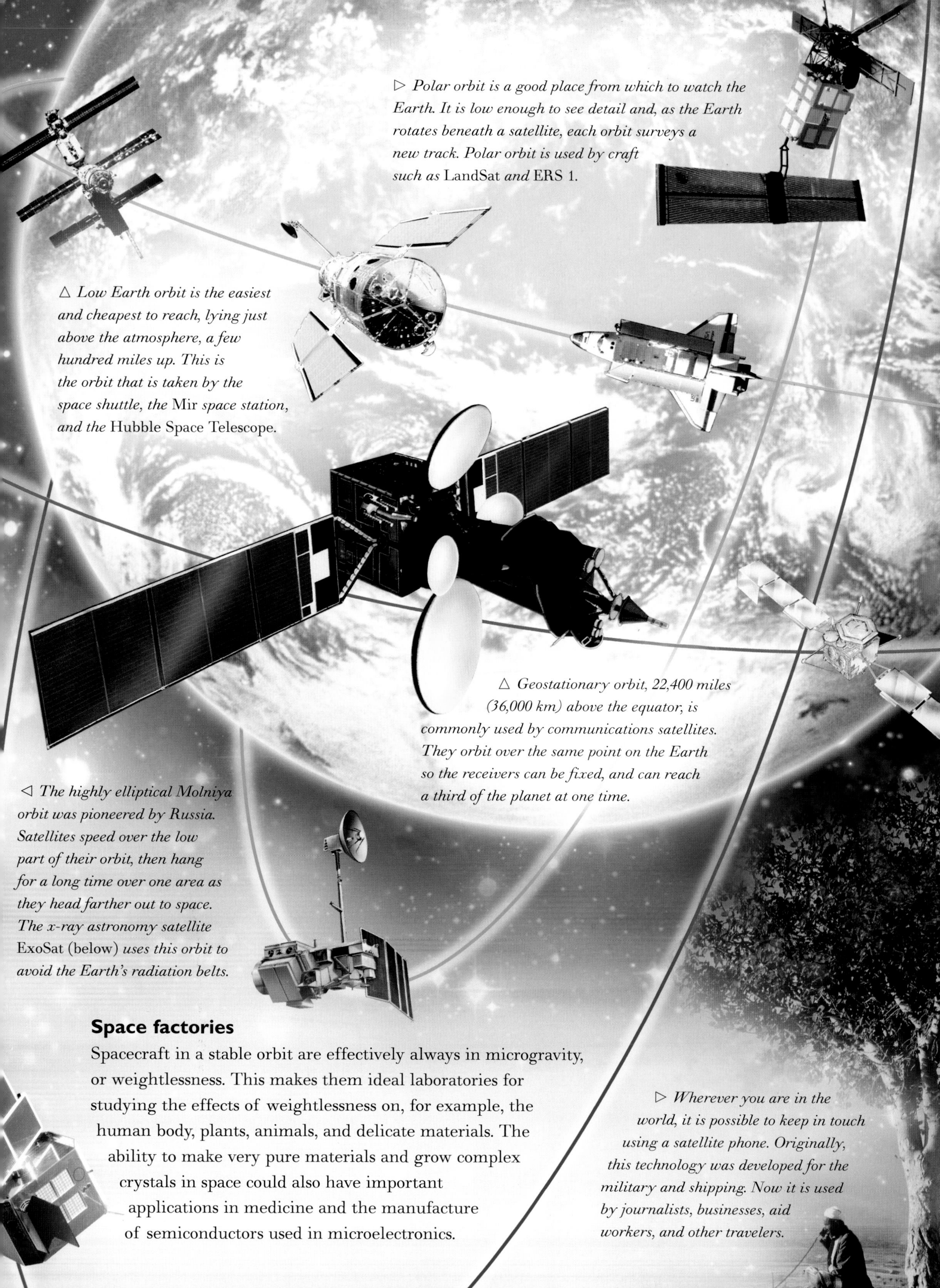

▷ *Polar orbit is a good place from which to watch the Earth. It is low enough to see detail and, as the Earth rotates beneath a satellite, each orbit surveys a new track. Polar orbit is used by craft such as* LandSat *and* ERS 1.

△ *Low Earth orbit is the easiest and cheapest to reach, lying just above the atmosphere, a few hundred miles up. This is the orbit that is taken by the space shuttle, the* Mir *space station, and the* Hubble Space Telescope.

△ *Geostationary orbit, 22,400 miles (36,000 km) above the equator, is commonly used by communications satellites. They orbit over the same point on the Earth so the receivers can be fixed, and can reach a third of the planet at one time.*

◁ *The highly elliptical Molniya orbit was pioneered by Russia. Satellites speed over the low part of their orbit, then hang for a long time over one area as they head farther out to space. The x-ray astronomy satellite* ExoSat (below) *uses this orbit to avoid the Earth's radiation belts.*

Space factories

Spacecraft in a stable orbit are effectively always in microgravity, or weightlessness. This makes them ideal laboratories for studying the effects of weightlessness on, for example, the human body, plants, animals, and delicate materials. The ability to make very pure materials and grow complex crystals in space could also have important applications in medicine and the manufacture of semiconductors used in microelectronics.

▷ *Wherever you are in the world, it is possible to keep in touch using a satellite phone. Originally, this technology was developed for the military and shipping. Now it is used by journalists, businesses, aid workers, and other travelers.*

▷ *The Earth is ringed by a cosmic necklace of satellites, watching over it from a range of different orbits.*

△ *From low orbit,* Landsat 4 *passes over all on the Earth. This false-colo shows an area of cleare forest in Brazil w network of*

Earthwatch

Strangely, we sometimes need to go into space to see our own world more clearly. From the perspective of space it is possible to see the overall pattern without being confused by detail. As long ago as 1948, the astronomer Fred Hoyle commented that "when a photograph of Earth, taken from outside, is returned, an idea as powerful as any in history will be let loose." To a great extent, he was right. Astronauts comment on how fragile the Earth appears from space. Scientists use observations to build up a picture of the complex systems on the Earth and how our environment is changing. Satellite pictures can inspire a sense of wonder, which may generate a new ecological awareness. Space also provides a window for monitoring military activities, along with disaster relief, peacekeeping, and humanitarian operations.

△ *Meteosats hang in geostationary orbit above the Atlantic watching weather systems such as this hurricane forming. This* Meteosat Second Generation Craft *is designed to help forecasters predict weather in the new millennium.*

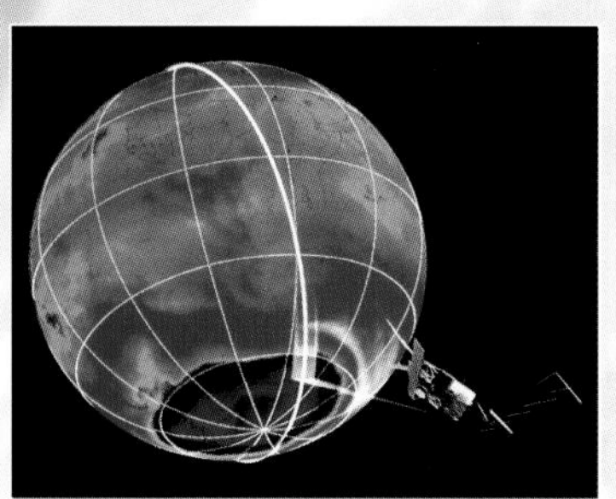

△ *The* ERS-2 *satellite measures ozone in the upper atmosphere. Here an ozone hole (in blue) is clearly seen above the Antarctic.*

And now for the weather ...

Satellite images are used in weather forecasts to show us what weather to expect. Weather satellites monitor wind speed, cloud temperat and height, sea temperature, and many other factors. Computers then produce detailed forecasts up to a week ahead. These are vital farmers, sailors, and even ice-cream makers. This data can also help predict climate chang such as global warming, decades into the futu

△ The space shuttle sometimes carries remote sensing instruments for monitoring the Earth. These two images were taken by cloud-penetrating radar. They reveal new flows of ash and lava on Mount Pinotubo, an active volcano in the Philippines.

RS satellites use
ır, ultraviolet, and infrared to monitor the Earth. Here, two
bined images show ground movements after an earthquake.

△ Spy satellites often use powerful telescopes to watch for potential threats. Here, a train carrying Iraqi tanks can be seen heading toward Kuwait in 1994.

pping the Earth

ı few 90-minute-long orbits, a satellite can produce a logical survey of an area of remote and mountainous ntry that would take years to map on the ground. By ting at the ground, not in just the few colors our eyes see but using hundreds of different bands of the ctrum, it is possible to reveal mineral deposits, polluted as, and analyze rocks and soil. Satellites can reveal orestation or the health of crops. They even measure ks deep inside the Earth in the search for new oil fields.

Spy in the sky

One of the first uses of space was for military purposes. Many rockets were developed to deliver long-range missiles, and more spy satellites may have been launched than any other type. Many take photographs, others monitor radio messages or look for signs of missile launches or bomb tests. In the 1980s, the United States planned a space-based defense system, called "Star Wars." Before the technology and finance could be resolved, the Cold War ended and the project was canceled.

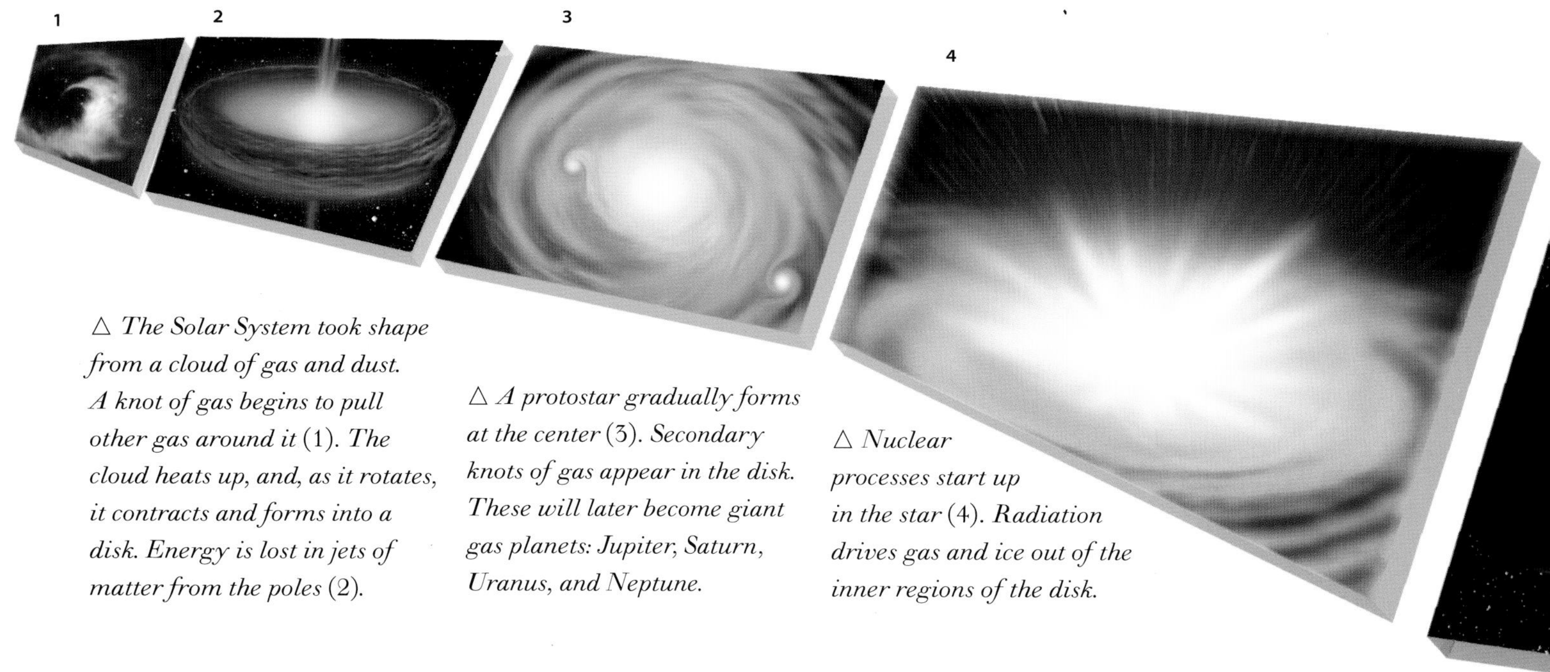

△ *The Solar System took shape from a cloud of gas and dust. A knot of gas begins to pull other gas around it (1). The cloud heats up, and, as it rotates, it contracts and forms into a disk. Energy is lost in jets of matter from the poles (2).*

△ *A protostar gradually forms at the center (3). Secondary knots of gas appear in the disk. These will later become giant gas planets: Jupiter, Saturn, Uranus, and Neptune.*

△ *Nuclear processes start up in the star (4). Radiation drives gas and ice out of the inner regions of the disk.*

The Solar System

The Solar System is dominated by the Sun, our local star. The Sun is circled by nine planets and their moons, together with countless asteroids and comets. The four planets closest to the Sun—Mercury, Venus, Earth, and Mars—are small, rocky worlds. The next four planets—Jupiter, Saturn, Uranus, and Neptune—are huge and composed of gas. Finally comes Pluto, the smallest of the planets, with a diameter of 1,367 miles (2,200 km). Jupiter is the largest, with a diameter of almost 88,860 miles (143,000 km). But the Sun dwarfs everything else in the Solar System. If the Sun were the size of a soccer ball, then Earth would be smaller than a pea in comparison. Even if all the matter in all the planets were gathered together into a single ball, you could still fit 700 planets inside the Sun and have room to spare.

△ *The Solar System is nea formed. The Sun is beginn shine strongly through its dusty shroud (5). Planets formed, but the building r is still flying around and bombarding the planets.*

Dusty birthplace

About five billion years ago, the material that now ma up the Sun and planets was a great cloud of gas and d called the solar nebula. This material was composed o mixture of light elements, mostly hydrogen and heliu that had been left over from the formation of our Mil Way Galaxy, and heavier elements spewed out by an earlier generation of short-lived stars. A shock wave m have passed through the nebula as it crossed a spiral ar of the galaxy, or as a nearby star exploded. As a result, the nebula began to condense into a nursery of stars.

◁ *The inclined orbit of along with those of Nept Uranus, Saturn, and Jup are clearly visible. Much in are the inner planets— Earth, Venus, and Mercu*

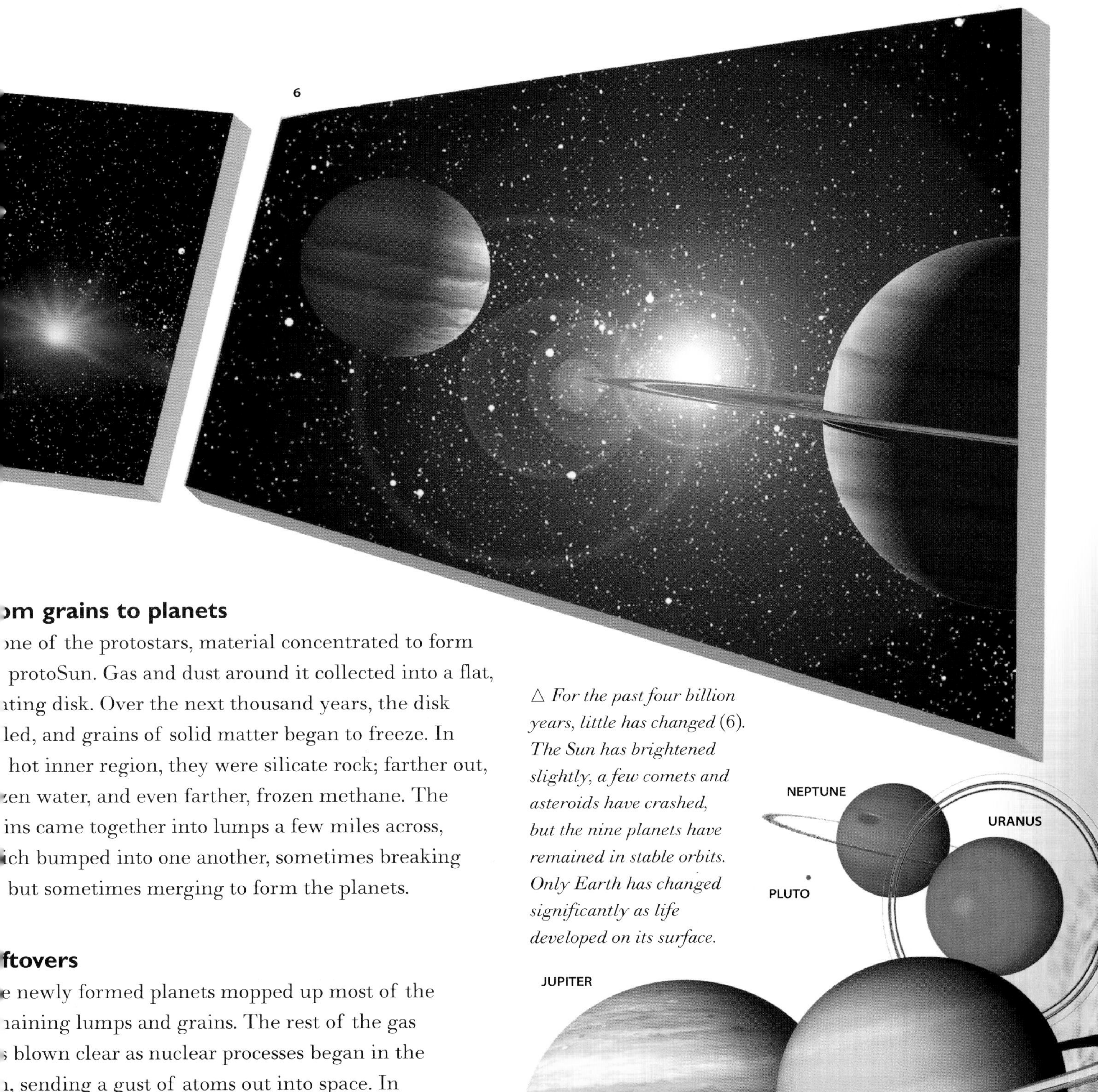

ɔm grains to planets

ɔne of the protostars, material concentrated to form protoSun. Gas and dust around it collected into a flat, ıting disk. Over the next thousand years, the disk led, and grains of solid matter began to freeze. In hot inner region, they were silicate rock; farther out, zen water, and even farther, frozen methane. The ins came together into lumps a few miles across, ich bumped into one another, sometimes breaking but sometimes merging to form the planets.

△ For the past four billion years, little has changed (6). The Sun has brightened slightly, a few comets and asteroids have crashed, but the nine planets have remained in stable orbits. Only Earth has changed significantly as life developed on its surface.

ftovers

e newly formed planets mopped up most of the naining lumps and grains. The rest of the gas s blown clear as nuclear processes began in the ı, sending a gust of atoms out into space. In outermost reaches of the solar nebula, the icy toplanetary material was spread so thinly that id not form planets, but remains to this day ast cloud of potential comets.

Iere, the Sun and planets are shown to scale. · Sun dwarfs everything else in the Solar System, ıding Jupiter and Saturn.

Mercury

Mercury, named after the Roman winged messenger of the gods, is an elusive planet. Small, fast-moving, and lying closer to the Sun than any other planet, it is only visible from the Earth just after sunset or just before dawn. Mercury is the second smallest planet and only slightly larger than our Moon. It takes just 88 Earth days to orbit the Sun. Its distance from the Sun varies from 29 million miles (46 million km) at its closest to 43 million miles (70 million km) at its most distant. The Sun's strong gravitational tug on Mercury has dramatically slowed the planet's rotation on its axis. This has the result that a day on Mercury lasts the equivalent of 176 Earth days—twice as long as its quicksilver 88-day year.

△ *Almost everything we know about Mercury comes from one space probe,* Mariner 10, *which flew past the planet in 1973, 1974, and again in 1975. Here,* Mariner 10 *is shown above a false-color image of Mercury's cratered surface.*

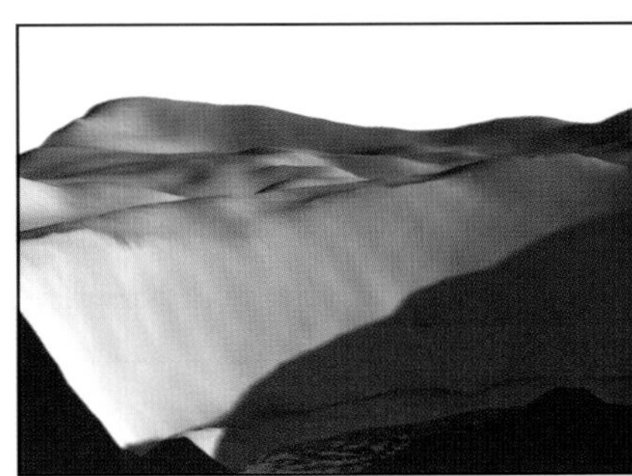

△ *There is evidence from radar on Earth that there may be ice in craters near Mercury's poles. In deep craters, icy deposits—possibly leftover material from comet impacts—would remain hidden from the Sun's intense heat.*

Unchanged features

The surface of Mercury is very similar to the Moon's. It is heavily cratered, with evidence of ancient lava flows. With no atmosphere or water to erode them, the craters look almost as fresh as the day they formed. Yet that must have been more than 4 billion years ago, when debris left over from the formation of the planets was still flying around in the Solar System. This rubble crashed into the surface, throwing up circular craters with characteristic central peaks.

▽ *Mercury's dry and airless surface creates a very bleak landscape. Pockmarked with impact craters, during the day it is baked by radiation and heat from the nearby Sun.*

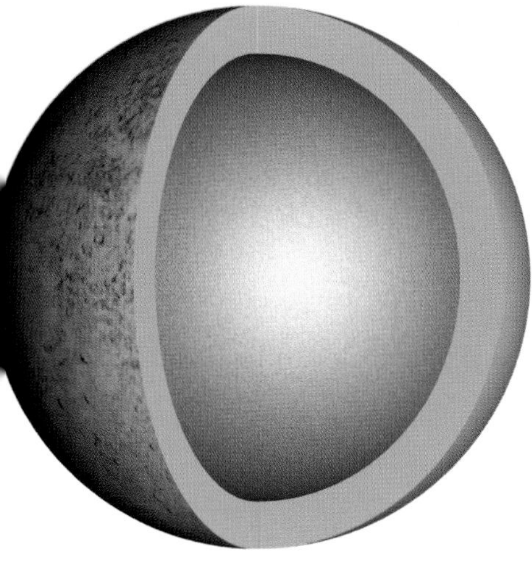

△ *Although only about a third the size of the Earth, Mercury is almost as dense. This suggests that a core of iron-nickel takes up about 70 percent of the interior, with a mantle of silicate rock surrounding it. The outer part of the metal core may still be molten.*

World of extremes

Mercury has no atmosphere (except for a trace of helium given off by the rocks), so there is no wind or rain. There is also no protection against the Sun's searing heat by day, and no blanket to keep the surface warm at night. Days and nights each last about three Earth months. With the planet swinging closer and farther from the Sun, temperatures can range from 788°F (420°C) to –292°F (–180°C). These extremes are hot enough to melt some metals or cold enough to freeze air.

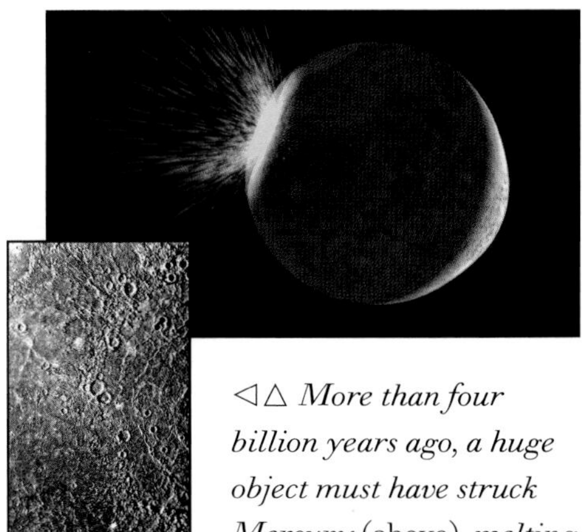

◁△ *More than four billion years ago, a huge object must have struck Mercury* (above), *melting part of the surface and causing ridges and hills to form on the opposite side of the planet. The ridges around the impact crater, called the Caloris Basin* (left), *were photographed by* Mariner 10.

izened world

urprise discovery by *Mariner 10* was a gnetic field on Mercury. The planet had been ught to rotate too slowly for it to generate agnetic field. The answer may lie in the net's large core. If the outer part is still lten, currents in it could produce a weak gnetic effect. A big iron core could also explain rcury's wrinkles. As it cooled and solidified, iron shrank, making the planet contract and ducing a wrinkled appearance on the surface.

Venus

△ *Bands of thick, swirling clouds circle Venus at speeds of up to 225 mph (360 km/hr). This ultraviolet picture was taken by* Mariner 10 *in 1974.*

Venus, the brightest planet visible from Earth, is named after the goddess of beauty. The planet has also been called the Earth's twin. It is almost exactly the same size, is only slightly less dense, and is made up of volcanic rocks, but there the similarity ends. The thick atmosphere on Venus means that it is always cloudy, and the pressure on the surface is 90 times greater than on Earth. The dense atmosphere consists mostly of carbon dioxide, and this traps the planet's heat, causing a runaway greenhouse effect that makes the worst predictions of global warming on Earth seem chilly by comparison. The surface temperature is 896°F (480°C), and if oceans ever existed on Venus they have long since boiled away. If you could withstand the searing heat and bone-crushing pressure on this hostile planet, you would see an orange sky. If it ever rained, you would be drenched in a lethal downpour of sulfuric acid.

△ *Four Russian Venera probes have landed on Venus and sent back images. In 1982, close-ups taken by* Venera 13 *revealed flat, eroded terrain southeast of a volcanic region called Phoebe Regio. The edge of the Venus lander and its lens cap can also be seen in the picture.*

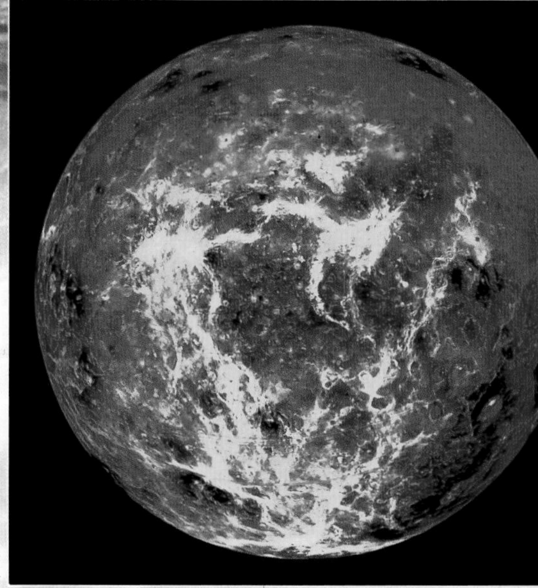

△ *The* Magellan *radar mapper revealed that the surface of Venus has rough, mountainous terrain (bright areas) and smoother plains (darker areas).*

Global warming

The dramatic contrast with the Earth could simply be because Venus is closer to the Sun. As the young Sun warmed, more carbon dioxide was released from volcanoes and the surface temperature climbed. The seas began to evaporate, the water vapor adding to the greenhouse effect. Without oceans and plants, carbon dioxide could not be removed as the heat output of the Sun continued to grow. On the Earth, billions of tons of carbon are locked up in limestone and chalk. On Venus it is all still in the atmosphere.

Revealing geology

The radar mapper on the *Magellan* space probe indicated clear evidence of volcanic activity, including domes of thick or viscous lava and vast floods of liquid basalt. However, it did not detect any drifting plates, which on Earth create great chains of volcanoes. There must be other forces at work on Venus, still to be identified.

▽ *The background landscape is a computer-generated view of Maat Mons, 5 miles (8 km) high and one of the largest volcanoes on Venus. This image was created by data sent back by the* Magellan *probe. Fresh lava flows around the volcano suggest that it is still active.*

▷ *The* Magellan *probe, seen here as it was released from the space shuttle in 1989, was made up of spare parts from other missions.*

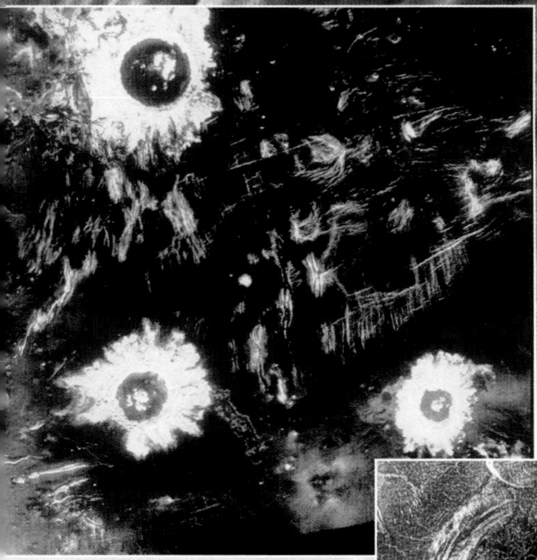

'he existence of uneroded ers on Venus indicates that e parts of the surface are h older than areas covered olcanic lava. The largest er (top left) *has a diameter 0 miles (50 km).*

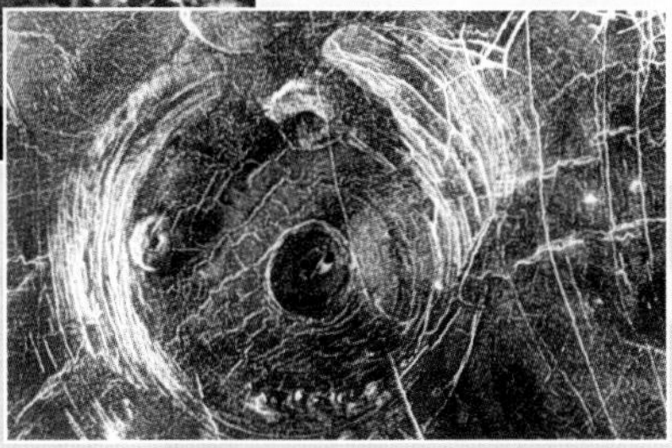

△ *This corona, or circular feature, is 125 miles (200 km) across. It was probably caused by a rising dome of lava from deep below the surface.*

△ *Like the Earth, Venus has a rocky mantle and a crust. Inside is an iron core that may be partly molten. Because the planet rotates very slowly (unlike the Earth), there is no noticeable magnetic field.*

◁ *The atmosphere of Venus is 96 percent carbon dioxide. Nitrogen, water vapor, and traces of gases such as sulfur dioxide are also present.*

ngthy days

us is best seen from Earth with the naked eye just after set or before dawn. Like the Moon, Venus has phases as Sun illuminates a crescent, half, or full disk. Venus has a v rotation from east to west. In fact, its rotation rate of Earth days makes a day on Venus longer than the planet's r—the time it takes to revolve once around the Sun.

The Moon

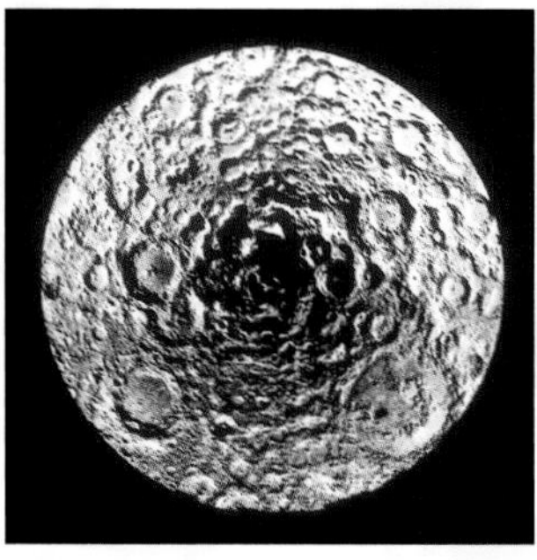

△ *This mosaic of 1,500 images shows the south pole of the Moon. The dark crater in the center is permanently in shade and contains an icy layer.*

The Moon is the most spectacular object in the night sky, and it is the only world beyond Earth so far on which people have walked. It is our closest neighbor, orbiting our planet with the same face always pointing toward us. The far side is often called the dark side, because it cannot be seen from Earth. In its monthly orbit, the Moon seems to change shape as different areas of its surface are lit by the Sun. The Moon's five distinct phases are called new, crescent, quarter, gibbous, and full. When the side we see is dark (a new Moon), the far side is in full sunshine. The Moon is close enough to the Earth for its gravity to pull the water in our oceans toward it, causing the tides.

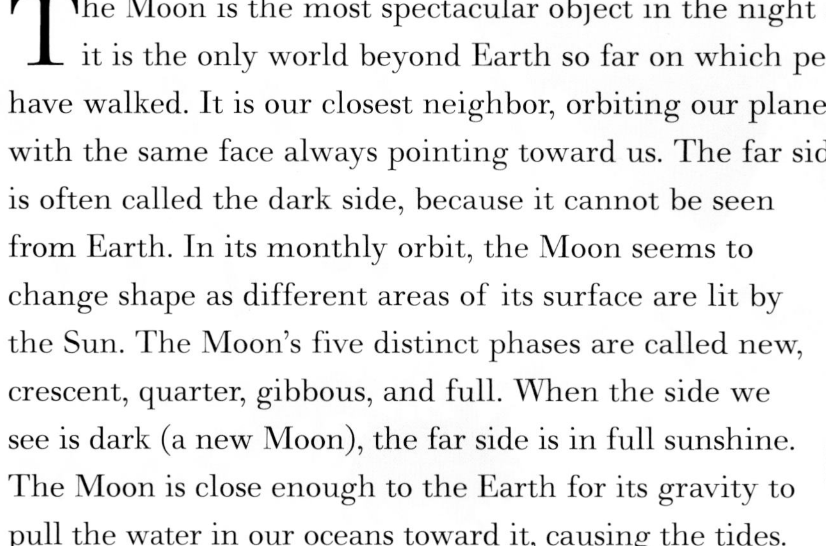

▷ *On the left is the Moon as seen from Earth, with its highlands and dark, flat* maria. *On the right is part of the heavily cratered far side.*

How the Moon formed

There are several theories to explain how the Moon formed. It may have formed together with the Earth from the solar nebula, or perhaps it spun off from a bulge at the Earth's equator. The most popular theory, derived from analysis of Moon rock and computer simulations, is that the early Earth was hit by a protoplanet the size of Mars. Some of the resulting debris merged to form the Moon.

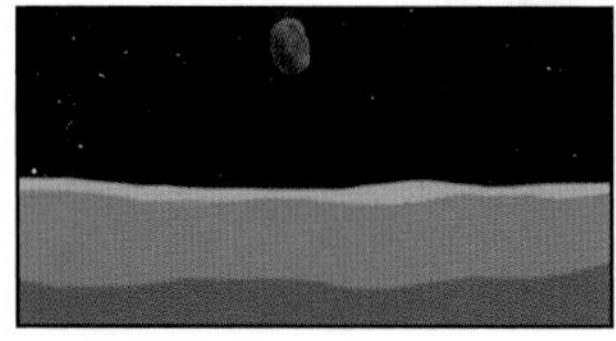

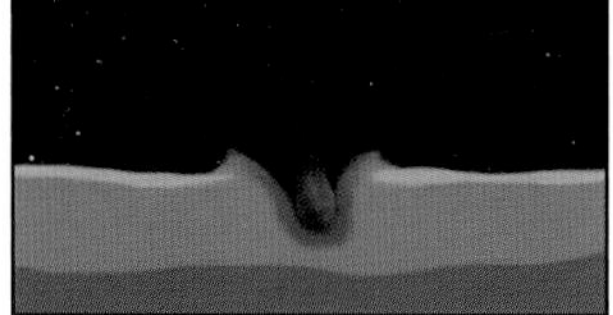

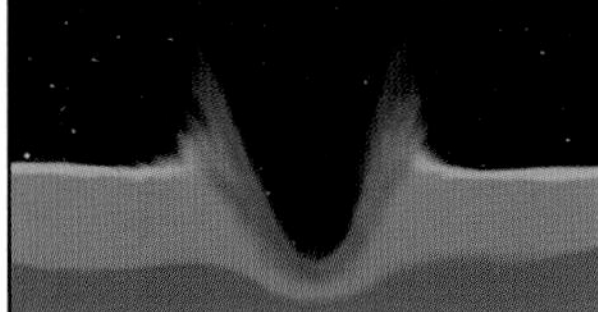

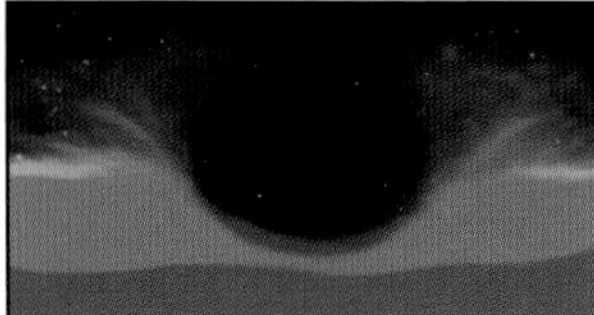

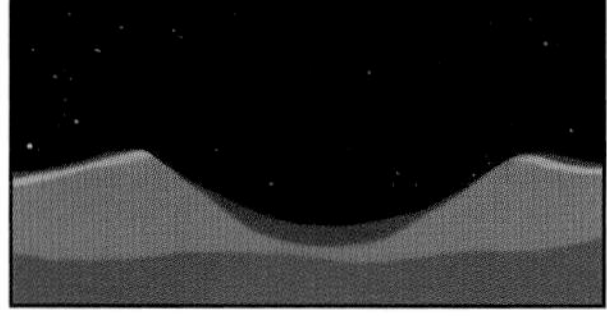

△ *Craters were formed when asteroids plunged into the lunar surface. They can be anything from a few yards to hundreds of miles across.*

△ *This view of the Moon's craters, lit by sunlight at a low angle, was taken from* Apollo 13 *in 1970.*

The Moon's surface

The lunar highlands are more than 4.2 billion years old and heavily cratered. Collisions with asteroids were violent enough to melt parts of the Moon's surfac flooding the impact basins with lava and creating grea dark regions called *maria*, or seas. Strangely, there are almost no such features on the far side of the Moon. About 3.8 billion years ago, the asteroid bombardment virtually ceased, aside from the creation of a few crater such as Copernicus. Without wind and water to erode the surface, the Moon has remained the same ever sinc

▷ *The five different phases of the Moon depend on the direction from which it is illuminated by the Sun. During each monthly cycle it goes through nine different stages.*

NEW MOON

WAXING CRESCENT

FIRST QUARTER

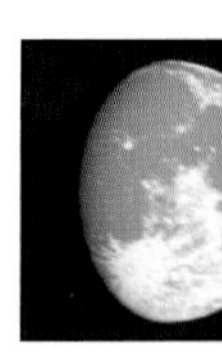

WAXING GIB

▷ The Moon was probably formed 4.5 billion years ago when a rocky protoplanet as big as Mars crashed into the newly formed Earth. Both bodies became molten, and their cores merged.

▷ The vaporized rock and fragments from the collision formed a ring around the Earth. Some of the material combined to make an object massive enough to sweep up the debris with its gravity. Finally, only two bodies remained in this area of the Solar System—the Earth and its new Moon.

Tomorrow's Moon

Twelve men have walked on the Moon, leaving landers, rovers, flags, and footprints behind. And it is still the goal of many scientists and commercial enterprises. With only one-sixth of the Earth's gravity, the Moon would be a very good place to mine bulk materials for launch into space. With permanently dark skies, no atmosphere, and no radio noise, it would also be an excellent site for setting up telescopes. Water, discovered frozen in the rocks of the south pole, could be used to supply moonbases. The main obstacle, at the moment, is the cost.

◁ The Moon's low gravity would make moonbases good staging posts for interplanetary journeys in the future. And its airless surface and dark skies would make an excellent laboratory for astronomers and scientists.

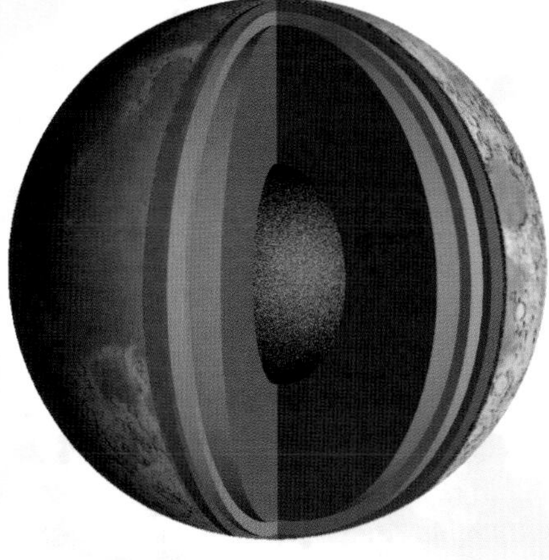

△ There is a thin crust of light colored, granitelike rock on the highlands of the Moon, above a thick, dark, and dense rocky mantle.

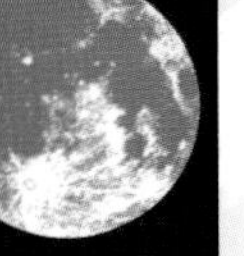

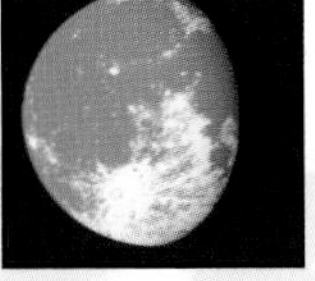

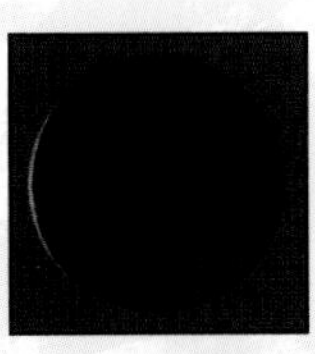

JLL MOON WANING GIBBOUS LAST QUARTER WANING CRESCENT OLD MOON

Mars

Mars is smaller, darker, and slightly more distant than Venus. It is also the most Earthlike of the planets and has always attracted humans. Mars's reddish color (with its associations of blood) led to it being named after the Roman god of war, and Martians have featured in countless science fiction stories. Speculation about life on Mars was reinforced by changing hues on the surface and reported sightings of canals. When the first Mariner probes flew past in the 1960s, however, all they saw was a barren, cratered surface, somewhat like the Moon, beneath an atmosphere one hundredth the density of the Earth's. In 1971, *Mariner 9* (the first craft to orbit a planet other than the Earth) explored Mars's fascinating geology. As the dust from a violent storm settled, a giant volcano was revealed, followed by valleys and canyons.

△ *This picture of Mars was taken by the* Hubble Space Telescope *in 1990. It reveals wispy storm clouds around the north pole and thin dust clouds in the south.*

△ *The* Mars Global Surveyor *arrived at Mars in September 1997 to begin mapping the planet with high resolution cameras, lasers, and radar.*

Heat and dust

Like Earth, Mars has a 24-hour day, although its year is nearly twice as long. The thin atmosphere is made almost entirely of carbon dioxide. Cloud swirls are often visible and, in winter, polar caps of water ice and frozen carbon dioxide form. Temperatures range from a comfortable 77°F (25°C) in summer to a bitter −184°F (−120°C) on winter nights. Although it no longer rains, there is clear evidence that water once flowed on Mars, scouring out deep channels. Today, strong winds whip up dust storms, which sometimes envelop the whole planet.

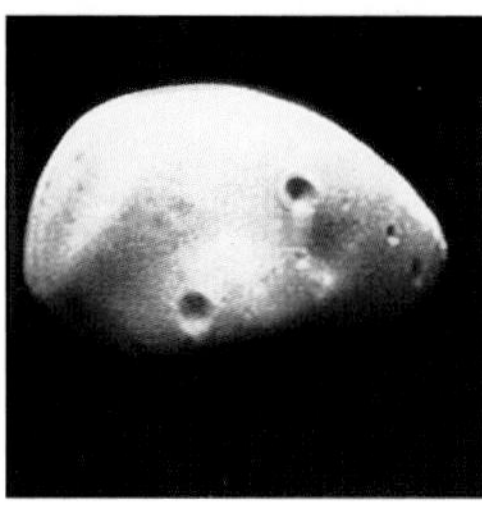

◁ *Mars has two tiny moons, Phobos* (top) *and Deimos* (bottom). *Both are probably captured asteroids. Phobos is heavily cratered. Deimos is smoother and darker.*

△ *Mars has a weak magnetic field, suggesting that its core must be solid. The thick rocky mantle may circulate slowly beneath a thin, hard crust.*

◁ *The Martian atmosphere is only one hundredth the density of the Earth's. Although it is 95 percent carbon dioxide, it does little to insulate the planet.*

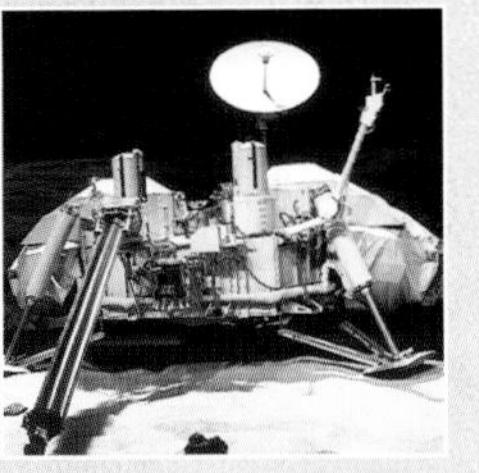

◁ *Two Viking Landers touched down on Mars in 1976. The sampling arm* (front left) *scooped up soil for analysis. The two cylinders with vertical slits are stereo cameras.*

Jnlike Mars's south pole, which is mostly en carbon dioxide, its north pole is mostly er ice. Every summer it shrinks, leaving a al pattern, probably due to wind erosion.

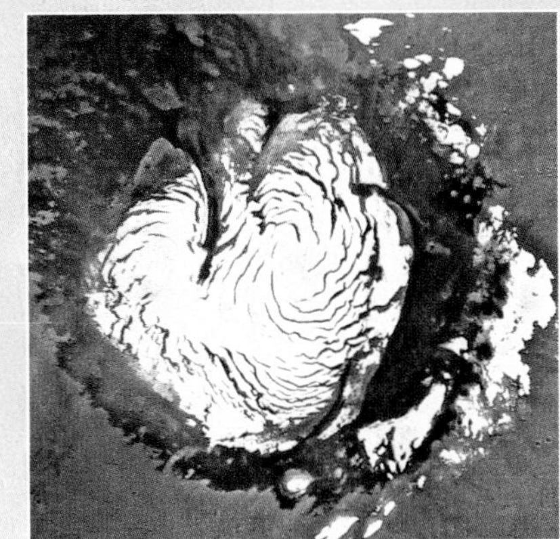

Evidence vs that water flowed down valley in the es Marineris.

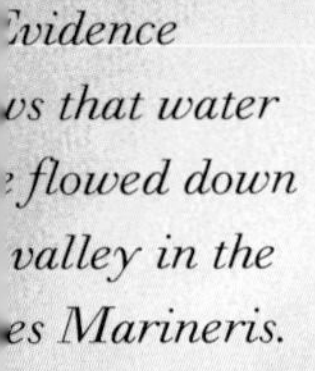

▷ *Lava flows on the flanks of the volcano Alba Patera produced this unusual pattern, photographed by* Viking 2*'s orbiter.*

The Ophir Chasm, in the Valles Marineris, formed by geological faulting. Its 13,000-foot 00-m) cliffs have seen major landslides, including walanche that traveled 40 miles (65 km).

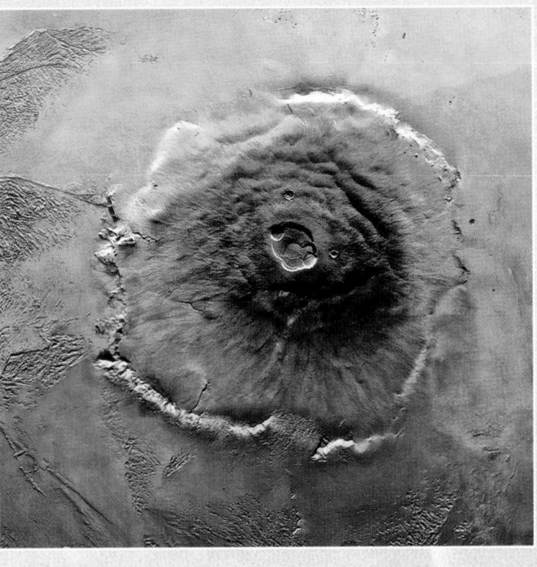

△ *The biggest volcano on Mars, and in the Solar System, is Olympus Mons at 86,600 feet (26,400 m) high. Like the Earth's biggest volcanoes, it is shield shaped, and once erupted runny, black, basalt lava.*

kings invade Mars

the 1970s, it was clear that Mars was ther covered in lush vegetation nor pulated by Martians. But there might be croscopic life (bacteria or algae) in the soil. 1976, two Viking space probes set out to estigate. Each comprised an orbiter and a der. Both landers contained miniature oratories to test Martian soil samples for ns of life. They fed nutrients into the soil d, when a gas was given off, this suggested t living organisms were using up the trients. But the process slowed and stopped. entists concluded that all they had ected were lifeless chemical reactions.

The Martian landscape

Some parts of Mars are heavily cratered and very old. Other parts have been smoothed over by newer lava flows from volcanoes. Cracks and canyons indicate past earthquakes. The Valles Marineris (*below*) is four times deeper and six times wider than the Grand Canyon in the United States. It has large areas of windblown sand dunes. Dust storms change the surface dramatically, covering or exposing rock underneath. Signs of water erosion suggest past flooding along channels and plains. This water may have escaped to space or lie frozen underground.

△ *A panorama taken by* Viking 2 *in the Utopia Planitia region. The sloping ground is strewn with angular lumps of dark, volcanic rock and frosted with a thin layer of water ice.*

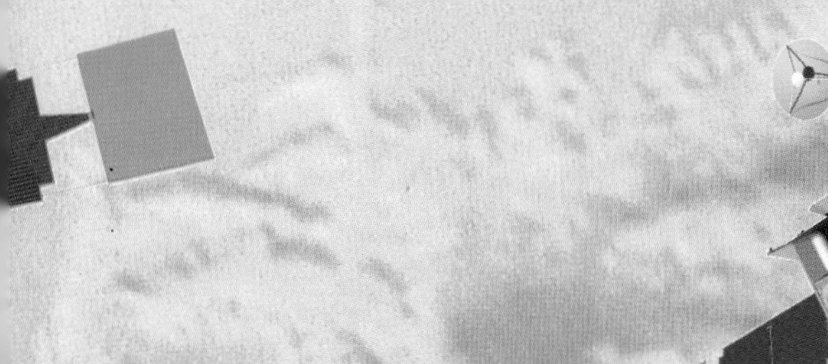

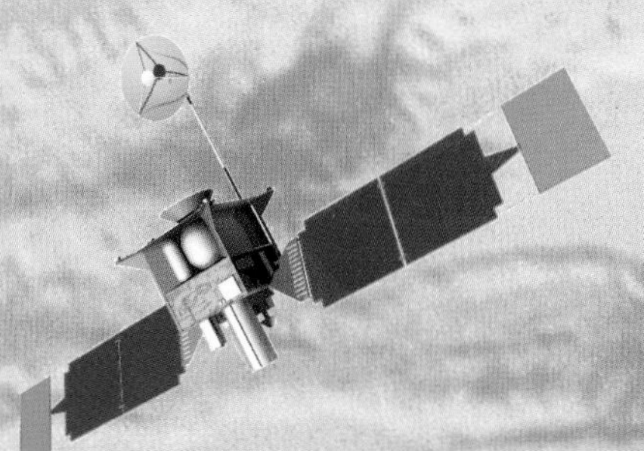

Mission to Mars

△ *As* Mars Pathfinder *neared the surface, the tether to its parachute was cut and balloons inflated. The craft bounced to a standstill and opened up to reveal instruments, solar cells, and a little rover* (inset below).

The year 1997 marked the return to the red planet. For almost twenty years, every Mars mission ended in failure. The two Russian *Phobos* crafts failed, the U.S. *Mars Observer* exploded as it prepared to enter the planet's orbit, and the mighty Russian *Mars '96* craft did not escape from the Earth's atmosphere. But finally, on Independence Day, 1997, *Mars Pathfinder* parachuted down to Mars, and its new landing technology proved to be a success. A little six-wheeled rover, *Sojourner*, spent nearly three months analyzing Martian rocks before the battery went flat. More missions have been planned, including a mission to return rock samples to Earth, and ultimately one to land the first humans on Mars.

Where did all the water go?

Great floods of water once washed down from the Martian highlands and fanned out onto the plains below. Now all the water has escaped to space, or lies frozen underground, or in the icecaps. For water to flow, Mars must once have been warmer, with a denser atmosphere. About three billion years ago all that changed. The once-molten iron core may have solidified, or the planet may have been struck by an asteroid. Whatever the cause, it resulted in the cold, barren world we see today.

Meteorite from Mars

In 1984, a grapefruit-sized lump of roc was found in Antarctica. After years of careful research, scientists were able to tell its story. It had formed on Mars 4.5 billion years ago, when the planet still young. Then, 16 million years ago, an impact threw it out into space, and 13,000 years ago, it landed on Earth. The meteorite contains chemicals and microscopic structures that some NASA scientists suggest are evidence of life—fossils from another world.

▽ Mars Pathfinder *landed in a wide flood plain. The camera revealed a panorama of low hills and a surface littered with rocks of all sizes and textures for the rover* Sojourner *to analyze.*

▷ *A Martian hand reaches out from a spaceship in the film* The War of the Worlds.

◁ Sojourner *used an x-ray spectrometer to measure the composition of rocks. Here, it is examining the rock given the name "Barnacle Bill."*

◁ *The six-wheeled* Sojourner, *the size of a microwave oven, moved from rock to rock, navigating with its own camera and laser, as well as instructions from Earth.*

△ *AH84001* (left) *is a Martian meteorite that was found in Antarctica. It contains possible fossil evidence of life. Under a powerful electron microscope, a segment of rock reveals structures that could be tiny fossil bacteria* (above).

Alien invaders

vidence on Earth suggests that life n endure extremes of temperature ıd even survive in cracks within rocks. lthough Mars appears to be a barren anet, life may once have thrived there similarly hostile conditions. Fossil ınters of the future will want to explore ıy ancient hydrothermal springs they ay find on Mars. Returned samples e likely to be put into quarantine— st in case microbes are still alive ıd choose to invade the Earth!

Home from home

Sending people to Mars—and returning them to Earth—might be more feasible if the fuel for the return journey were to be made on Mars. A robot craft could make propellant from the Martian atmosphere before astronauts arrived. A more fantastic idea is using orbiting mirrors to warm the south pole of Mars. This would release more carbon dioxide and warm the planet. Bacteria might release oxygen and ultimately make the atmosphere breathable for human colonists.

▽ *In the distant future, Mars may be made more Earthlike. A thicker atmosphere and warmer climate will allow liquid water to remain on the surface—just as it did some four billion years ago.*

▽ The asteroid belt, be Mars and Jupiter, conte rocks of all sizes. Altho they frequently collide break up, the belt is ma mostly of empty space. together, the asteroids w form an object smaller than the Moon.

Asteroids & Meteorites

△ On June 30, 1908, a huge fireball flattened 1,200 sq. miles (3,000 sq. km) of forest near Tunguska, Siberia. It was probably caused by an asteroid exploding in the atmosphere.

Between the orbits of Mars and Jupiter is a gigantic belt made up of more than 4,000 lumps of rock. They range in size from several feet across to the biggest, called Ceres, which is about 620 miles (1,000 km) across. These chunks of rock are called asteroids. Scientists believe they were formed from material similar to that of the rocky planets, such as the Earth and Mars. Stirred up by the immense gravitational influence of Jupiter, this material was unable to stick together to form a single planet. However, mini planets with iron cores may have formed, only to be smashed up by impacts with smaller debris. Collisions between asteroids are thought to be frequent. Some of the asteroids are composed mostly of iron, like the core of the Earth.

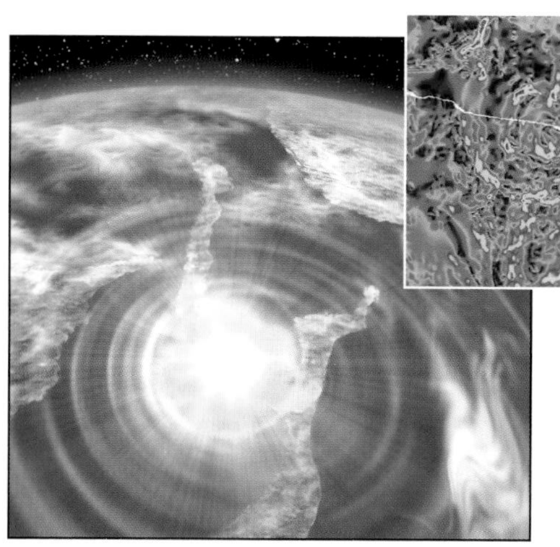

◁ When a 19-mile (30-km) asteroid hit Central America 65 million years ago, it caused a huge fireball and climate change that may have ended the age of the dinosaurs. A map (inset) *of Mexico's Yucatan Peninsula shows the crater left by the impact.*

A big impact

Not all asteroids remain in orbit between Jupiter and Mars. Some have elliptical orbits that bring them clo the Earth. Craters on the Moon were caused by asterc impacts. Evidence of asteroids bombarding Earth has mostly worn away, but geologists have identified trac of enormous ancient craters. One, in the Gulf of Me was caused by an asteroid 19 miles (30 km) across tha fell 65 million years ago. It threw up thousands of to of water and rock, blocking out the Sun and contribu to the extinction of the dinosaurs.

ould it happen again?

ccasionally, asteroid-sized rocks still hit the Earth. Small teroids strike once every 100 years, probably over ıinhabited land or sea. A 1-mile (2-km)-sized object may t only once in a million years, but it could change the climate and, indirectly, kill millions of people. Telescopes now look out for rocks that pose a threat, in the hope that missiles or lasers can be used to deflect them.

▷ *Wolf Creek crater* (above) *in Western Australia was formed about 10,000 years ago and still looks fresh. Deep Bay* (below) *in Reindeer Lake, Canada, is 150 million years old. It is so eroded that it was not thought to be an impact crater until 1957.*

Meteorites

1

2

3

4

Hundreds of tons of rock hit the Earth each year, but most burn up in the atmosphere to form shooting stars. Lumps that reach the surface are called meteorites. A few are chips off comets, the Moon, or even Mars, but most are asteroid debris. Collectors scour Australia and Antarctica to recover them. Even the bigger ones, which vaporize on impact, leave traces. They can enrich sediments many miles away with the element iridium.

'he most common meteorites stony ones made of silicate s (1). *Glassy tektites* (2) *form npact from vaporized rock. eorites made of iron* ıd 4) *are more rare.*

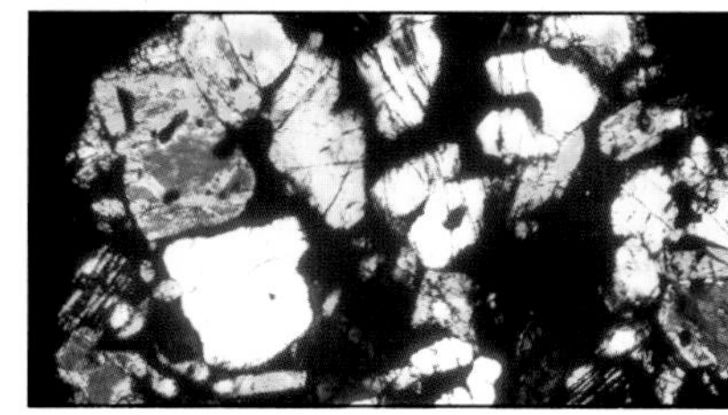

△ *Small metallic asteroids may be very valuable due to the iron, copper, cobalt, and nickel they contain. This imaginary scene shows one captured for mining in orbit around Earth.*

◁ *Under the microscope, a thin slice of meteorite reveals its component minerals. Crystals formed at high temperatures are surrounded by dark material formed at lower temperatures.*

Jupiter

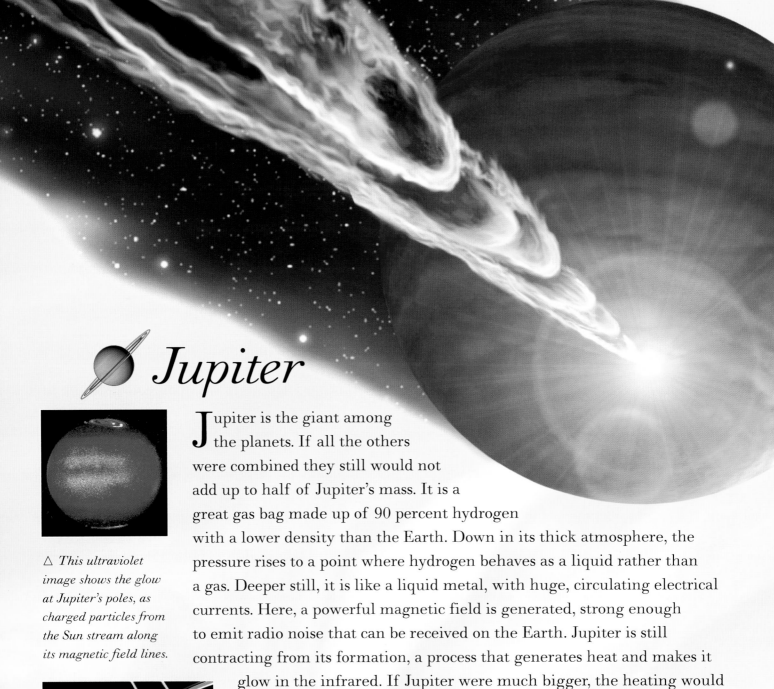

Jupiter is the giant among the planets. If all the others were combined they still would not add up to half of Jupiter's mass. It is a great gas bag made up of 90 percent hydrogen with a lower density than the Earth. Down in its thick atmosphere, the pressure rises to a point where hydrogen behaves as a liquid rather than a gas. Deeper still, it is like a liquid metal, with huge, circulating electrical currents. Here, a powerful magnetic field is generated, strong enough to emit radio noise that can be received on the Earth. Jupiter is still contracting from its formation, a process that generates heat and makes it glow in the infrared. If Jupiter were much bigger, the heating would start nuclear fusion in its core, and the planet would become a star.

△ *This ultraviolet image shows the glow at Jupiter's poles, as charged particles from the Sun stream along its magnetic field lines.*

△ *This photo shows Jupiter's thin rings, as seen by* Voyager 2 *from a distance of 901,030 miles (1,450,000 km).*

Turbulent planet

Jupiter's incredibly fast 9 hour and 55 minute rotation (or day) makes it bulge 5,592 miles (9,000 km) wider at its equator than its poles. It whips up violent winds and stretches the clouds into bands parallel to the equator. Essentially, there are about 14 alternating bands of dark, low pressure regions that circulate with the planet's rotation, and light, high pressure regions that blow the other way. Swirling storm systems form where they meet, especially in the turbulent polar regions. High, white clouds of ammonia ice are tinted yellow and orange lower down by sulfur compounds.

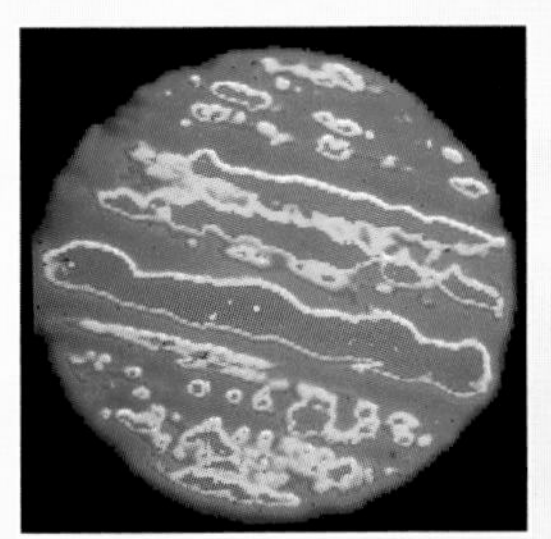

△ *The red bands in this infrared image are gases from the deeper atmosph[...] heated by the planet's continued contraction.*

◁ *Voyager 2 went on a grand tour of the giant planets, passing Jupiter in 1979, Saturn in 1981, Uranus in 1986, and Neptune in 1989.*

△ *The Red Spot, a 24,856-mile (40,000-km) storm system, has been raging for over 300 years. It has a dramatic effect on surrounding weather systems* (inset). *Nearby white ovals are huge temporary storms.*

Cosmic fireworks

In 1993, comet hunters David Levy and Gene and Carolyn Shoemaker spotted a strange comet. It had come so close to Jupiter that gravitational forces had torn it into what looked like a long string of pearls. Calculations showed that the fragments would crash into Jupiter (*left*) in July 1994. No one knew what to expect. The impacts would be just out of sight over Jupiter's horizon, so perhaps nothing would be seen. In fact, the fireballs were clearly visible and, when the impact sites rotated into view, they appeared as great brown marks, larger than the Earth.

Visitors to Jupiter

e spacecraft have visited Jupiter. *Pioneer 10* and *11* and *Voyager 1* and *2* sped past, giving valuable but tantalizingly brief glimpses. (*Voyager* discovered a thin ring of particles as fine as smoke.) But in December 1995, *Galileo* went into orbit around the giant planet. On arrival, it released a probe that descended into Jupiter's atmosphere before being destroyed by the heat. The probe found less water than was expected, but it may just have missed the moist clouds. Although the spacecraft's main antenna failed to open properly, *Galileo* has still returned spectacular pictures and data.

△ *Jupiter's clouds lie in a thin layer on the surface. Below this, the atmosphere of hydrogen and helium is compressed until it behaves like a liquid metal. Inside is a compressed rocky core, slightly bigger than the Earth.*

The southern part of Jupiter, photographed in July 1994 by Hubble Space Telescope. *Dark chemicals welling up from deep in the atmosphere mark the impact sites of fragments of comet* Shoemaker Levy 9. *Each mark lasted for several months.*

◁ *The highest clouds in the atmosphere are made of white ammonia ice crystals. Deeper down, they are tinged with sulfur compounds made from traces of hydrogen sulfide. Even deeper may be water vapor clouds like those on Earth.*

Jupiter's Moons

△ *A faint greenish light penetrates cracks in the ice. Some scientists think that under the ice there could even be liquid water.*

When Galileo first looked at Jupiter through his telescope in January 1610, he saw three, then four, tiny starlike objects moving close to the planet. He quickly realized that these were moons orbiting Jupiter. Each of these moons—Callisto, Ganymede, Europa, and Io—is a world in its own right. We now know of 12 other moons. These include four that orbit inside Galileo's moons. Beyond them lie four more, 7 million miles (11 million km) from Jupiter. Finally, at twice that distance, are another four. These may have been passing asteroids, captured by Jupiter's gravity.

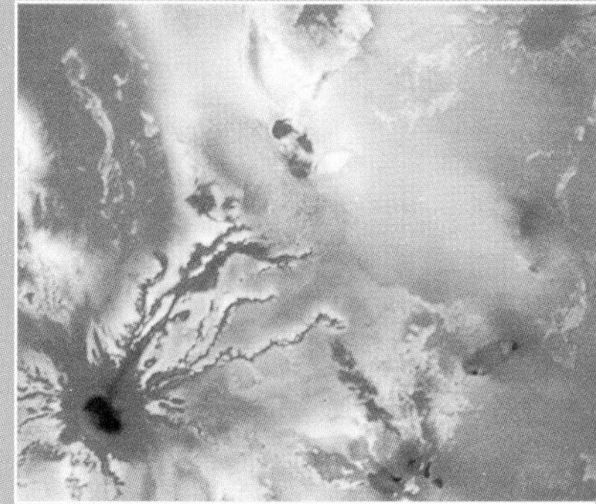

△ *The orange, sulfurous surface of Io is churned up by Jupiter's gravity resulting in these fresh lava flows from a volcanic crater. The volcanic gases escape into space to form a ring around Jupiter.*

Callisto and Ganymede

Callisto is the same size as Mercury and is covered almost entirely with craters. One huge impact structure, called Valhalla, consists of rings up to 1,900 miles (3,000 km) across. Its dark, dirty crust is a mixture of ice and rock and may be 190 miles (300 km) deep, with water or slush lying underneath. Ganymede is the largest moon in the Solar System at 3,279 miles (5,276 km) across. Its icy surface has lar dark patches that are heavily cratered. Ganymede's magneti field raises the possibility that it still has an active interi

◁ *The grooved surface of Ganymede appears to be made up of separate slabs of icy material.*

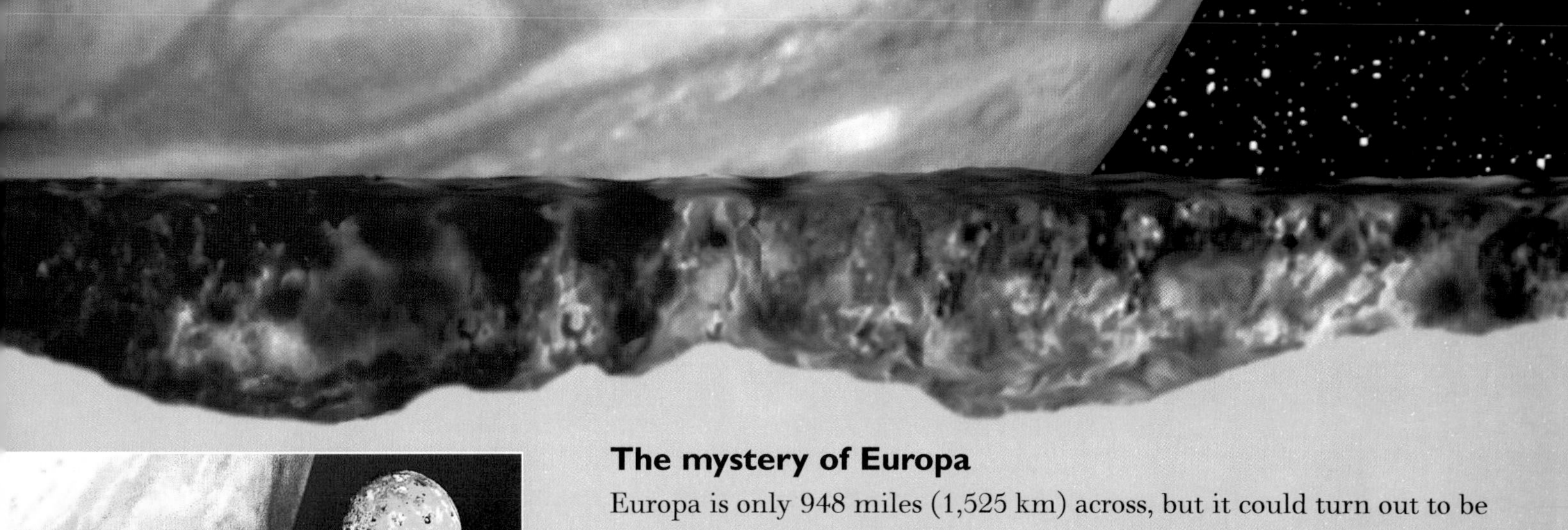

The mystery of Europa

Europa is only 948 miles (1,525 km) across, but it could turn out to be the most exciting of Jupiter's moons. The smooth, white surface has very few craters, but is crazed by numerous cracks. The cracks look very similar to those in pack ice on Earth. This suggests that the ice is floating on an ocean of liquid water. Hydrothermal vents in the ocean floor might provide energy as they do on Earth, and it is just possible that life could have developed in the cold, dark water.

Io, world of fire

Io is the most volcanically active world in the Solar System. It is tugged so hard by Jupiter's gravity that tidal forces churn up the surface and interior, keeping the moon partly molten. The Voyager craft saw eruptions taking place, with sulfur dioxide spewing 190 miles (300 km) up into space. Other volcanoes have left dark lava flows and red and yellow patches of sulfur, making this moon look like a moldy orange.

This composite picture shows Jupiter varfing its four main moons. Closest to the eat planet is Io (top), *followed by Europa, anymede—the largest moon—and Callisto.*

If oceans do exist beneath Europa's icy rface, there is also the possibility of life urishing in the cold water. Volcanic vents the ocean floor could provide the energy to support life, whatever form it might take.

△ Voyager 2 *revealed the cracked, icy surface of Europa. In close-up the structures resemble those found in pack ice around the Earth's poles, with tilted slabs, cracks, and icebergs.*

▷ *Callisto's ancient surface is pockmarked by billions of years of impacts.*

Saturn

△ Voyager 1 *found dark lines running across Saturn's rings, like spokes on a wheel. Since the rings orbit at different speeds, the spokes were difficult to explain. They are now thought to be caused by ice crystals charged with static electricity.*

After Galileo discovered Jupiter's moons he turned his attention to what appeared to be a triple planet. Then the objects to the sides seemed to disappear, making him suspect they were gas clouds. It was a Dutch astronomer, Christiaan Huygens, who finally realized, in 1675, that Saturn was a ringed planet. Just under 200 years later it was shown that the rings could not possibly be solid disks, but must be made up of millions of smaller particles of rock or ice, each acting like a tiny moon. When space probes *Pioneer 11* (1979), *Voyager 1* (1980), and *Voyager 2* (1981) flew past Saturn, it became clear that there are thousands of separate bands of different densities within the main rings (which are named A, B, C, D, and E). There is also a very thin F ring outside these, its particles kept in line by two tiny moons. The rings are less than 98 feet (30 m) thick, and may have formed from the breakup of a giant comet that strayed too close to Saturn.

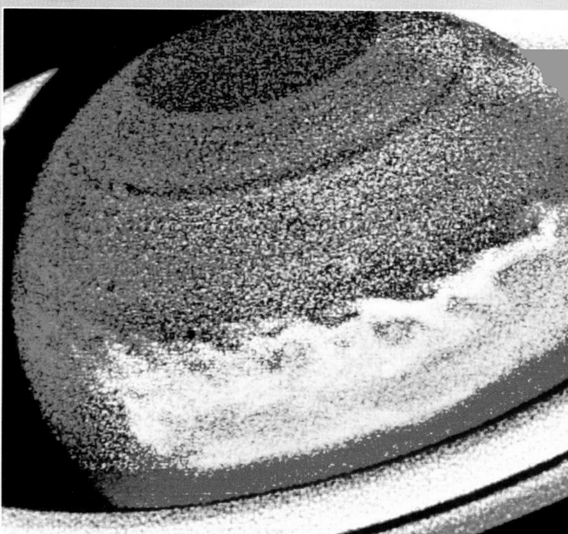

△ *An image, taken by the* Hub Space Telescope *in 1990, enhan to show the clouds. An elongate Great White Spot of ammonia crystals has formed high up in atmosphere. The false colors pic out the top of the spot in red.*

△ *As* Voyager 2 *drew away from Saturn, it photographed the rings illuminated from behind. By tracking a star as it passed behind the rings, thousands of individual ringlets were recorded.*

Stormy weather

A constant dull yellow haze of high ammonia clouds masks the deeper structure of Saturn's atmosphere. Occasionally, telescopes can make out a huge, swirling, white storm system. Computer enhancement of the Voyager images revealed circulating bands of clouds similar to Jupiter's. The fastest winds race around Saturn's equator, reaching up to 1,100 miles (1,800 km) per hour. To the north and south of the equator are alternating bands of slow and fast winds.

▷ *Two pictures of Saturn taken by the* Hubble Space Telescope. *In the top picture, the shadow of the rings and Titan, Saturn's largest moon, are visible. In the bottom picture, Saturn appears with its rings tilted.*

'oyager 2 27 million es (43 million away from urn when it rded this image 981. Computers e enhanced the dull 'ow clouds to reveal ds in the atmosphere vinds up to 1,100 mph (1,800 /h) encircle the planet. A double m system is visible in the thern hemisphere.

△ Saturn's atmosphere may be 1,200 miles (2,000 km) deep with liquid hydrogen reaching down another 20,000 miles (32,000 km).

◁ Beneath a yellow haze, the Voyager probes identified three layers in Saturn's atmosphere. The outer layer has clouds of ammonia, followed by ammonium sulfide, and finally clouds containing water.

netary structure

e Jupiter, Saturn does not have a solid surface, although ronomers think it has a small, rocky core at its center. e planet is 75,000 miles (120,000 km) across (without its gs) and 95 times Earth's mass. Hydrogen makes up percent; the rest is helium, with traces of ammonia, thane, and other gases. Also like Jupiter, most of the erior is liquid hydrogen, which deep down becomes an ctrically conducting, metallic liquid. Electrical currents e generate a strong magnetic d. A day at the equator lasts a ef 10 hours, 15 minutes.

Last bus to Saturn

Since the Voyager flybys, only one probe has been sent to distant Saturn. *Cassini* is the size of a bus and packed with instruments. Launched in 1997, *Cassini* will arrive in 2004 and go into orbit, surveying the planet, its rings, moons, and magnetic field for at least three years.

During the six-year journey to Saturn, Cassini*'s ectory will include two Venus flybys, flyby of the Earth, and of Jupiter.*

Saturn's Moons

Saturn is at the center of a solar system in miniature. Besides the billions of particles making up its rings, 23 different moons have been identified. Some are lumps of rock only a few miles across that lie close to the planet and shepherd the rings into place. Saturn's most distant moon, Phoebe, is nearly 8 million miles (13 million km) from the planet. The biggest of all the moons is Titan. At 3,200 miles (5,150 km) across, it is bigger than Mercury and has a thick atmosphere. It is the only atmosphere astronomers know of, aside from the Earth's, that is made up mostly of nitrogen. The surface of Titan is very cold—about –292°F (–180°C)—and the atmospheric pressure is double that of our own planet. Titan's atmosphere resembles the early Earth's, but kept in frozen lifelessness.

△ *Discovered by Christiaan Huygens in 1655, Titan is the second largest moon in the Solar System.* Voyager 2 *saw only this orange ball of smog, made by the action of sunlight on Titan's atmosphere.*

△ *In November 2004, after a seven-year journey, the* Huyge *probe will be released above th clouds of Titan from the* Cassi *Saturn orbiter. After an initial fiery entry, the heat shield wil fall away, and the probe will parachute down to the surface of the moon.*

A giant among moons

The interior of Titan is probably a mixture of rock and ice, with a rocky core that has an ice mantle. The ice could never melt, but there may be lakes or seas on Titan, not of water but of liquid natural gas or methane. Methane rain or snow may fall from the clouds. The Voyager probes were unable to see any features on Titan because it is wrapped in a thick, butterscotch yellow, chemical smog.

▽ *High in Titan's nitrogen atmosphere is a layer that absorbs ultraviolet rays. A thin blue haze of carbon chemicals sits above an unbroken layer of orange smog. Below this, the sky may have clouds of methane.*

Mysterious worlds

Saturn's other large moons are equally strange. Enceladus has an ancient, cratered landscape, with signs of newer activity in the form of smooth plains and a series of ridges. Iapetus, the outermost of Saturn's big moons, is a little denser than water, suggesting it is mostly ice. One side is bright and cratered but the opposite side is as black as anything in the Solar System. Dione has light, wispy markings that may be trails of frost sprayed out from ice volcanoes. Mimas, just outside the rings, has an enormous crater, like a huge black eye. Tethys is made up mostly of pure ice and has a crack, 60 miles (100 km) across and 3 miles (5 km) deep, running almost pole to pole.

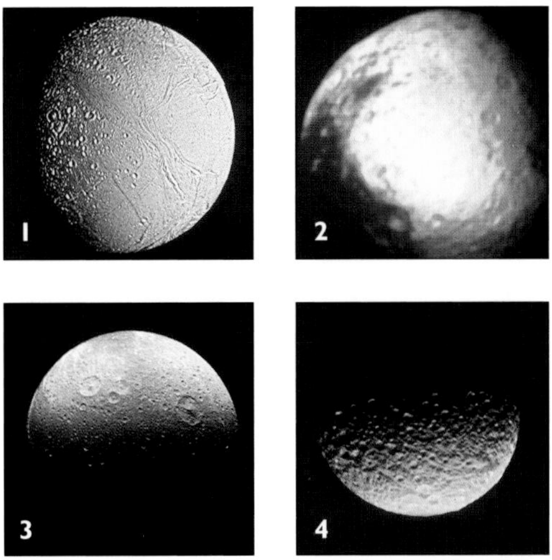

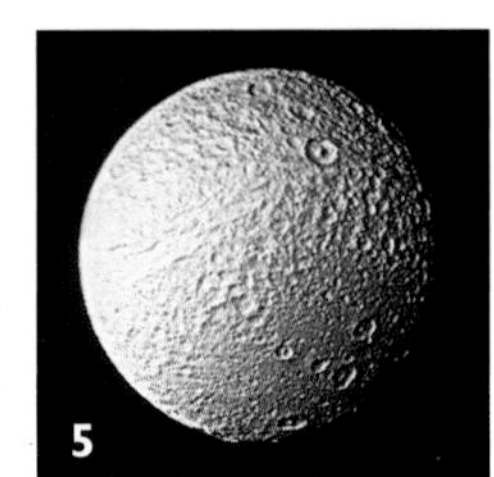

△ *These* Voyager *images show five of Saturn's large moons: Enceladus* (1), *Iapetus* (2), *Dione* (3), *Mimas* (4), *and Tethys* (5).

Landing on Titan

On November 27, 2004 the *Cassini* Saturn orbiter will release the *Huygens* probe above the clouds of Titan. No one knows what the probe will find. It may land on rock or ice, or even in a sea of liquid methane. If waves do not sink it, the probe will use sonar to measure depths, as well as recording temperatures and composition. It may even find the basic chemicals needed for life, suspended in a deep freeze.

▽ *The* Huygens *probe will have 2.5 hours to make its readings as it descends through the smog of Titan. It is designed to survive landings on both solid and liquid surfaces.*

Uranus

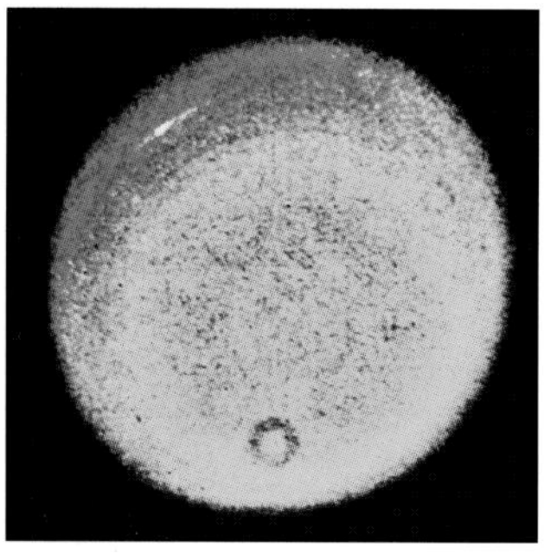

△ *By using computers to stretch blues and greens into a wider spectrum, scientists were able to see white clouds of methane near Uranus's equator* (top left).

Mercury, Venus, Mars, Jupiter, and Saturn are all visible to the naked eye and have been known since ancient times. Uranus was the first planet to be discovered through a telescope. One March night in 1781, the astronomer William Herschel noticed what he described as "either a nebulous star or perhaps a comet." He actually had become the first person to discover Uranus. Although it is four times the size of the Earth, Uranus is twice as far away as Saturn and, even through a telescope, only appears as a tiny greenish disk. Herschel wanted to name the new planet after the English king, George III, but in the end it was named after Uranus, the Greek god of the sky.

Cloudy world

Only one probe, *Voyager 2*, has visited Uranus, on January 24, 1986. No one knew what it would find, as the planet appears totally featureless through telescopes on the Earth. When the probe's pictures were enhanced, they revealed clouds on the surface. These show that the planet rotates once every 17 hours, 14 minutes, with winds blowing at up to 190 mph (300 km/h).

▽ *Combining images taken by* Voyager 2 *through orange, blue, and green filters revealed Uranus as a featureless blue ball.*

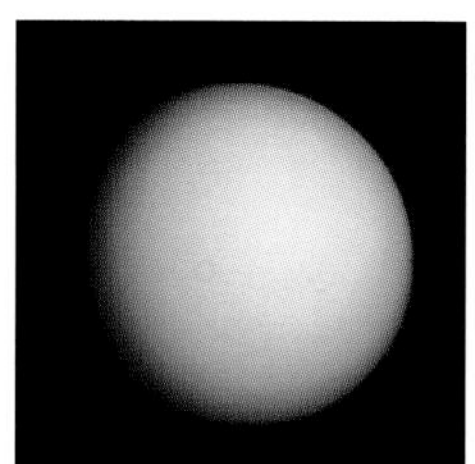

Surprise discovery

In March 1977, astronomers noticed a star passing behind Uranus. Hoping to record how it dimmed as it disappeared behind the atmosphere, they tracked it with an infrared telescope. To their amazement, the star flickered on and off. The only explanation was that Uranus is also encircled by rings.

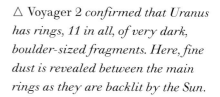

△ Voyager 2 *confirmed that Uranus has rings, 11 in all, of very dark, boulder-sized fragments. Here, fine dust is revealed between the main rings as they are backlit by the Sun.*

◁ *This color-enhanced picture, taken as* Voyager 2 *approached Uranus's south pole, indicated that a high-altitude haze had formed during the southern hemisphere's 42-year-long summer.*

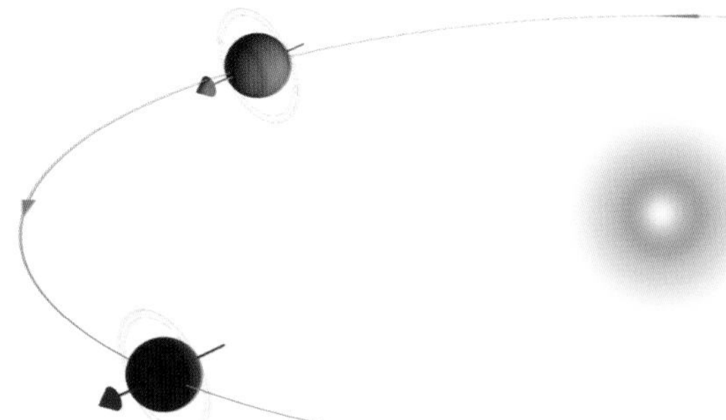

◁ *Miranda, only 300 miles (480 km) across, has a varied landscape with old, cratered plains and ice cliffs. Regions like the Chevron* (below) *suggest the moon was once almost completely shattered by a major impact.*

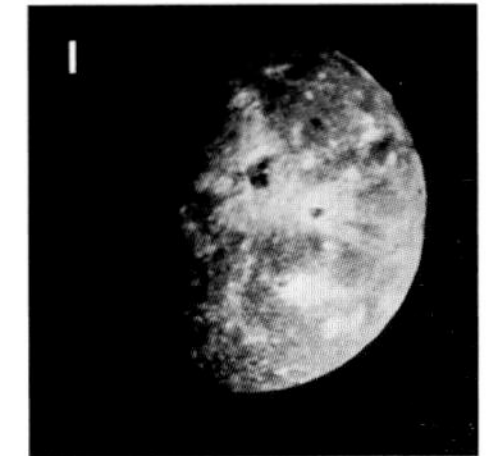

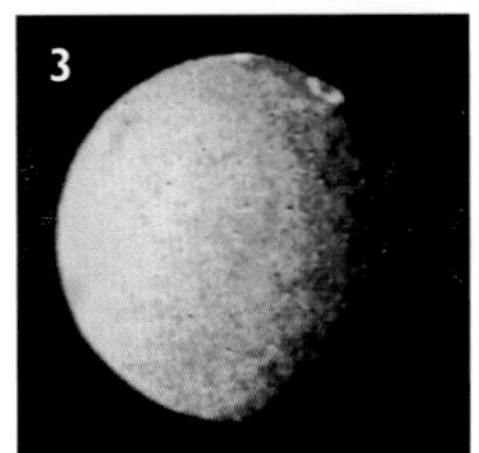

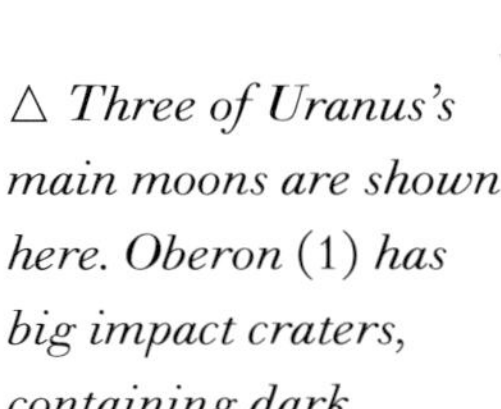

△ *Three of Uranus's main moons are shown here. Oberon* (1) *has big impact craters, containing dark, carbon-rich material. Ariel* (2) *is covered in places by small craters and resurfaced in others by eruptions of lava or water. Umbriel* (3) *has a dark, cratered surface, but no signs of geological activity.*

Multiple moons

Until the *Voyager 2* mission, Uranus was known to have five moons: Oberon, Titania, Umbriel, Ariel, and Miranda (all named after characters from English literature). As *Voyager 2* approached, another moon was spotted and named Puck. A further nine small, dark moons also were found. The two innermost moons, Cordelia and Ophelia, on opposite sides of the outer ring, help shepherd the ring particles into line. One astronomer commented that God must have taken a shaker and scattered moons in all directions.

◁ *The atmosphere of Uranus is made up of hydrogen, helium, and a small percentage of methane. It has very few cloud markings.*

△ *The blue-green gas giant Uranus is four times the size of the Earth. It has a strange magnetic field aligned at 60° to the rotation axis and off-centered 6,200 miles (10,000 km) from the heart of the planet. It may be generated by electrical currents in the watery mantle.*

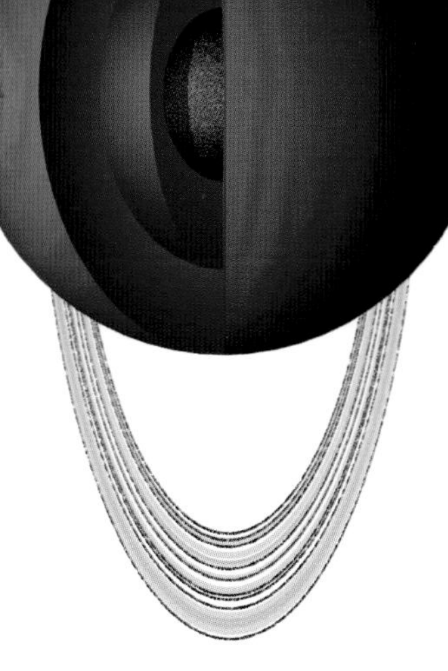

◁ *Uranus probably has a rocky core with a mantle of ammonia, methane, and water ice that may be partially liquid.*

trange rotation

ılike the other planets' axes, Uranus's axis of rotation .t right angles to its orbit around the Sun. So, as *vager 2* approached Uranus's south pole, the rings and ons seemed to circle the planet like a target. This also es Uranus very strange seasons. The poles are the warmest places on the planet. The south pole has a summer lasting 42 years, when the Sun never sets, while the opposite pole is plunged into total darkness for 42 years.

◁ *Uranus rotates at an angle of 97° to the Sun during its 84-year orbit.*

▷ *The orbits of Uranus's five main moons are shown here. From the outside in they are: Oberon, Titania, Umbriel, Ariel, and Miranda. They orbit in circular paths in the same direction as the planet's rotation.*

Neptune

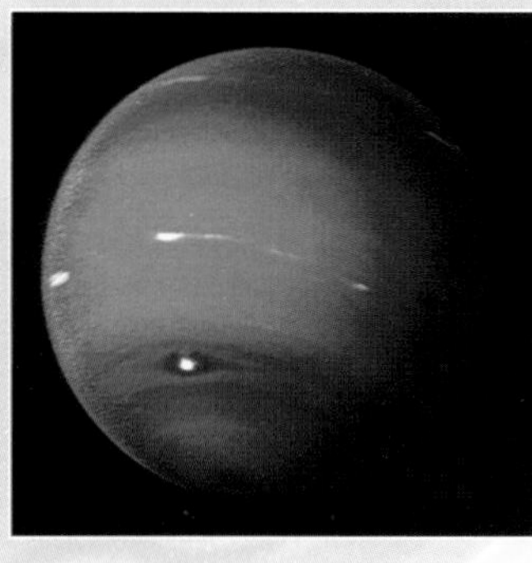

△ *This image, made by* Voyager 2 *in 1989, has been enhanced to reveal a haze above the atmosphere and white clouds of methane ice.*

After the discovery of Uranus, astronomers were unable to make sense of its orbit around the Sun—it seemed as if something was pulling it off course. In 1845, Cambridge graduate John Couch Adams suggested this movement was being caused by an eighth planet, and a year later his professor, James Challis, began a search. In France, Urbain Leverrier had made similar predictions and, although Challis had seen the new planet without recognizing it, Berlin astronomers used the French predictions to discover Neptune in 1846. They named the blue-green planet after the Roman god of the sea. It is 2.8 billion miles (4.5 billion km) from the Sun and takes 165 years to orbit it (a Neptunian year).

◁ *The Great Dark Spot, fringed with methane ice clouds, is as big as the Earth. It travels around Neptune backward. The Solar System's fastest winds blow around it at 1,240 mph (2,000 km/hr).*

△ *Neptune is mad up of a thick mantl of liquid water and gases around a roc core. It has a magn field inclined at 50 its axis and 6,200 n (10,000 km) off cen It has rings made u of large particles and broad bands of finer dust.*

Weather forecast

Neptune's atmosphere is 85 percent hydrogen, 13 percent helium, and 2 percent methane. It is bitterly cold (the cloud tops are –346°F [–210°C]), but heat is produced in the interior. Neptune is very active. Clouds of methane rise through the atmosphere and violent winds blow at over 620 mph (1,000 km/hr). One cloud pattern, the Scooter, speeds around the planet passing another feature, the Great Dark Spot, every few days.

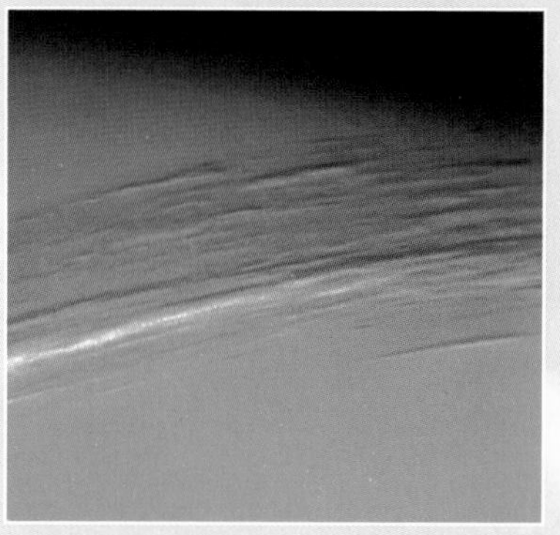

△ *The atmosphere is topped by a thi haze with cirrus clouds of methane ic Sunlight causes reactions in the meth producing hydrocarbon snow. As this it reverts to methane gas and rises ag*

◁ *High-speed winds have stretched o these high cirrus clouds of methane in streamers. They cast shadows onto th main cloud deck, 30 mi. (50 km) bene*

◁ *Neptune's two main moons, Triton and Nereid, have very different orbits. Nereid's long elliptical orbit lasts 360 days. Triton's 5.9-day orbit circles the planet backward. Both may have been caught by Neptune's gravity as they passed.*

Rings and moons

Before *Voyager 2*'s flyby of Neptune in 1989, only two moons and partial rings were known to astronomers. The craft's cameras confirmed complete rings, bands of dust, and six new moons. The largest is Proteus. It is 271 miles (436 km) across and has a giant 93-mile (150-km) crater. Then comes Larissa at 129 miles (208 km). The other four moons lie between the rings. The outermost moon, Nereid, may be a captured comet. Neptune's largest moon, Triton, is 1,681 miles (2,706 km) across. With no high mountains and few craters, its surface may have been flooded by eruptions of liquid water and ammonia. Most of its surface is ice, but the poles are capped with a pink snow of frozen nitrogen.

▽ *Triton's south pole is capped by a light, pinkish substance that is probably frozen nitrogen accumulated during its long winter in shadow. The grooved and wrinkled surface to the north has a red tint, possibly due to hydrocarbons produced by the action of sunlight.*

This imagined view from the surface of Triton shows Neptune ·he horizon and an active nitrogen geyser erupting from the face. Pressure keeps nitrogen liquid deep below the ground. As it rises, it explodes as ice crystals and vapor. The eruption carries this 18.5 miles (30 km) high, before it blows away in the thin wind, raining a dark streak of dust down onto the surface.

Pluto

In order to explain the orbit of Uranus, astronomers realized they had to discover something else. An American astronomer, Percival Lowell, predicted a planet larger than Earth and searched for it in vain. (Pluto appeared on his photographs, but he failed to recognize it.) However, Clyde Tombaugh, a successor at the observatory Lowell founded in Arizona, painstakingly compared star after star and finally found one that moved. Named Pluto (Greek god of the underworld) at the suggestion of an 11-year-old girl, it is 3.7 billion miles (6 billion km) from the Sun and one four-hundredth the mass of Earth.

△ *This image of Pluto is made up from measurements taken by the* Hubble Space Telescope. *The lightest patches may be nitrogen ice.*

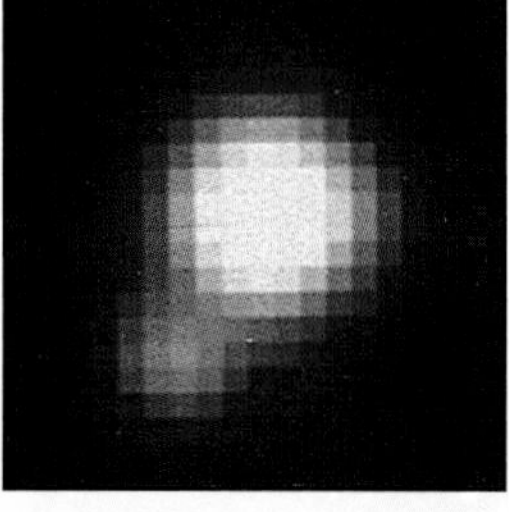

△ *Even the most powerful Earth-based telescopes can only just make out the faint disk of Pluto. No probe has visited Pluto, and it will be many years before one will be able to fill in the details.*

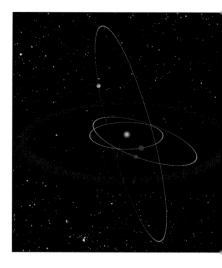

△ *Pluto is usually the farthest planet from the Sun, but its elliptical orbit* (orange) *briefly brings it closer than Neptune* (blue). *Some astronomers predict that a Planet X* (green) *follow a steeply inclined orbit far outside Plu The Kuiper Belt—a ring of small, icy objects—lies beyond the planets.*

▽ *Icy Pluto hangs just above the horizon in this imagined view fr its moon, Charon. The Sun is t bright star in the sky to the ri Charon is half the size of Plu and twenty times closer than the Moon is to the Earth. Its permanently frozen surface m have a solidified sea of metha*

Seeing double

When it was first discovered, Pluto's mass and density were unknown, so no one knew if it was the final explanation for the outer planets' orbits. If Pluto had a moon, however, the masses could be calculated from that moon's orbit. There the matter rested until 1978, when James Christy was trying to make precise measurements of Pluto at the U.S. Naval Observatory. At first, his picture seemed pear shaped. Suddenly, he realized he was seeing not one object, but two. He named the second moon Charon for his wife, and also for the mythological ferryman to the ancient Greek underworld.

▷ Both Pluto and Charon are denser than the other outer planets and their moons. They must have big, rocky cores covered by thick layers of water ice, frozen methane, and nitrogen.

This picture shows Pluto and Charon. Pluto at 1,400 miles (2,300 km) across is far smaller than our Moon, while Charon is less than 750 miles (1,200 km) across.

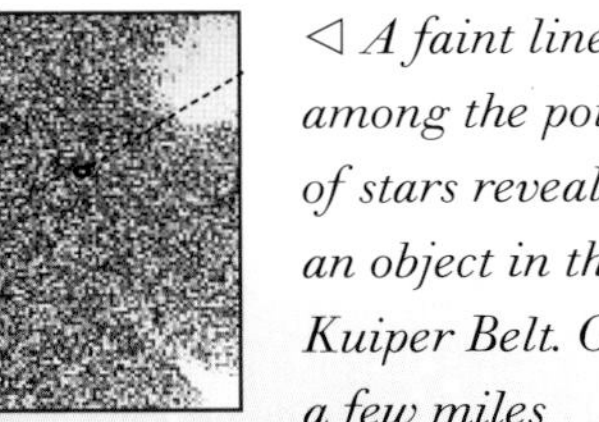

◁ A faint line among the points of stars reveals an object in the Kuiper Belt. Only a few miles across, a few hundred of these objects have been observed with powerful infrared telescopes.

Planet X and beyond

Pluto, however, did not account for all the discrepancies in Uranus's orbit, and astronomers started searching for a tenth planet, Planet X. Clyde Tombaugh searched for 13 years, plotting the positions of 45 million stars and identifying 775 asteroids in the process. Some people predicted that a planet would be found in an orbit angled to the other planets, while others thought that the Sun had a distant, dark companion. There may also be billions of comets beyond the planets adding their gravitational effect. A belt of icy objects known as the Kuiper Belt has been discovered far beyond Pluto. Each object is only a few miles across, and they may be the frozen leftovers from planetary formation.

△ Pluto has a thin atmosphere of nitrogen and methane. It thickens as the planet warms slightly, when its elliptical orbit brings it nearer the Sun. Polar caps of methane ice may be deposited as Pluto cools again.

Comets

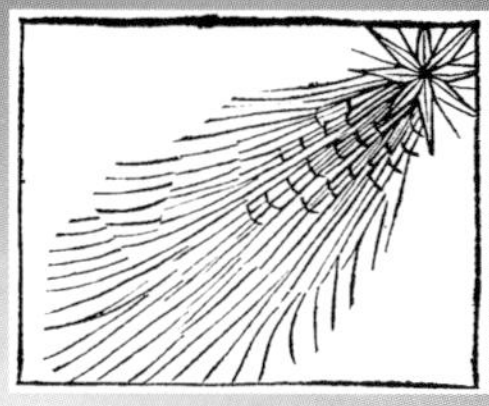

△ *This engraving from the* Nuremberg Chronicle *(published in 1493) depicts the sighting of Halley's Comet in A.D. 684.*

Comets are among the most beautiful and exciting sights in the sky. They are made all the more mysterious by their unpredictability, leading people in the past to think that they were omens of either good or evil. Five hundred years ago, they were thought to be part of the atmosphere. Then, in 1577, Danish astronomer Tycho Brahe figured out the distance to a comet and showed that they came from beyond the planets and rounded the Sun before returning to deep space. We now know that there must be a vast number of comets in the outer regions of the Solar System, far beyond the planets. In fact, there could be billions waiting in the deep freeze of space.

△ *In the* Adoration of the Magi *by Giotto, Halley's Comet is shown as the star of Bethlehem, above the stable.*

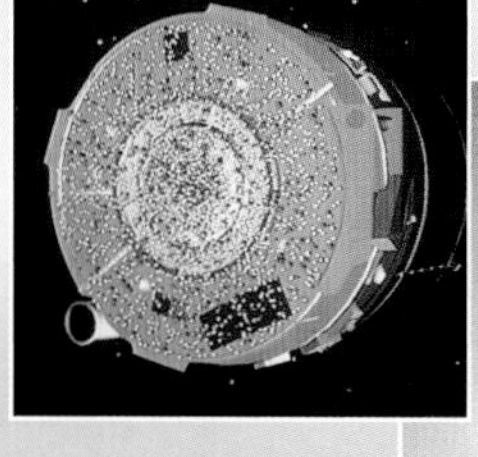

△ *This computer simulation shows how the front dust shield of* Giotto *looked after speeding past the nucleus of Halley's Comet. Dust particles punched holes in the metal.* Giotto *took a close-up picture of the comet's dark nucleus* (right) *silhouetted against brighter jets of gas.*

Halley's Comet

Edmond Halley studied the records of comets and realized that the comets of 1531, 1607, and 1682 were actually the same object. He predicted correctly this comet's return in 1759, although he never lived to see it. In fact, Halley's Comet has been seen 30 times since 240 B.C. It is depicted in the Bayeux Tapestry, which shows the Norman Conquest of England in 1066, and in a painting of the Nativity by the Italian artist Giotto, based on his sighting of the comet in 1301. In 1986, a probe named *Giotto* visited Halley's Comet.

▽ *In 1997, Comet Hale-Bopp gave a great display. Its nucleus was unusually large and it started to brighten beyond Jupiter's orbit.*

△ *This image of Comet Hale-Bopp, taken in 1996, is colored to show the bright coma as well as the dark nucleus embedded deep within it.*

The core of a comet

Comets are all show and little substance. At the center is a small nucleus, only a few miles across, like a dirty snowball. It may contain lumps of rock, but they are loosely bound by ice, so comets often break up. As the nucleus approaches the inner Solar System, the ice begins to vaporize, creating the bright coma (a sphere of gas and dust around the nucleus) and tail, which can be millions of miles long. A crust of black, carbon-rich material covers the surface with jets of gas breaking out through cracks. Each time a comet passes the Sun it loses millions of tons of ice, eventually leaving a dead, dark nucleus or just a trail of dust.

'he nucleus of a comet is like a e, dirty snowball. Jets of gas and escape through fissures in its black, altlike surface, blown by the solar d to form a tail. Here, the surface has cut away to reveal the icy interior, ounding a loosely bound, rocky core.

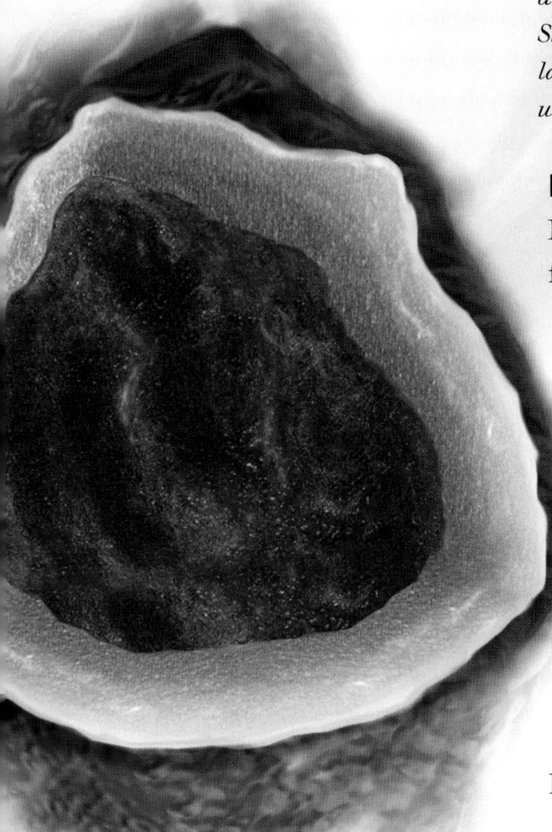

△ *Comets have two tails. Electrically charged ions of gas always point directly away from the Sun. The yellower dust tail lags slightly and curves with the comet's motion.*

△ *Blown back by the solar wind (a constant stream of electrically charged particles emitted by the Sun), a comet's tails always point away from the Sun. The tails are longest closest to the Sun, when gas production is at its highest.*

Dead comets and shooting stars

Long after a comet has run out of bright gas and faded for good, anything that is left of the nucleus, along with a stream of dusty particles, continues in the same orbit. When the Earth passes through this orbit, thousands of the particles burn up as shooting stars in the atmosphere. These are the meteor showers that seem to radiate out from the same place in the sky at the same time each year. Spectacular storms look as if they emerge from particular constellations. For example, the Perseid shower, which follows Comet Swift-Tuttle, appears from the constellation Perseus, while the Orionids, which follow Halley's Comet, seem to come from Orion.

e Oort Cloud

out, on the edge of the Solar System, lies a gigantic ıd of billions of frozen comets called the Oort Cloud. ne comets are concentrated in a disk beyond the orbit Pluto, while others are randomly distributed up to a ıt year or more away. The gravity of nearby stars ocks" these comets from their orbits so that they fall ard the Sun. About ten comets a year are newcomers he inner Solar System, where many become trapped. Oort Cloud may be debris left over from when the ır System formed. If so, comets may be able to tell vhat conditions were like when the Sun was born.

△ *An exposure of only a few seconds captured the bright streaks of the Leonid meteor shower, which seems to radiate from the constellation Leo and follows Comet Tempel-Tuttle.*

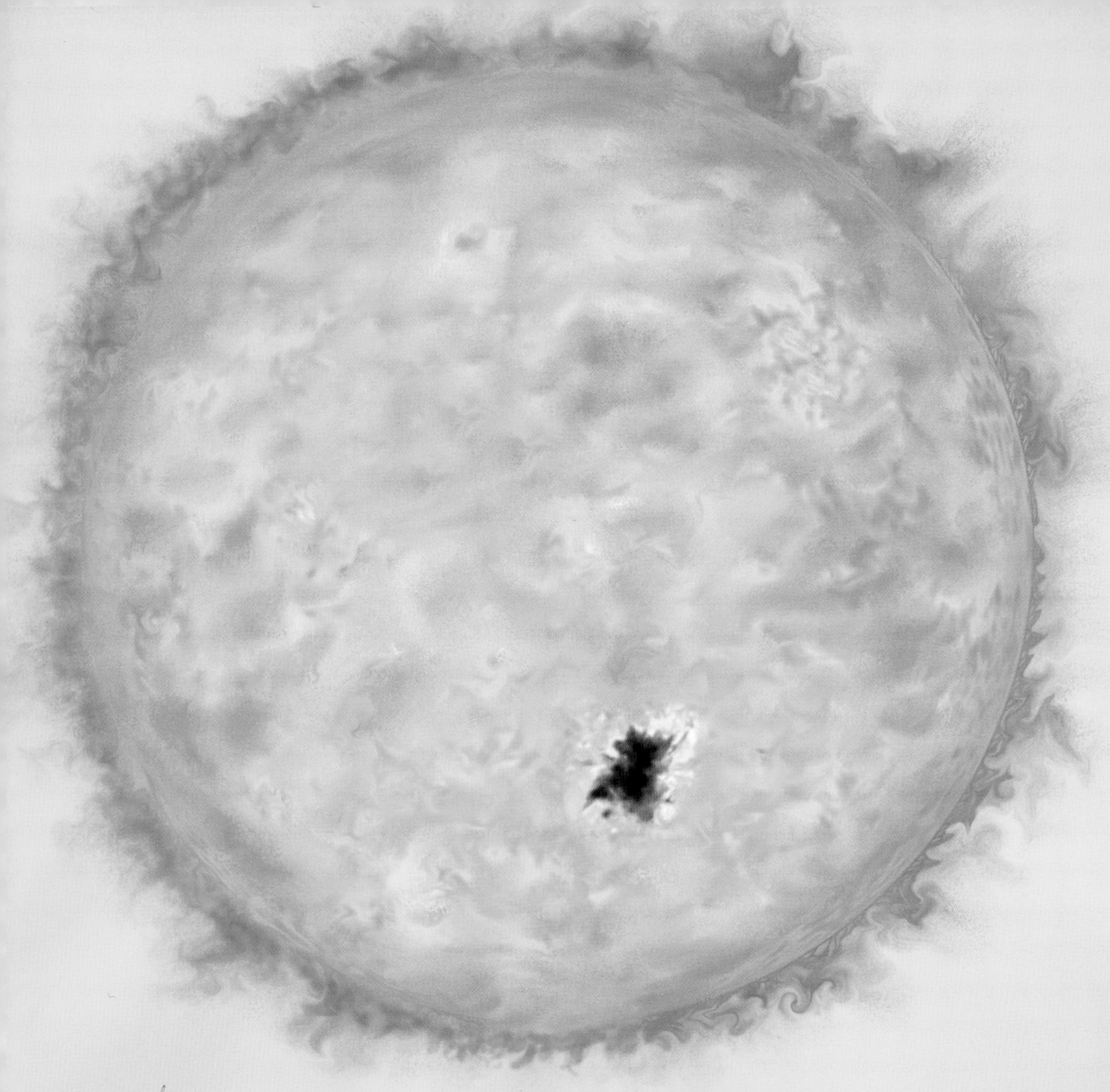

◁ *The Sun has been burning for abc five billion years. Like all stars, it is huge ball of very hot gas. Its constan stream of sunshine keeps our planet warm, enables plants to photosynthes and ultimately sustains all life.*

The Active Sun

△ *Sunlight scatters off dust and clouds in Earth's atmosphere to produce spectacular sunrises and sunsets.*

The Sun is our nearest star, the center of the Solar System, and the source, directly or indirectly, of almost all the energy we use. The Sun is extremely hot—about 10,800°F (6,000°C) at the surface, or photosphere, and 27,000,000°F (15,000,000°C) at the core. The core temperature and pressure are high enough for an energy-generating process called nuclear fusion to take place. Protons, the nuclei of hydrogen atoms, fuse together to make deuterium or heavy hydrogen, then helium. At each stage, mass is lost in the form of energy. Altogether the Sun loses 4 million tons of mass every second, which is converted into the 400 quintillion megawatts of energy it needs to support itself and to shine. Most of the energy radiates as heat, light, and gamma rays, taking thousands of years to reach the surface. But some escapes straight through the Sun, carried by ghostly particles called neutrinos, produced in the nuclear reactions.

▽ *During a total eclipse, the corona—the outer layer of th Sun's atmosphere—becomes visible. It c reach temperatures of up to 3,600,000°F (2,000,000°C).*

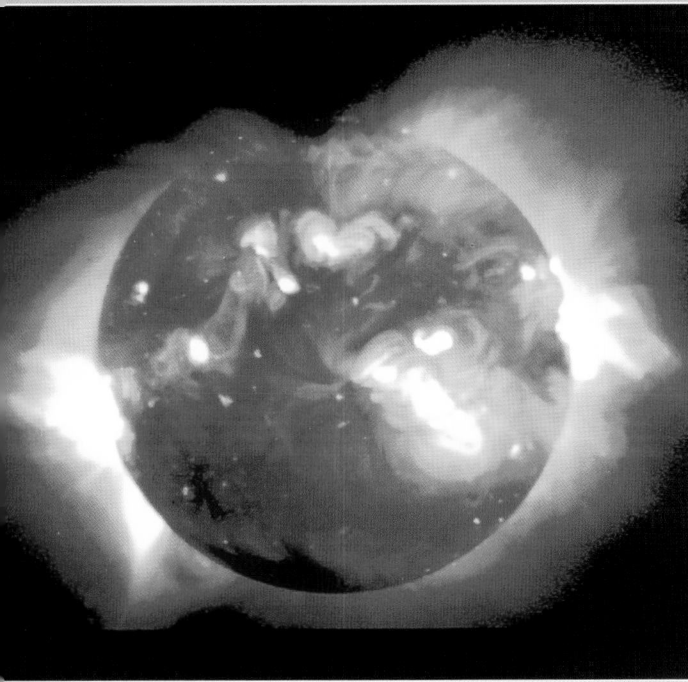

'his x-ray image of the Sun and its corona was recorded by Japanese satellite Yohkoh *in 1992. The brightest and hottest ɪs occur above sunspots, where hot gases flare up.*

lipse!

ɔut once a year, the Moon comes between the Sun ɪ Earth, casting a shadow. When the Moon is close ɪugh to Earth in its orbit, it masks the Sun's disk irely, causing a total eclipse.

'During a total eclipse, part of the ·ld is plunged into darkness. People he outer shadow see a partial eclipse.

▷ *Nuclear reactions take place inside the Sun's core, and the energy slowly radiates out to a distance of about 370,000 miles (600,000 km). Huge bubbles of hot gas continue the transfer of energy to the surface.*

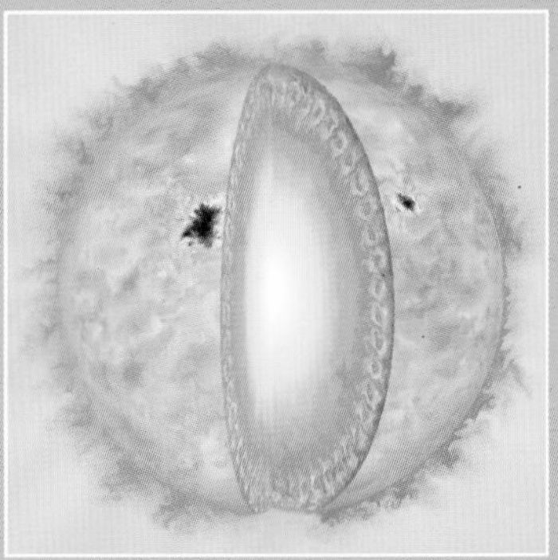

Observing the Sun

You should not look at the Sun directly, and certainly never through a telescope or binoculars—you risk being blinded for life. It is possible, however, to project an image onto a sheet of paper using binoculars, a lens, or even a pinhole in a sheet of cardboard. This is essentially what solar astronomers do, focusing the light down long tubes, through filters, and onto an observation table.

Unobstructed view

The Sun is best viewed from beyond our turbulent atmosphere. From space, the Sun can be seen in other wavelengths such as x rays, revealing the superhot flares that leap from the surface. Several spacecraft have studied the Sun directly, including *Skylab* in the 1970s and *SolarMax* in the 1980s. *Ulysses* has left the plane of the planets to study the magnetic field and solar wind above the poles of the Sun. And Europe's *SOHO* hangs between Earth and the Sun looking at sunquakes and flares and spotting storms of particles on their way to Earth.

△ *The Sun is ringing like a bell. Scientists can record the vibrations by seeing how the movement stretches or compresses light from different regions. The sound waves are created in the solar convective zone, or the outer layer of the Sun.*

△ *The McMath Solar Telescope in Arizona focuses the Sun's image down a 499-foot (152-m) diagonal tube to instruments below.*

Outside the Sun

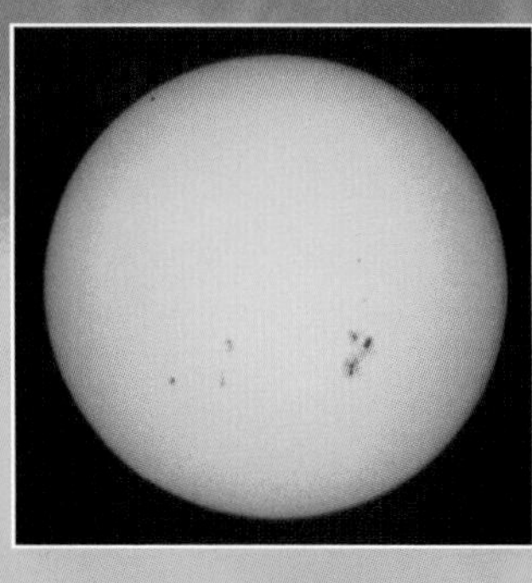

△ *A visible light image of the Sun, taken using the McMath Solar Telescope in Arizona. Several sunspots can clearly be seen on the photosphere, or the visible surface of the Sun.*

The hot, electrically charged gas within the Sun generates very powerful magnetic fields. Where these break the surface, huge jets or loops of hot gas called prominences lift off into space. Dark, relatively cool patches on the Sun's surface are called sunspots. These form in pairs or groups, and represent points where the magnetic field lines leave and rejoin the surface. Rapid eruptions called solar flares also arise along these lines. They usually last no longer than ten minutes, and release the energy equivalent of a million hydrogen bombs. Together with the solar wind (a constant stream of charged particles flowing from the Sun), they create a vast envelope, known as the heliosphere, around the Solar System.

△ *Prominences of hot gas brea free from the Sun's surface and leap out hundreds of thousands of miles into space.*

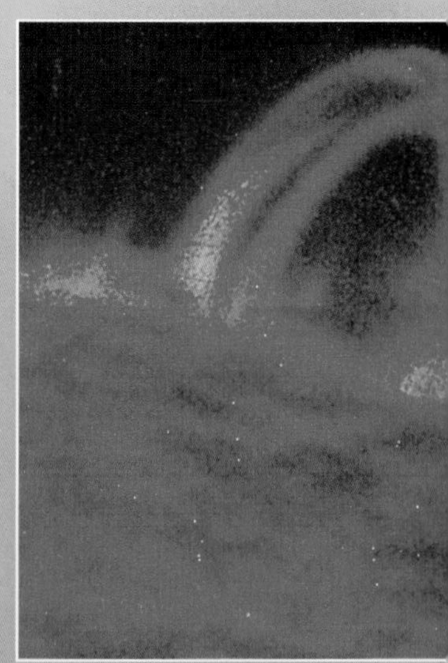

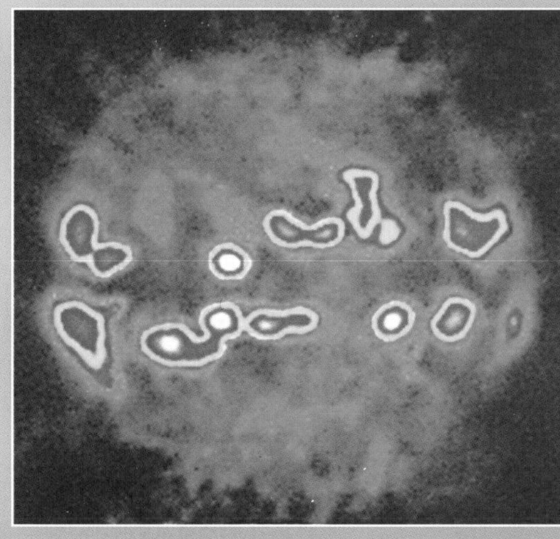

△ *The Sun broadcasts strong radio signals that were first noticed in the 1940s. The brightest areas in this radio image occur where gas flares off into space above pairs of sunspots.*

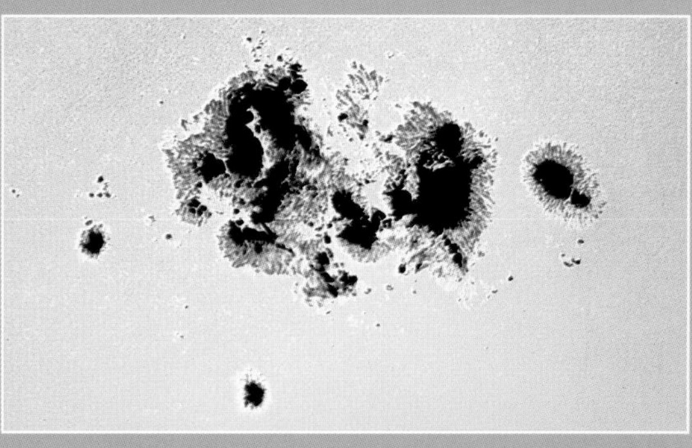

△ *This false-color photograph shows a group of sunspots. The spots form in pairs with opposite magnetic poles. The dark centers of the spots are the coolest, lowest regions where strong magnetic fields slow the upward flow of heat. Around them, bubbles of gas rise, cool, and move away.*

e changing Sun

e Sun is not as constant as it appears. By tracking spots, it is clear that it rotates at the equator once ry 25 days, and at the poles once every 35 days. This 'erence results in magnetic field lines getting wrapped und the Sun until they break through the surface at spots. The pattern of sunspots changes in a cycle of ut 11 years. At the start of the cycle, spots begin to ear near the poles. As they fade, spots appear nearer and nearer to the equator, where they cause a peak of solar activity.

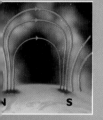

◁ *Magnetic field lines snake out from a sunspot with north polarity and reenter a spot with south polarity. The magnetic lines form tubes along which hot gas flows.*

Solar weather

There are less dramatic changes, too. Between 1645 and 1715, there were virtually no sunspots. This period coincided with extreme winters in Europe, and sometimes is known as the "Little Ice Age." Evidence from other Sunlike stars suggests that, for up to 20 percent of their time, they have no sunspots.

◁ *These loops of hot gas were photographed in ultraviolet by* Skylab *in 1973. Great loops arch up between pairs of sunspots and can remain relatively stable for many hours or even days.*

The end of the Sun

It probably took the Sun 3.5 billion years to reach its present brightness, during which time plants were slowly using up carbon dioxide from Earth's atmosphere, reducing the greenhouse effect and keeping our climate roughly constant. The Sun probably will continue to shine at its present level for another two billion years. But in about six billion years' time, hydrogen will begin to run out at the core, and the Sun will begin to expand rapidly and cool as it becomes a dying star called a red giant. This will engulf the inner planets, including Earth.

△ *In about six billion years' time, Earth's atmosphere and oceans will boil away as the dying Sun becomes a red giant. As this giant star expands, the baked husk of our planet will be swallowed up and become part of a new generation of stars and planets.*

▽ *Swirling nebulae of dust and gas are the nurseries of stars. Often, they are themselves the ashes of earlier generations, cooked and spewed out from short-lived, massive stars.*

△ *Knots form in the gas as gravity pulls it together. As th compresses, it begins to heat u*

Star Birth

△ *Below the line of three stars that form the belt of Orion is Orion's Sword. At its center lies the distinctive Orion Nebula, a birthplace of stars.*

The backdrop of stars used to be thought of as constant and unchanging. Over human lifetimes, there is little detectable change; but over the billio of years of galactic life, stars are born, live their lives, grow old, and die. Space by human standards, appears very, very empty. But collect together all the gas dust of supposedly empty space, and there is more matter than all the stars an planets put together. It is out of these thin clouds, or nebulae, that new stars a born. Over 12 billion years ago, when the Universe itself was young, clouds of hydrogen and helium created the first stars to ever shine. Now, all kinds of other elements are mixed in, the ashes of earlier generations of stars. These combine to make the stars we see forming in dusty nebulae today.

Conception!

Stars tend to be born not singly but in nurseries, where sufficiently dense clouds of gas have accumulated. Star formation can be triggered simply by the gravitational pull of the gas, or when a shock wave passes through it from, for example, a nearby exploding star or intergalactic collision.

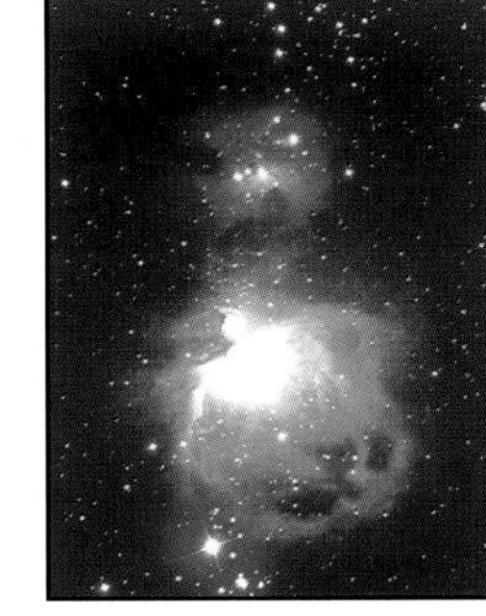

▷ *Altogether, 700 young stars have been spotted in the dust and gas clouds of the Orion Nebula, illuminated here by visible and ultraviolet light.*

◁ *An infrared image* (left) *of th Orion Nebula take by the* Hubble Space Telescope *reveals that n young stars lie inside the tee mass of gas and dust* (above).

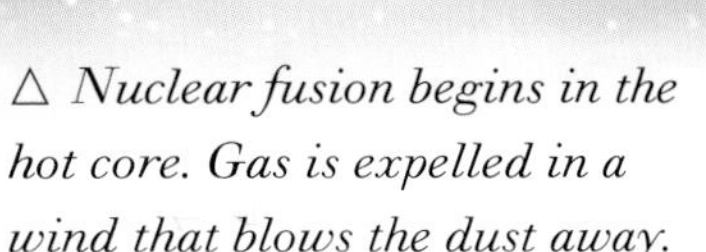

The gas begins to spiral in *sk. The protostar expels* *of gas from its poles.*

△ *Nuclear fusion begins in the hot core. Gas is expelled in a wind that blows the dust away.*

△ *Finally, the star begins to shine steadily.*

Baby stars hatch from EGGs (Evaporating Gaseous Globules), fingerlike tips emerging from this pillar of gas in the Eagle *bula. This picture was taken by the* Hubble Space Telescope.

The Hubble Space Telescope *has revealed more than 150 of these* *like knots in the Orion Nebula. They provide the best evidence* *ar that planetary systems can form at the same time as stars.*

Getting warm

As knots of gas inside the cloud become compressed, they begin to warm up. As it contracts, the cloud rotates faster, making the gas form into a disk. Matter falling inward from the disk is ejected in jets from the poles. Eventually, the central protostar becomes so hot and compressed that the process of nuclear fusion begins at its core. This in turn causes more material to be blown off and, finally, the remains of the disk blow away—apart from any lumps that are forming into planets—and the new star shines into clear space.

Seeing cool, seeing deep

At the different stages of a star's birth and life cycle, matter glows with different wavelengths. When stars begin to form, warm gas radiates in the infrared wavelength, while cooler dust and molecules glow at the submillimeter radio wavelengths. Infrared and radio waves can also penetrate the thick clouds, so it is at these wavelengths that astronomers peer into the nebulae and watch stars being born.

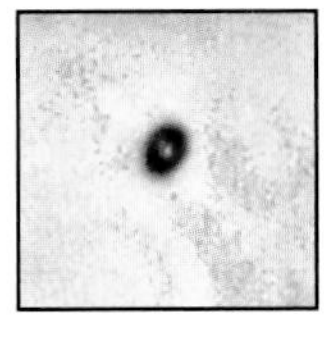

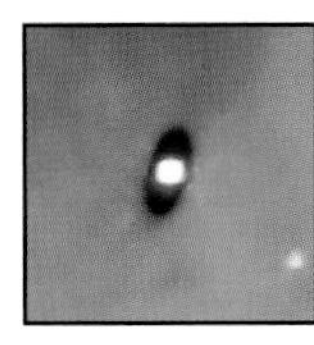

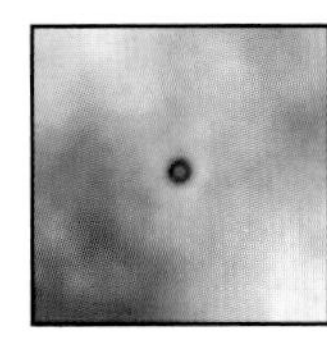

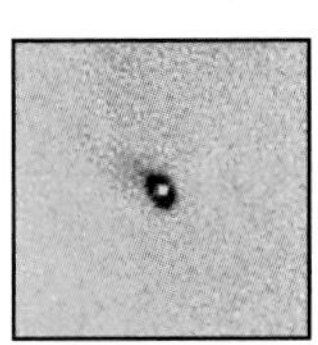

Star Life

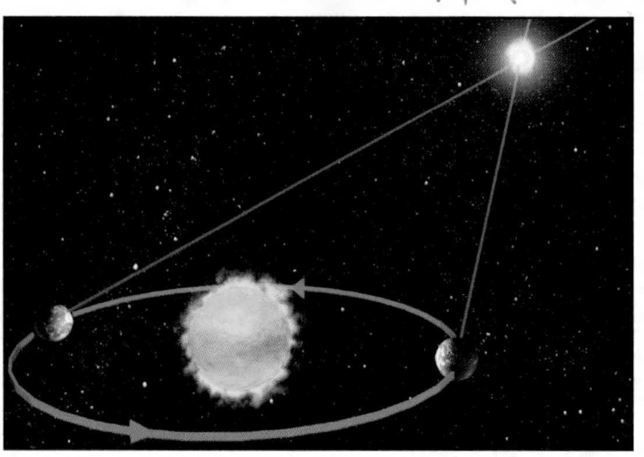

△ *As Earth moves in its orbit around the Sun, nearby stars appear to move against the distant background. This displacement is called "parallax," and it is used to measure the distances to stars.*

Stars come in all sizes and colors. Look up on a clear, dark night and you will see hundreds, perhaps thousands of star Look with a powerful telescope and you will see millions, or ev billions. Some are bright, others faint. Some look blue, others w yellow, or red. There are stars that are bright simply because the are nearby. Certain stars are, in absolute terms, hundreds of tir brighter than the Sun; others are thousands of times dimmer. star's color reflects its surface temperature. Blue stars are very while red ones are cooler. Their ages vary as well. Some are alm as old as the Universe; others are babies in comparison. It is the little ones that live longest. Big stars burn up their nuclear fuel much faster and only last a few million years.

The main sequence

This is a fixed relationship between the temperature and brightness of most stars. They begin as red dwarfs and become hotter and brighter. The period of a star's life when it is shining almost constantly is known as the "main sequence." How long this lasts depends on the star's mass. When the hydrogen burning in its core runs out, the star expands and cools into a red giant, leaving the main sequence. Eventually, the star sheds its outer layers, leaving a slowly cooling white dwarf.

▷ Hipparcos, *the European satellite, has measured the precise position of more than 120,000 stars. It found that some are closer than we previously thought.*

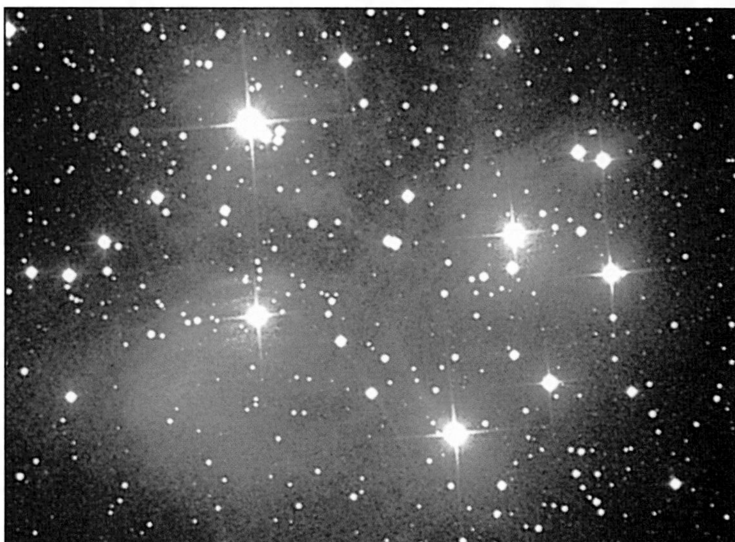

△ *The Pleiades open cluster of stars is sometimes known as the Seven Sisters, after the seven stars clearly visible to the naked eye. This cluster contains, in fact, almost 500 young, blue stars.*

How far to the stars

The brightest star in the sky, Sirius, is close (8.6 light years), and, although it is in reality 26 times brighter than the Sun, it is not nearly as bright as some more distant stars. To find out how bright a star really is, you need to know how far away it is. The first step in figuri out the distance of a star is to measure its position. By doing this twice, six months apart, when the Earth is o opposite sides of the Sun, a nearby star's distance can b calculated by using parallax. Move your head from side side. Objects close to you seem to move against the mor distant background. Earth's orbit is equivalent to movi your head; and the apparent motion of stars against the distant background gives a measure of distance.

sense of scale

e distance to the stars is vast. Proxima Centuri, the rest, is 25,000,000,000,000 miles (40,000,000,000,000) away, while others are hundreds of times farther out. arly, miles are not very convenient units of measure. So, onomers use light years—a measurement of distance, time. One light year is the distance light travels in year. Proxima Centuri is 4.2 light years away.

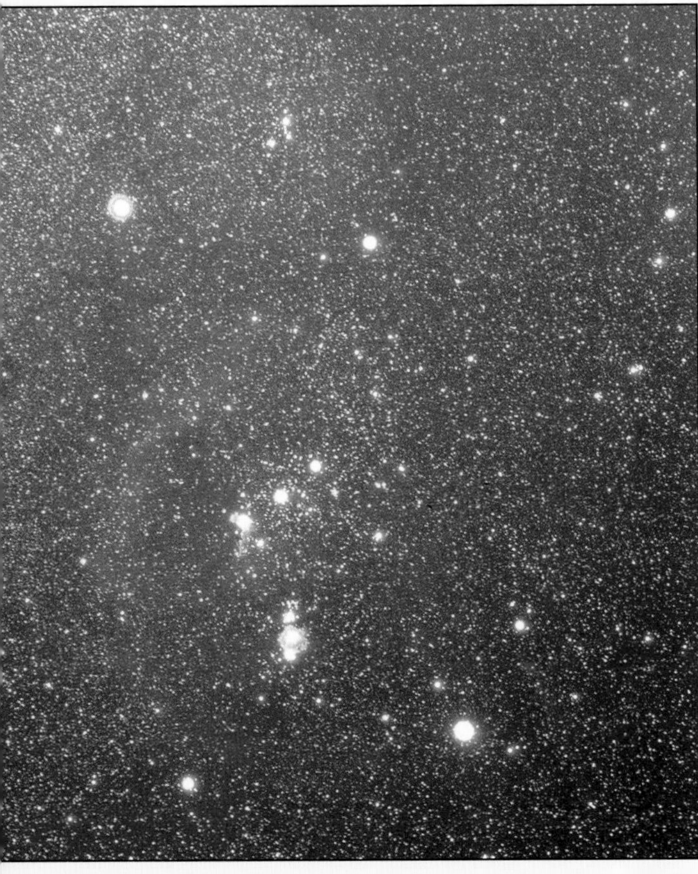

One of the best-known constellations is Orion the hunter. ontains stars at all stages of life, including newborn stars in Orion Nebula (lower center), *bright blue-white Rigel* (lower nt), *and red giant Betelgeuse, near the end of its life* (top left).

irs and clusters

r Sun shines alone in space, but most stars are members groups. Frequently, they are in pairs known as binaries. ne are in less stable groups of three, or in double aries of four. Stars turn up in larger groups, too, such the Pleiades. Some of the most closely packed groups stars, called globular clusters, may contain millions of rs, light months rather than light years apart.

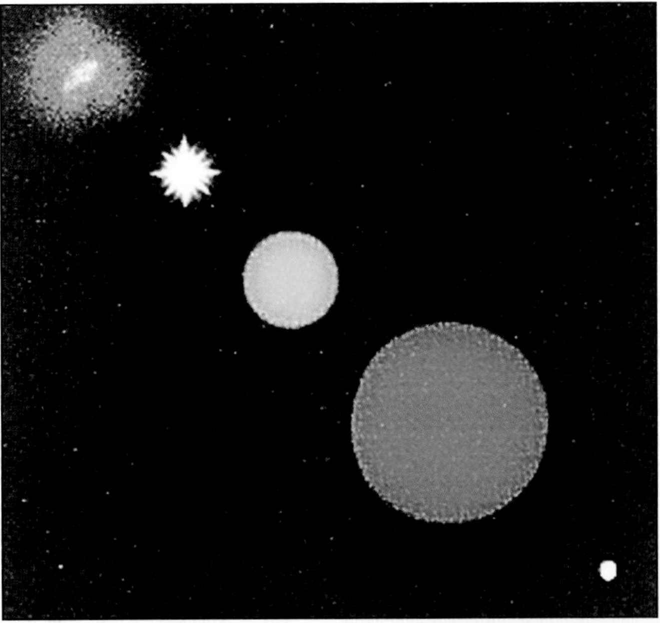

△ *The life story of a star like the Sun begins in a cloud of gas from which a bright, young protostar condenses. For eight billion years it shines as a yellow star, then expands into a red giant before becoming a white dwarf.*

Variable stars

Some stars appear to vary in their brightness, either erratically, or in a regular cycle. Sometimes it is because they are in binary pairs and one eclipses the other. Young and unstable stars flare out great masses of hot gas into space, while old, red supergiants send out black, sooty clouds of carbon. Others pulsate regularly. One type, the so-called Cepheid variables, alternately inflates and contracts, brightening and fading at a rate directly related to its overall brightness. This makes these stars useful for measuring distances in the Universe.

▷ *This globular cluster in our neighboring galaxy, Andromeda, has at least 300,000 stars. From the amount of helium that has built up, astronomers have estimated that the stars are almost as old as the Universe itself.*

Star Death

△ *The Egg Nebula consists of concentric shells of gas ejected by a red giant star near the end of its life. The "searchlights" are areas where light and jets of particles penetrate gaps in the swirling clouds of dust.*

Stars the size of our Sun swell up as hydrogen runs low in their core and they shed layers of gas to form what are known as planetary nebulae. Left behind at the center is a white dwarf star, which slowly cools to a cinder over billions of years. Bigger stars live more brief and violent lives. Within them, a constant battle rages between the pressure of the heat holding them up and the crushing force of gravity. If a star's mass is over 40 percent greater than the Sun's mass, not even electrons can hold it up when its nuclear fuel runs out. Electrons in the core are squashed so hard that they fuse with protons to make neutrons. The resulting matter has a density of 4.8 billion tons per cubic inch and forms a star no bigger than a city, but weighing more than the Sun. The energy released as the core collapses tears through the outer layers of the dying star in a huge supernova explosion.

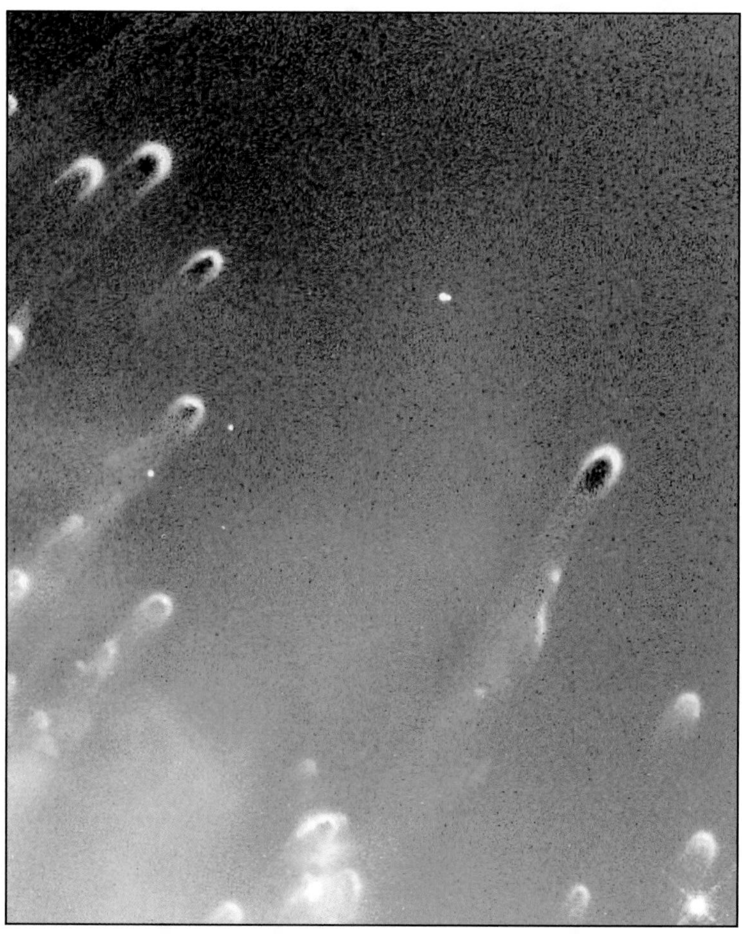

△ *Tadpolelike knots of material in the Helix Planetary Nebula plow into gases ejected earlier from a dying star. Each knot is larger than our own Solar System.*

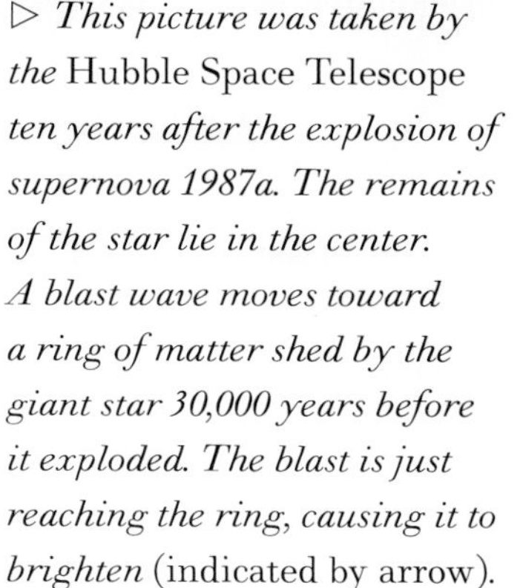

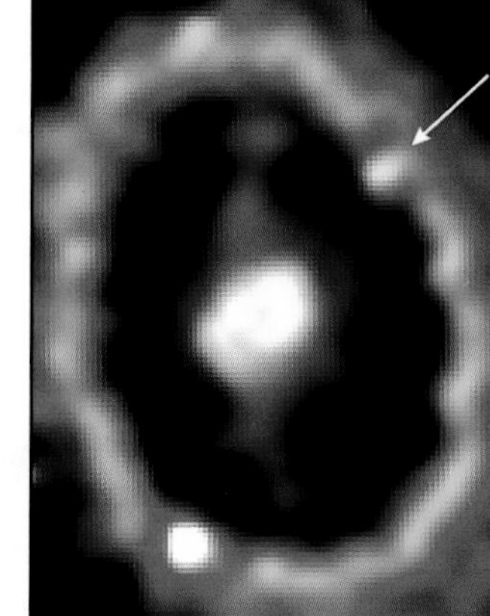

▷ *This picture was taken by the* Hubble Space Telescope *ten years after the explosion of supernova 1987a. The remains of the star lie in the center. A blast wave moves toward a ring of matter shed by the giant star 30,000 years before it exploded. The blast is just reaching the ring, causing it to brighten* (indicated by arrow).

Going supernova

On February 23, 1987, Canadian astronomer Ian Shelto[n] was making routine observations using a telescope in Chile when he noticed a very bright star that he did not remember seeing before. He soon realized that he had spotted an exploding star—a supernova lying 170,0[00] light years away. A few hours earlier, special undergrou[nd] detectors in the United States and Japan had picked up a pulse of ghostly *neutrinos*, particles created when the iron core of a giant star collapses and a neutron star form[s]. The process had caused a tremendous explosion that tor[e] the star apart in a blaze of hot new radioactive element[s]

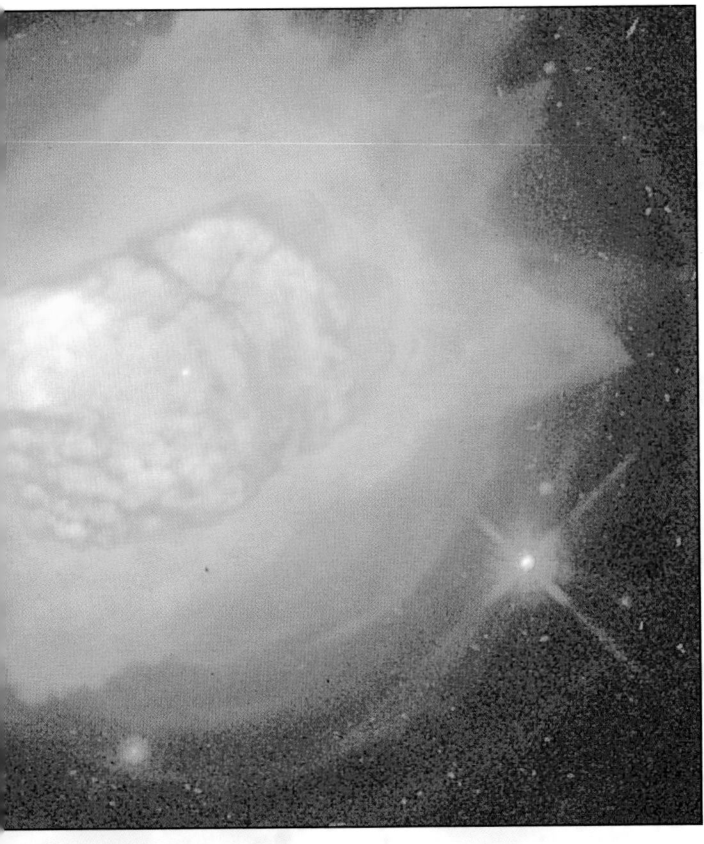

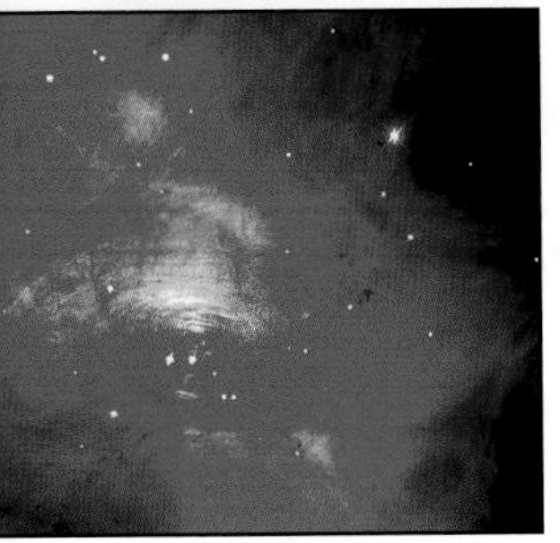

◁ *The Crab Nebula is the remnant of a star that exploded in A.D. 1054. At its center is a tiny, superdense neutron star, pulsing as it spins thirty times a second and ejecting particles that interact with the gas.*

lsars

ery year, several supernova explosions are spotted in tant galaxies, and there is plenty of evidence for past plosions nearer home. In A.D. 1054, Chinese astronomers orded a bright new star, or nova, in the direction of the nstellation of Taurus. Today, it is still visible as the Crab bula, a bright, expanding shell of radioactive gas and oris. At its center is a small white star sending out radio shes thirty times a second. When it was discovered in 55, it was given the name LGM1 (L for little, G for een, and M for man). This is not an alien distress beacon. s a pulsar—an ultradense neutron star, flashing a beam radiation as it spins. Hundreds have been found since, ne spinning up to a thousand times per second.

◁ *When the star NGC 7027 swelled into a red giant, it started to shed gas and formed the blue, spherical shell. As the process became more violent, it produced the red and yellow material.*

▷ *The Hourglass Nebula has formed around a star reaching the end of its life. A stellar wind has blown out from the poles creating the double ring.*

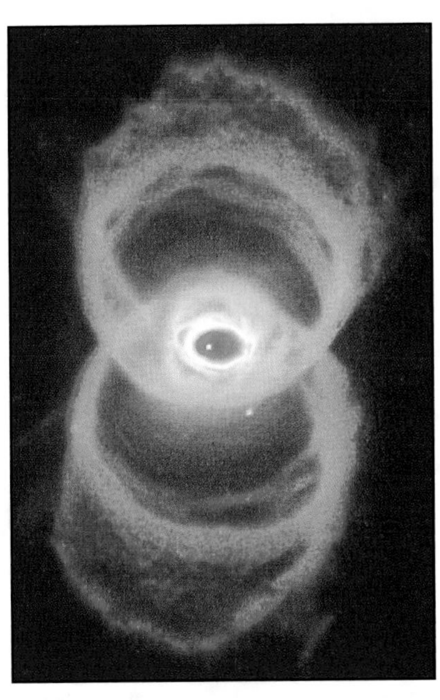

The stars, our ancestors

The first matter in the Universe was almost all helium and hydrogen. All the other elements around us today, including carbon, silicon, oxygen, and nitrogen, were cooked up in the nuclear furnaces of stars, scattered into space, and reformed into solar systems such as ours. All elements that are heavier than iron were created and spewed out in supernova explosions. Our world and even our bodies are made, quite literally, of stardust.

△ *The bright ray of a pulsar sweeps across space as a neutron star spins on its axis. Escaping electrons are funneled by the intense magnetic field, which emits radiation and light.*

◁ *"Oh my ears and whiskers, how late it's getting!" At least both Alice and the White Rabbit agree what time it is, as Alice sets out on a journey into a black hole.*

Black Hole!

While some dying stars turn into superdense neutron stars, others collapse even further. In a star that is more than three times the Sun's mass, gravity violently crushes matter inward. It continues to collapse before disappearing into an incredibly dense but dimensionless point called a singularity. A black hole is the space around a singularity, and nothing that falls in can ever go fast enough to escape—not even light. Black holes vary in size—the bigger the singularity, the wider the black hole.

△ *Gas is dragged off a massive star* (above right), *and spirals violently into a black hole. The spinning disk heats up until it emits x rays, and a jet of hot matter shoots from the poles.*

Time for a change

A black hole plays strange tricks on the fabric of space and time, curving it in on itself. If you were able to watch someone falling toward a black hole's outer edge, or event horizon, you would see their watch ticking slower and slower. At the same time, they would become redder and redder, until they faded from view.

The long stretch

If you were the unfortunate person falling into a black hole, your watch would seem to tick normally and you would remain your usual color. But you would have other things to worry about. The gravity would pull so hard that it would stretch you out like spaghetti. Your remains would rapidly spiral in, like water down a cosmic drain, and friction would heat them up until they gave off x rays.

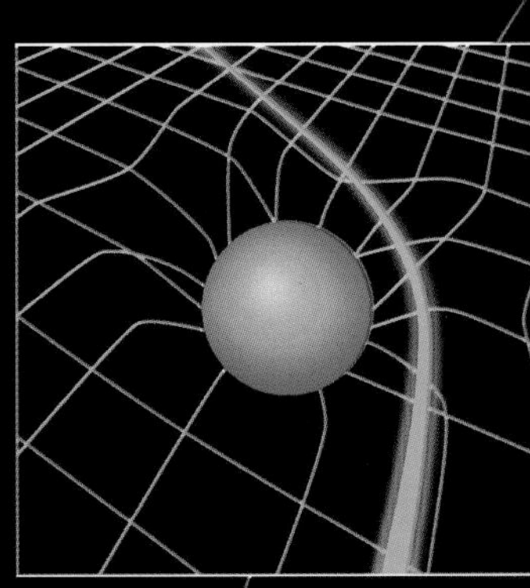

▷ *The gravitational well of a black hole or even a massive star distorts the fabric of space-time. A ray of light traveling from a star to Earth is bent as it shines past, changing the apparent position of the star.*

s Alice gets close to the black its gravity begins to act more er feet than her head and she s to stretch. It also stretches the , and her feet grow redder. e notices no change in the rate vatch ticks, but already the bit sees her watch running slow.

Hunting the invisible

Although astronomers cannot see black holes directly, they can detect them through their effects. Stars often come in pairs, and if one of the pair has collapsed into a black hole it may also pull in gas from the companion star. As the gas spirals in, it emits x rays. By looking at these x-ray sources, astronomers can study the invisible black hole.

▽ *In what to Alice are the next few seconds, she will be beyond the point of no return—the event horizon. Meanwhile, the Rabbit is getting later and later.*

ow Alice really has ems. She becomes "spaghettified" gravitational forces begin to pull her . Compared to the Rabbit's watch, me is running slower and slower.

e great escape

10ugh you could never escape from a black e, something does emerge from them. Pairs of ticles, created on the event horizon itself, end up h one falling in, one coming out. The loss of rgy is known as "Hawking radiation." It is so faint, vever, that it would take 100 billion billion billion ion billion billion years for a black hole with mass of our Sun to evaporate.

The Milky Way

△ *This fish-eye view of the entire night sky above Australia is dominated by the billions of stars that make up the Milky Way.*

We have seen how ideas have changed from the ancient notion of our Earth as the center of the Universe to one where the Sun rules the planets. Today, we know that the Sun is just one among about 200 billion stars in the great star city of our galaxy, the Milky Way. The whole galaxy is like a vast disk with a bulge in the middle (somewhat like two fried eggs, put back to back), with great spiral arms of stars. About three-quarters of the way out along the Orion Arm is our local star, the Sun. The Milky Way is about 100,000 light years across (the Solar System is only about 12 light hours across) and rotates in space, spinning fastest at its center.

Highway of stars

Look up at the sky on a clear, dark night, away from city lights, and you can see the great highway of stars that is the Milky Way. It is most dense toward its center, in the constellation of Sagittarius. You will see nearby bright stars, clusters of stars, and a faint haze of millions of distant stars. The darker patches that look like holes are really huge clouds of dust. The faint remains of ancient supernova explosions show up as a wispy structure of gas all around us.

△ *This near-infrared view of the Milky Way clearly shows the central bulge of the galaxy from our position within it.*

Among the crowd

We cannot see the center of the galaxy (it is shrouded in gas and dust), but infrared and radio waves can penetrate the clouds, giving hints of violent processes at work. It is a very crowded place, with millions of stars and immense quantities of gas. There is a barlike structure, and clouds of molecules. Strong magnetic fields have drawn gas out into thin filaments, and a fountain of antimatter rises thousands of light years from the galactic plane.

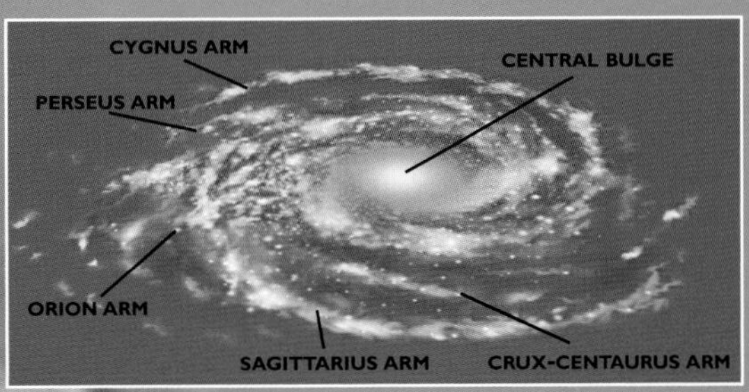

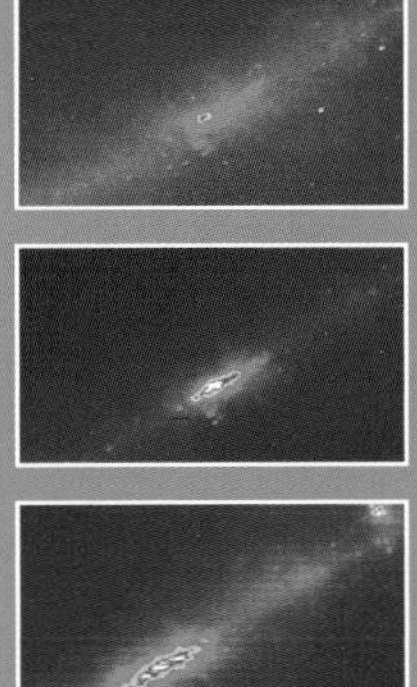

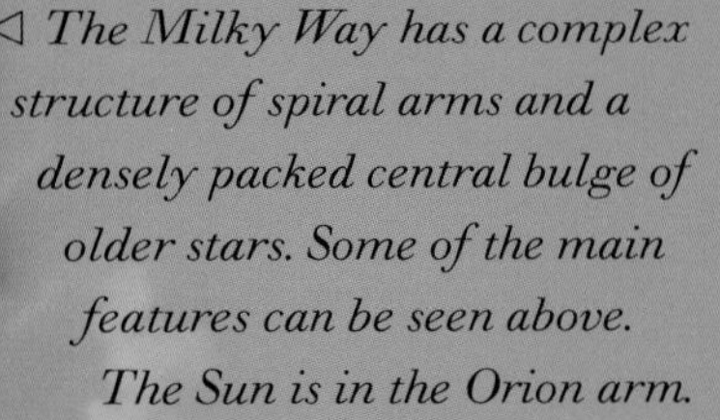

◁ *The Milky Way has a complex structure of spiral arms and a densely packed central bulge of older stars. Some of the main features can be seen above. The Sun is in the Orion arm.*

△ *Infrared images can see through the clouds of dust and give a tantalizing glimpse of the Milky Way's center, where a black hole may lurk.*

Shifting heart

Three hundred light years from the galaxy's core lies a gamma-ray source called the Great Annihilator. Once thought to be the center of the Milky Way, it produces jets of antimatter and emits gamma rays. It is probably a black hole. The true center is now known to be Sagittarius A*. This may be a monster black hole more than a million times the mass of the Sun. But if it is, the beast at the center of the galaxy appears to be sleeping right now.

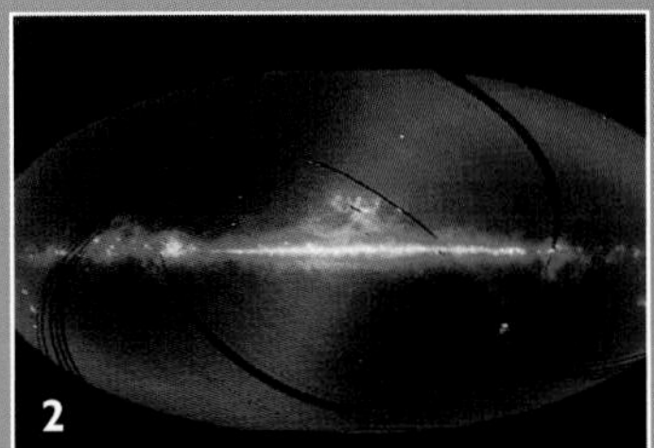

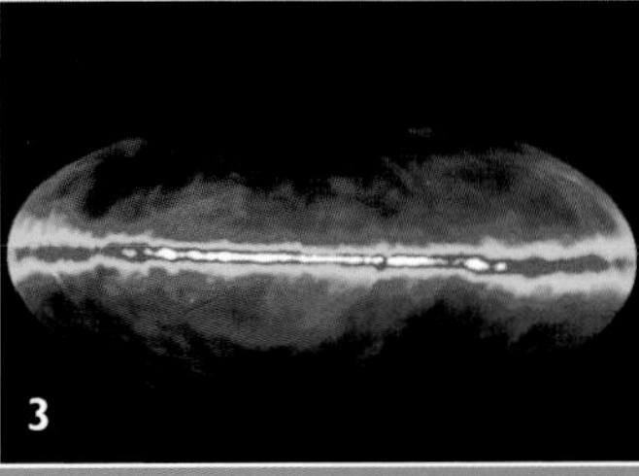

△ *The 28-inch (73-cm) wavelength radio map* (1) *reveals high-velocity electrons moving in a magnetic field. It helps astronomers to plot the magnetic field of the galaxy. The infrared map* (2) *is especially bright where there are dust clouds warmed by hot new stars. The blue "S" is dust in our Solar System. The 8-inch (21-cm) radio map* (3) *reveals atomic hydrogen in gas clouds between stars. The gas emits a very precise frequency, helping scientists to trace its motion in the rotating galaxy.*

Our Local Group

The Milky Way and the Andromeda galaxies are immense spirals of stars, island universes in their own right. They are the two largest and most important members of the Local Group, a cluster of galaxies stretching five million light years across space. The Local Group contains some 30 galaxies, loosely bound together in each other's gravitational pull. Andromeda, which has twice as many stars as our own galaxy, is located near another small spiral. The other members of the group are even smaller, and are either irregular blobs of stars, like the Magellanic clouds near our own spiral galaxy, or even dwarf galaxies.

Cannibal galaxies

It appears that over billions of years, the big spirals, including our own Milky Way, have grown by eating up their neighbors. Some of the nearby dwarf galaxies will be gobbled up by our galaxy in a few million years' time. And even the great spiral Andromeda Galaxy itself is coming toward our own galaxy at about 186 miles (300 km) every second. It still has a long way to go, but eventually the two galaxies may pass through one another, or even merge. The distances between stars are so immense that few will collide, but great clouds of gas and dust might be stirred up into star formation.

▽ *In 1912, the American astronomer Henrietta Leavitt discovered that stars called Cepheid variables change their brightness in a predictable way.*

▽ *The Virgo cluster contai than 1,000 galaxies. Virgo i 50 million light years away is the center of our superclu*

△ *Henrietta Leavitt*

△ *Virgo cluster*

△ *Cepheid star* (center)

△ *Cepheid star* (cente

△ *The changing brightness of a Cepheid variable star, seen here on the left at its most dim, and on the right at its brighte allows astronomers to measure the distance to the galaxies. After the discovery of this type of star, the painstaking mapping of the Universe, galaxy by galaxy, could begin.*

△ *The Local Group consists of about 30 galaxies. Our own spiral galaxy, the Milky Way, is surrounded by dwarf galaxies and a few irregular galaxies. To the right is the great Andromeda Galaxy and its smaller companions, including the spiral M33. The other irregular galaxies are more isolated.*

TYPE OF GALA

Dwarf galaxy

Irregular gala

Spiral galaxy

ritz Zwicky discovered that ...xies are grouped in clusters, ...e of them thousands strong ... millions of light years across.

▽ *The* Hubble Space Telescope *revealed that the core of the Andromeda Galaxy has a double nucleus. This may have resulted from a merger with another galaxy.*

◁ *The Andromeda Galaxy has a spiral form similar to the Milky Way. Andromeda is 2.2 million light years away, and 150,000 light years across.*

△ *Andromeda Galaxy*

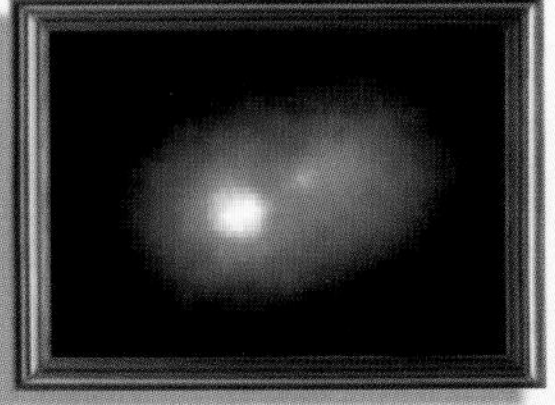

△ *Andromeda's core*

△ *Fritz Zwicky*

ANDROMEDA

M33

MILKY WAY

Rotating galaxies

The spiral shape of many galaxies gives the impression that they are rotating. However, it is not the stars that are going around and around, but the arms, with the stars passing through them. The arms rotate over hundreds of millions of years, their outside ends trailing behind the faster inner regions. In our own galaxy, it takes the Sun over 200 million years to complete an orbit and come back to the same position.

This period is sometimes called the cosmic year.

Superclusters

Even the vast Local Group is a small backyard on the intergalactic scale. We are part of a much larger grouping of other clusters, which together form the Local Supercluster. Our Local Group is being pulled by gravity toward the Virgo cluster, the center of the Local Supercluster (also known as the Virgo Supercluster), at a speed of 168 miles (270 km) per second. Superclusters are among the largest structures seen in the Universe, but even the Local Supercluster is just one of many others stretching billions of light years across the Universe.

Expanding Universe

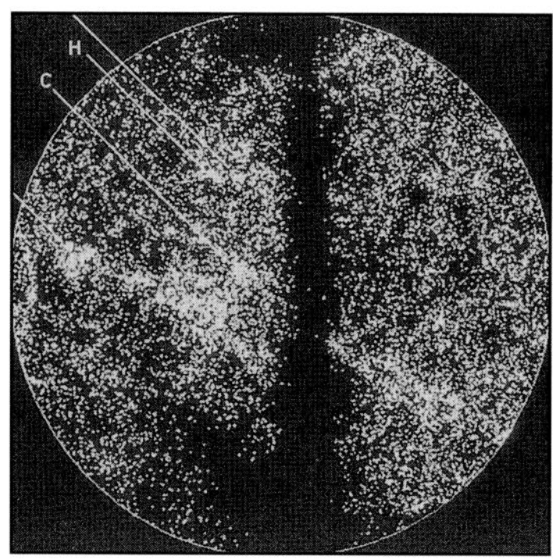

△ *The dark, vertical band in this map of galaxies is where our own galaxy, the Milky Way, blocks the view. We are moving at 373 miles (600 km) per second toward the Great Attractor, the dense, bright cluster near the center.*

The speed of galaxies is one of the easier things to calculate in the Universe. The light from stars and galaxies comes with a very convenient measure. If a galaxy is moving away from us, the wavelength of its light is stretched, or redshifted. If it is coming toward us, the wavelength gets squashed and shifted toward the blue end of the spectrum. In 1929, Edwin Hubble discovered that the more distant a galaxy is, the more its light is redshifted. And it soon became clear that the farther a galaxy is from our own, the faster it is speeding away. Hubble concluded that the reason for this is not that our galaxy is at the center of the Universe, but rather that the entire Universe is expanding. If this is so, then there must have been a time when all the galaxies were much closer together.

Mapping the Universe

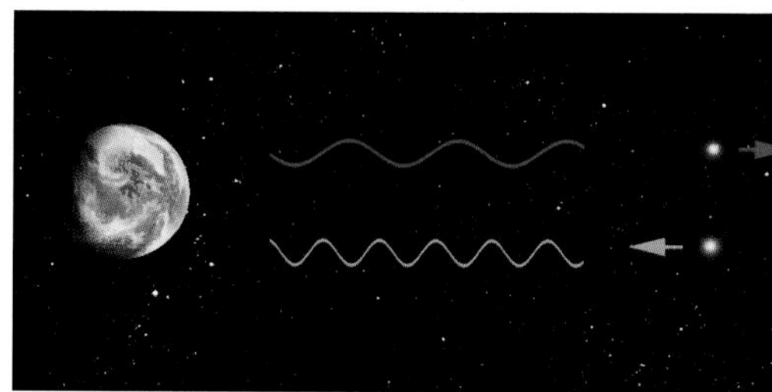

△ *If a galaxy or star is moving toward us, the waves in its light become squashed together, or blueshifted, so it looks more blue. If, on the other hand, the object is receding from us, the light becomes stretched, or redshifted.*

By using redshift to measure the distances to galaxies, astronomers have begun to map the Universe in three dimensions. It is an enormous task but already some very large structures have been revealed. Some areas are like voids or bubbles with very few galaxies in them. Around them are slabs and filaments rich in galaxies. One particular structure forms what has been called the Great Wall, and is at least a billion light years across. There might be a repeating structure of such walls, a bit like a picket fence, with walls about 400 million light years apart.

▽ *On the largest scale, the Universe is like a vast foam, with superclusters and walls of galaxies located along the boundaries of giant bubbles, or voids in space.*

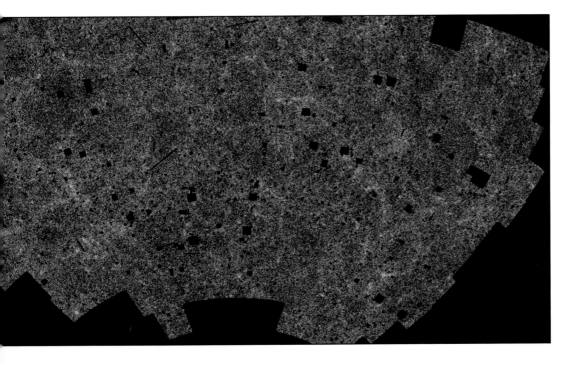

◁ *This slice through the Universe shows all the galaxies that have had their redshifts measured. Faint structures are visible. Black areas have not yet been fully surveyed.*

▽ *The* 2DF *instrument on the* Anglo-Australian Telescope *can measure the redshifts of up to 400 galaxies at once.*

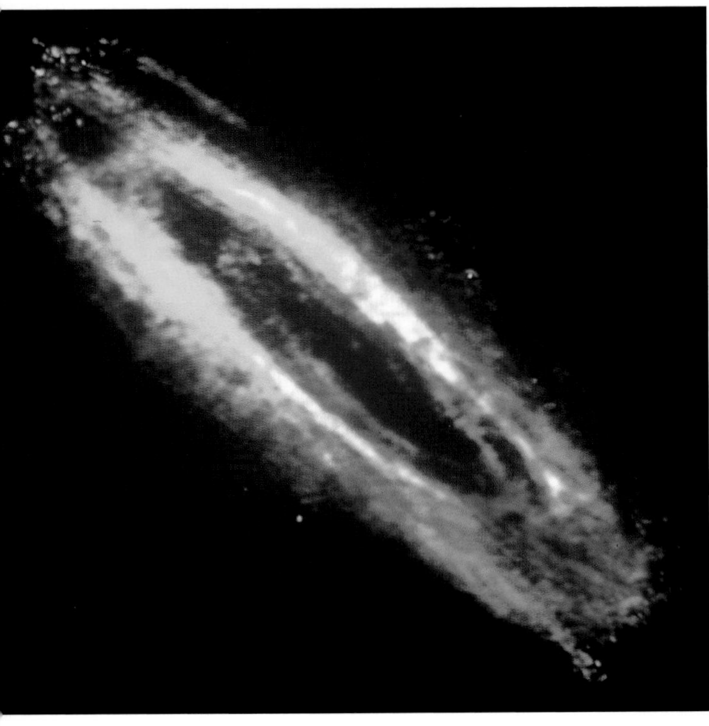

This image of the Andromeda Galaxy has en color coded to show the redshift and ueshift caused by the galaxy's rotation.

The Great Attractor

The Universe does not expand evenly in every direction. Huge concentrations of galaxies put a gravitational brake on the process. Whole streams of galaxies end up resisting the expansion—we are part of such a stream. Beyond the great Virgo supercluster, there appears to be something pulling us and thousands of other galaxies toward it. It has been called the Great Attractor, and it lies in the approximate direction of the constellation Perseus. It acts as if it has a mass of 50 million billion suns, equivalent to hundreds of thousands of galaxies. At one time it was thought that it might be a monster black hole or some other strange object. Now it is generally believed to be an irregularity, or a knot, in the clouds of galaxies. Even so, it has enough gravity to pull our whole local group of galaxies toward it at a velocity of about 373 miles (600 km) per second.

The Galactic Zoo

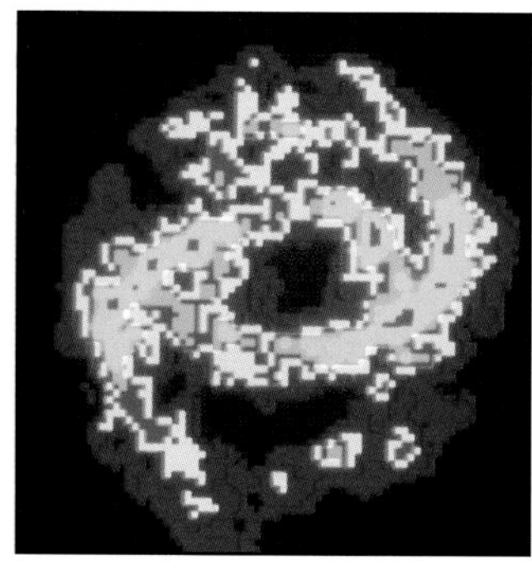

△ *Some galaxies, such as NGC 1300, appear to lose their tightly wound spiral structure as they evolve and develop a broad bar.*

The Universe contains around 100 billion galaxies, and each galaxy, on average, is made up of about 100 billion stars. Galaxies come in many different shapes and sizes. Spiral galaxies can be tightly wound or loose, while others have a broad bar across their center. Some galaxies have no obvious shape, and are classed as irregular. The largest of all galaxies are elliptical. Stars are no longer forming in elliptical galaxies. It could be that most galaxies begin as spirals but, as they interact with one another, all their gas is pulled into the stars. The spiral structure disappears and becomes an elliptical galaxy.

Looking back in time

The most distant galaxies ever seen are probably more than ten billion light years away. This means that light has taken ten billion years to reach us so what we are seeing is the light that left them when the Universe was ten billion years younger. By peering back across such distances, it is possible to see galaxies as they form. In one particular study by the *Hubble Space Telescope*, no fewer than 18 dwarf galaxies were spotted moving together under the influence of each other's gravity. This suggests that galaxies are formed when much smaller galaxies merge. The final stages of this process can be seen today in our own galaxy as it swallows up a few remaining dwarf galaxies.

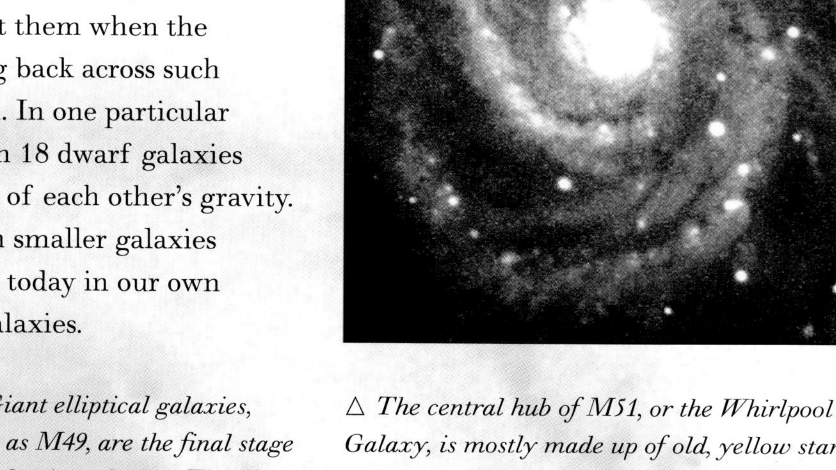

△ *The central hub of M51, or the Whirlpool Galaxy, is mostly made up of old, yellow stars. spiral arms contain young, blue stars, while a of gas and dust connects it to a second galaxy.*

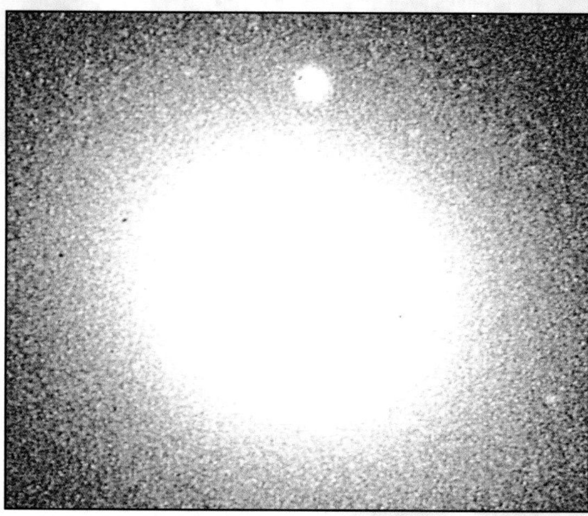

◁ *Giant elliptical galaxies, such as M49, are the final stage in galactic evolution. They contain almost no young stars.*

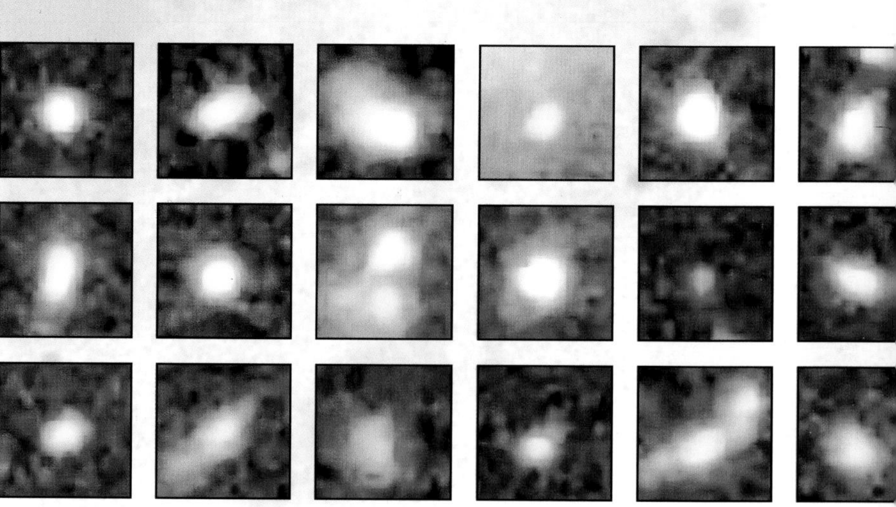

▷ *Astronomers believe that these faint smudges of star cluster, 11 billion light years away, are the building blocks that will merge to form the core of a new galaxy.*

M82 is a spiral galaxy, seen here from the *e. The disturbance at the center is probably* *sed by the galaxy plowing into a gas cloud.*

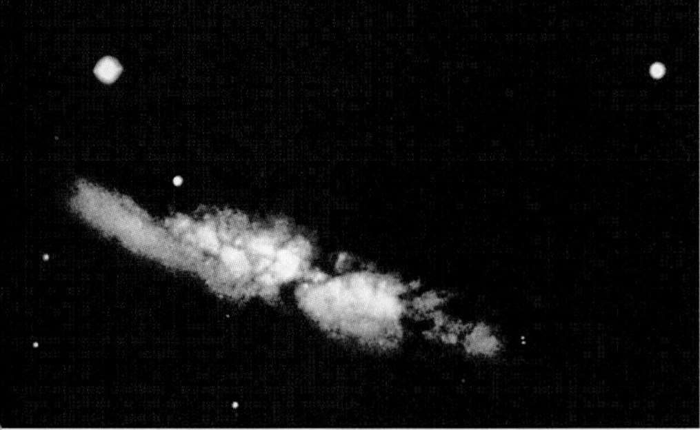

Starburst

There must have been a time when the first stars started to shine, a spectacular period in the history of the Universe, which had been dark since the Big Bang of creation. When astronomers peer through the great clouds of dust in which stars are made, they can see whole galaxies shining brightly with the sudden birth of millions of big, hot stars. More recent starburst galaxies are also seen where galaxies have smashed into one another, stirring up the dust lanes and triggering a new burst of star formation. In one of these, called Arp 220, the rate of star formation is probably a hundred times that of our entire Milky Way Galaxy, but concentrated into a nucleus a hundred times smaller.

This is what the Hubble Space Telescope *saw when it took a ten-day* *osure of a patch of sky close to the constellation of the Big Dipper.* *Hubble Deep Field is made up of 342 exposures and contains 1,500* *axies, some of them among the faintest and most distant ever seen.*

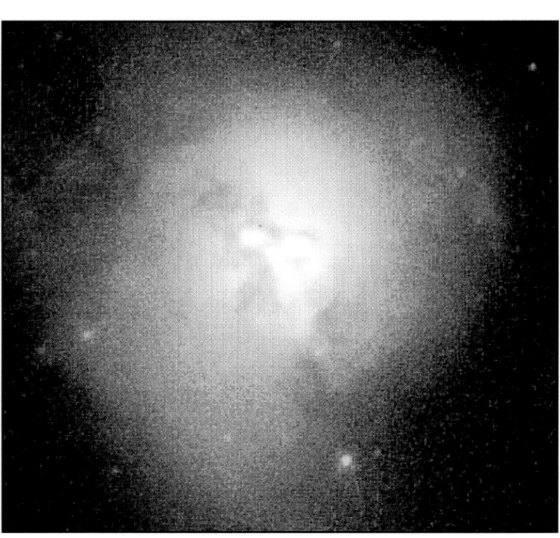

◁ *Arp 220 is a starburst galaxy, packed with very new, hot, young stars. It probably formed when two spiral galaxies merged.*

The Hubble Deep Field

In December 1995, the *Hubble Space Telescope* was pointed at a single stretch of sky for ten consecutive days. It revealed no fewer than 1,500 galaxies at various stages of evolution. Some are four billion times fainter than can be seen by the naked eye, and date back to near the beginning of the Universe. This so-called Hubble Deep Field is beginning to give astronomers clues about how many galaxies there are in the Universe, and how they formed.

Violent Galaxies

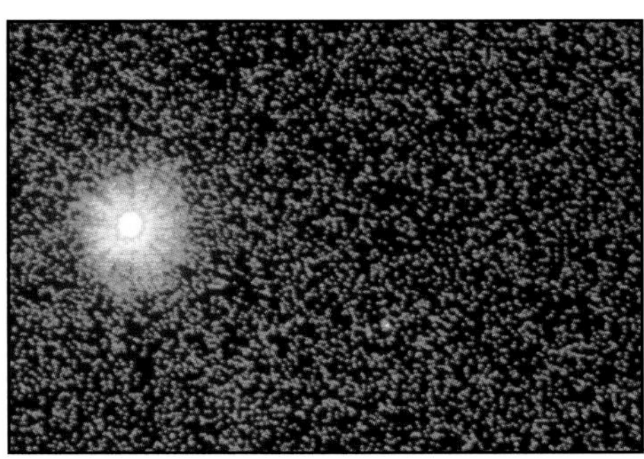

△ *The first quasar to be identified was 3C 273, viewed here in x rays. Although starlike in appearance, quasars are very distant and intensely active galaxies.*

In 1963, Maartin Schmidt, an astronomer in California, was examining the spectrum of light from a faint blue, starlike object known as 3C 273. To his astonishment, he realized that, although it w more than three billion light years away and moving away from Eart at almost 31,070 miles (50,000 km) per second, it was giving out inter radiation. These distant objects became known as quasistellar radio sources, or quasars for short. They appear starlike because they emit a hundred times more energy than our entire galaxy, but from an area not much bigger than our Solar System. The *Hubble Space Telescope* has revealed that quasars are, in fact, blindingly bright objects embedded in the centers of distant galaxies.

Monster black holes

There is only one power source that could generate the immense energy of quasars—black holes. Most quasars are found in colliding galaxies. As the galaxies merge, gas and stars are stirred up and begin to spiral around a black hole that lies at the center of one, or even both galaxies. As matter is sucked in, an accretion disk is created, similar to those around black holes formed from dying stars in our own galaxy. But in the case of quasars, the black holes must be incredibly massive, each perhaps a billion times the mass of the Sun.

▽ *The galaxy M87, in the Virgo cluster, sends out a narrow jet of matter from its core. The activity in this galaxy is probably caused by a giant black hole.*

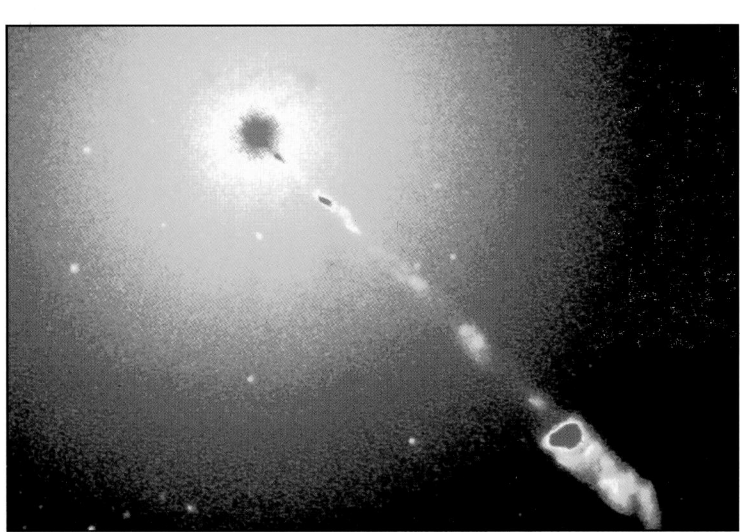

△ *A great cloud of swirling gas and star debris spirals down toward a black hole millions of times the mass of the Sun. At the same time, it gives out x rays and powerful jets of radio-emitting gas. Many of the violent processes taking place in the cores of galaxies are probably similar events seen from different angles.*

△ *In this computer simulation, two spiral galaxies have collided and passed one another. Spiral arms have been dragged out into a bridge of matter between them.*

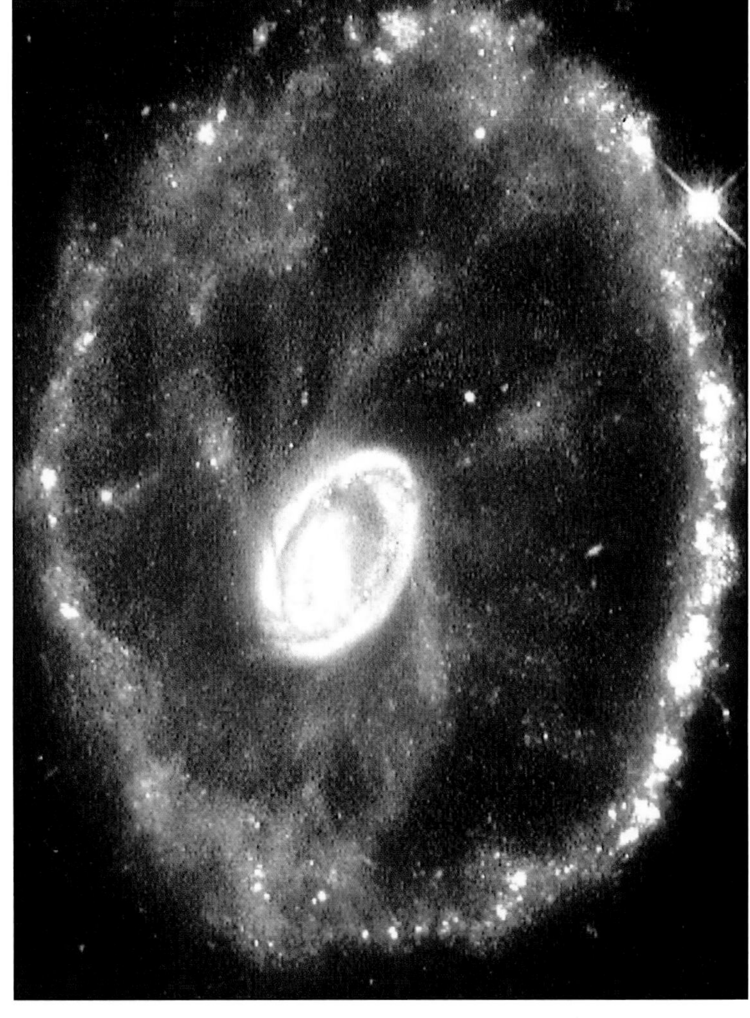

Galactic activity

Not all galaxies fit into the neat classification of spiral, elliptical, irregular, or even quasar. Many are being torn apart by immense explosions. Others, like M87 in the Virgo cluster, have a single great jet of matter spiraling out from the core. It seems likely that all these different galaxies have a massive black hole at their center. In some cases, the black hole becomes active each time it is fed with gas and stars. In other galaxies, the black hole remains dormant. There is good reason to believe that every galaxy, including our own, has a black hole at its center.

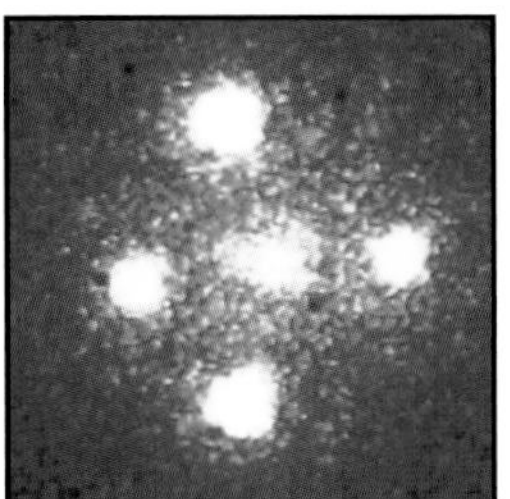

△ *The Cartwheel Galaxy is the result of a collision in which one galaxy passed straight through the middle of another spiral galaxy.*

◁ *Light bent by gravity creates the illusion of a cluster of five different quasars, when in fact there is only one. It is called Einstein's cross.*

Gravitational lens

When astronomers identified two identical quasars lying next to each other, they were puzzled. The explanation quickly dawned—it was something first predicted by Einstein, who realized that light is bent by a strong gravitational field. If there is a massive object such as a cluster of galaxies between us and the quasar, the light from the quasar becomes bent, as if through a lens. If the alignment is right, light will be bent through several routes to create a multiple image. This can take the form of a cross, for example, or even a clover leaf.

Echoes of Creation

The Universe is flying apart. Trace all the lines of the expanding galaxies back in time, and it appears they all originated from the same place. If so, they must have been blown apart by an incredible explosion. In the 1950s, the English astronomer Fred Hoyle and others suggested a different explanation. They argued that the Universe, though expanding, remains essentially the same, with new matter created to fill the expanding gaps. This is known as the Steady State Universe, and Fred Hoyle called the alternative the Big Bang Universe. The name stuck and some scientists predicted that we would find a way of proving that the Big Bang really happened. If the Universe did begin in an explosion, it would have left an echo. The incredible heat of the explosion would now have cooled to just a few degrees above absolute zero –460°F (–273°C), but even so it should be detectable.

◁ *The* Cosmic Background Explorer *satellite,* COBE, *was launched in 1990 to study the microwave background radiation left over from the Big Bang over 12 billion years ago. Scientists are now beginning to build up a very detailed map of the early Universe.*

▽ *You can listen to the sound of the Big Bang in your own home! If you tune your television between stations, the picture will "snow," and the sound will hiss. About one percent of this noise is from the microwave background, reaching us from the Big Bang itself.*

Whispers from space

When the first transatlantic communications satellite, *Telstar*, was launched in 1962, a big radio antenna was constructed in New Jersey to receive its signal. But the antenna also received a faint hiss that would not go away, even when two astronomers, Robert Wilson and Arno Penzias, removed pigeon droppings from the receiver! The hiss seemed to come from every direction and radiated energy at a temperature just 37 degrees above absolute zero. They realized that this must be the background radiation left from the Big Bang itself. To date, this is the best evidence that the Universe really did begin in a fireball.

The map of the cosmic background radiation is a true map, since some of the signal was due warmth in COBE's instruments. Even so, it firmed that the present structure of the iverse originated in the Big Bang. When the covery was made, the leader of the project cribed it as "like seeing the face of God."

Cosmic ripples

In 1990, NASA launched *COBE*, the *Cosmic Background Explorer* satellite. Its purpose was to stare at the microwave background. The first result was a spectacular confirmation that the radiation is a perfect example of so-called "black body" radiation—radiation simply due to heat. *COBE* then started to map it and look for features. The radiation turned out to be very, very smooth in every direction. Eventually, patterns began to emerge and, in 1992, scientists announced that they had seen ripples in the background. This caused a sensation. The fluctuations are only thirty millionths of a degree, but they provided the early Universe with enough variation in density for the very first stars and galaxies to be born. Without them, the Universe would still be a diffuse haze of gas.

▽ *Robert Wilson and Arno Penzias stand in front of the radio antenna with which they discovered the microwave background radiation in 1962. The antenna was originally designed to pick up signals from the communications satellite,* Telstar.

R

-0.27

rst light

ıe fireball of the Big Bang gave off no light. Light could not travel in aight lines without bumping into things—atoms had not yet formed d the Universe was a seething mass of particles. After about 300,000 ars, the Universe had cooled enough for atoms to form. The Universe came transparent and radiation could shine freely. The microwave ckground radiation is the cooled remnant of that first light.

The discovery of the background radiation sent out ripples ough astronomy. The theory of the Steady State Universe hich rejects the Big Bang theory) was finally discredited.

The Big Bang

Astronomers can trace the expanding Universe back to a time when all the stars and galaxies they can see must have been squashed together into a tiny space. They can look back directly to the cosmic background radiation emitted when our Universe was about 300,000 years old and only slightly larger than our own galaxy. To journey back farther, toward the Big Bang itself, it is necessary to turn to physics. Scientists have studied conditions back to within a hundredth of a billionth of a second of the start of the Universe by recreating them in high-energy particle colliders. And their theories take them even further.

A note on scale

The numbers in cosmology are so vast a[nd] the numbers in subatomic physics are so tiny that scientists use a special shorthan[d]. Ten multiplied by itself (i.e., a hundred) written as 10^2. A thousand is 10^3. Similar[ly] a tenth is 10^{-1}, a thousandth 10^{-3}, and so o[n].

1
2
3
4
5
6

E=mc²

△ *Einstein's famous equation $E=mc^2$ shows that it takes a lot of energy to make a little matter. In the first instant of the Big Bang* (1), *all four fundamental forces of nature act as one, and even space and time are unified.*

△ *By 10^{-32} seconds* (2), *the Universe is a hot, seething mass of particles, expanding at the speed of light. At 10^{-11} seconds* (3), *the weak nuclear force separates from electromagnetism. Quarks and antiquarks are spontaneously created and annihilate each other.*

In the beginning

The entire Universe may have been born from a single subatomic particle! Today, every speck of seemingly empty space is a seething well of potential energy. Physicists suspect that a whole range of particles are being born from it every instant. Usually, they die again before they have had time to do anything, go anywhere, or be seen by anyone. But, just occasionally, they can get trapped and become "real." No one really knows for sure, but this is possibly how the Universe came into being.

Superforce

There are just four fundamental forces at work in the Universe—gravity, the strong and weak nuclear forces, and electromagnetism. But they may all have been unite[d] into a single superforce that governed the Universe at th[e] moment of its birth. As the Universe cooled, each of the[se] forces separated. Gravity was the first to separate, at just 10^{-43} seconds after the start. The strong force followed at 10^{-35} seconds; the weak force and electromagnetism went their separate ways at 10^{-11} seconds.

After 300,000 years (6), radiation is no longer
ong enough to break up atoms. The Universe
comes transparent and light shines through it.
er one billion years (7), clumps of gas are
lling together to form protogalaxies. Inside
m the first stars are beginning to shine.

▽ *Today (8), after 12 billion years, clusters of galaxies have formed superclusters. Matter has been processed through several generations of stars to form the building materials for planets and life.*

8

7

At 10^4 seconds (4), the Universe is about the
of the Solar System, and the temperature
s fallen enough for quarks to form protons,
itrons, and other so-called baryons. After
) seconds (5), protons and neutrons link up.

△ *The background image shows the tracks of subatomic particles. Scientists create these high-energy collisions to explore conditions similar to those after the Big Bang.*

flation

process called inflation might explain how something
aller than an atom grew to a universe the size of a
apefruit in the first 10^{-32} of a second. If a little bubble
the Universe continued expanding after the strong
clear force should have separated from it, it might have
eated a false vacuum, a kind of antigravity. This would
ow the bubble to expand 100 times faster than the
eed of light. When inflation froze, it released so much
ergy that it produced all the matter in our Universe.

First atom

When the strong force separated, the Universe heated up to 10^{27} degrees. Matter and antimatter were created in equal proportions. An imbalance in the process led to a build-up of matter, which is why there are no antigalaxies today. The first particles were quarks and electrons. As the Universe cooled, quarks combined to form protons and neutrons. Some of them clustered together to make helium nuclei and, after 300,000 years, the electrons joined them to make the first atoms.

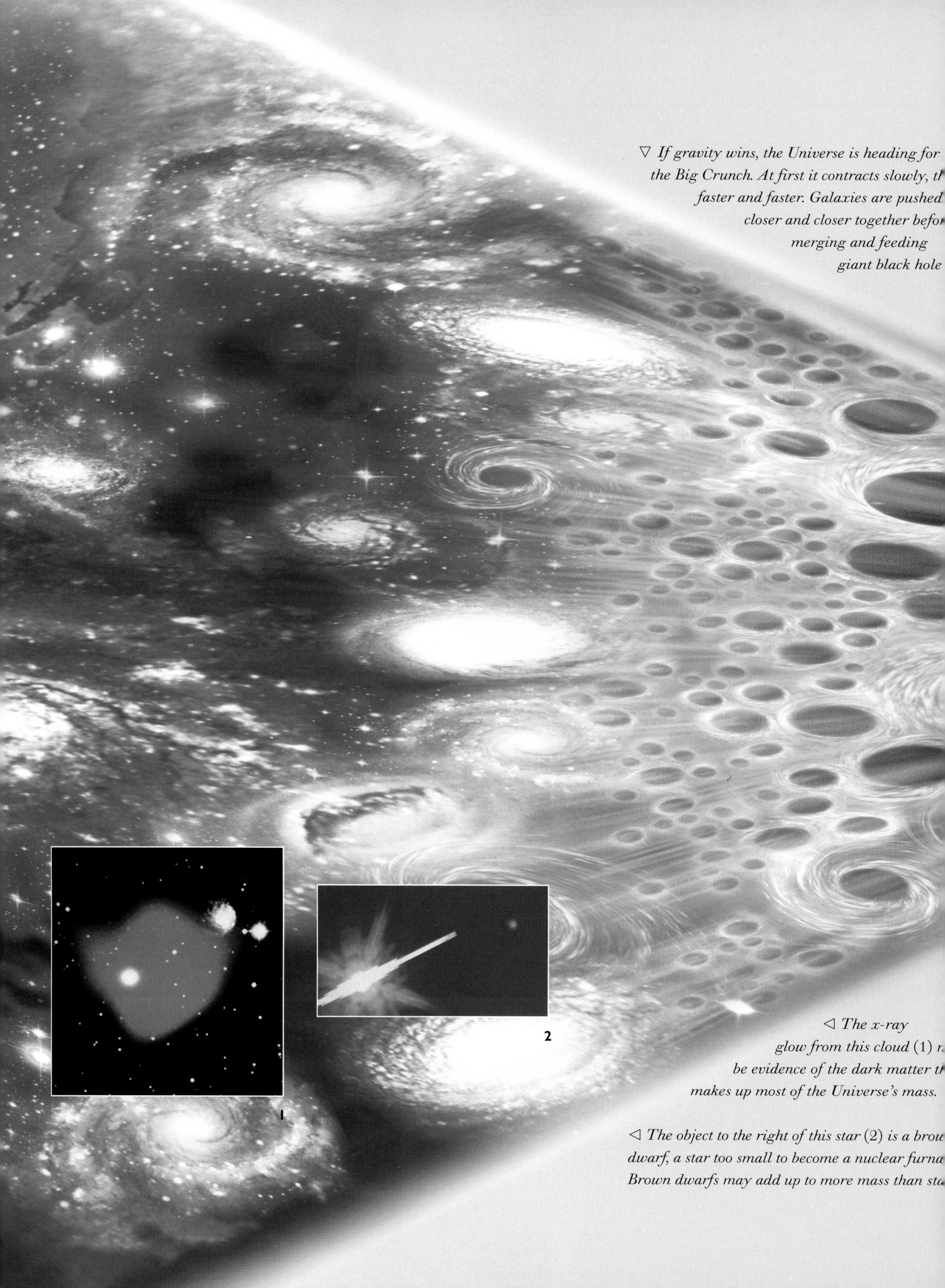

▽ *If gravity wins, the Universe is heading for the Big Crunch. At first it contracts slowly, th faster and faster. Galaxies are pushed closer and closer together befor merging and feeding giant black hole*

◁ *The x-ray glow from this cloud (1) m be evidence of the dark matter th makes up most of the Universe's mass.*

◁ *The object to the right of this star (2) is a brow dwarf, a star too small to become a nuclear furna Brown dwarfs may add up to more mass than sta*

The Great Unknown

There are some questions about the nature of the Universe that, until recently, seemed to be unanswerable. What akes up the Universe? How heavy is it? How old is it, and how ill it all end? Astronomers still do not have all the answers, ıt at last they feel able to begin researching the questions. ɔ do so will take some very strange telescopes. As well as ;ing the best measurements possible from optical, infrared, ıd radio telescopes on the ground and in space, astronomers also are using instruments deep underground to try to weigh the Universe and predict its ultimate fate.

△ *The Universe could end in three ways: The closed or Big Crunch Universe* (1) *is so massive it collapses under its own weight. In the flat Universe* (2), *expansion slows down, but never quite leads to collapse. The open Universe* (3) *expands forever.*

◁ *As the Universe approaches its end, the remaining matter spirals into black holes. Nothing can hold the Universe back from the final inferno. But perhaps it could bounce back in a new Big Bang.*

Dark matter

All that we can see is only a fraction of the Universe. Some matter is detectable only by its gravitational effects on the rotation of galaxies. This is called ɾk matter, and no one knows its material composition. ırk matter could be conventional matter, such as ,all stars called brown dwarfs, or even black holes.

ɦostly particles

ırk matter may also include neutrinos—ghostly ɾticles once thought to have no mass. These are so ımerous that any mass at all would make them far avier than all the stars. Other particles are predicted physicists, but have yet to be detected. If found, ɛy could make up 99 percent of the Universe.

The fate of the Universe

From its birth, now thought to be between 12 and 15 billion years ago, the Universe has continued to expand. The latest evidence suggests the expansion may even be accelerating. If the Universe contains one hundred times more matter than we can see, gravity might halt the expansion and make the Universe contract into a Big Crunch. This could be the end of everything or the start of a new Universe.

Heat death

If gravity cannot halt the expansion, stars will slowly age and die. Galaxies will fade away and even black holes will disappear. After billions and billions of years, the Universe will become a cold, dull place, containing only a few widely spaced particles.

△ *Alice enters a wormhole in space-time. It could take her to another time, or even into another universe.*

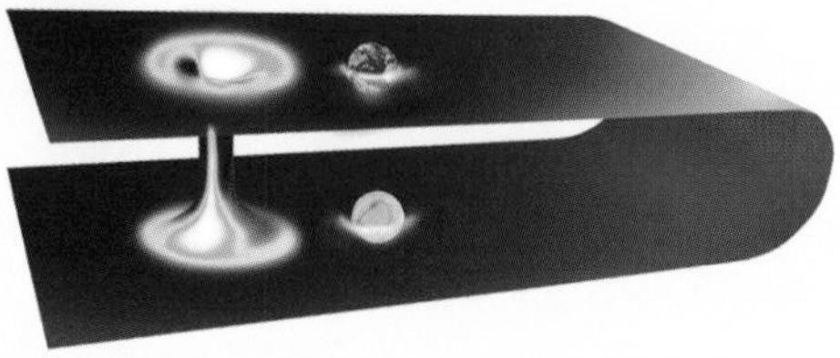

△ *Space itself can be curved, so a wormhole might act as a shortcut between two seemingly distant place*

Beyond Time

Time is relative. The rate your watch ticks relative to someone else's depends on how fast you are moving relative to each other. This was Alber Einstein's conclusion in 1905. He established that, as the speed of light must be the same for everyone, no matter how they are moving, then space and time themselves must be intertwined. Einstein developed these ideas in his general theory of relativity, taking gravity into account and showing how gravity bends space-time. Many science-fiction writers and some scientists have seized on Einstein's theories to show that one day time travel may just be possible.

△ *Time appears to run in one direction only. Broken eggs do not reassemble themselves. This tendency to disorder is one of the few natural arrows in time.*

Time's arrow

We all have a strong sense of passing time, and time always seems to run in one direction only. For example, people age, and cups of coffee cool off. However, according to the laws of physics, there is nothing to prevent most processes from reversing. In fact, in many processes, especially at the level of particles, there is no distinguishable arrow of time.

Warping space and time

The Universe's fundamental speed limit seems to be the speed of light—190,000 mil (300,000 km) per second. Even though a spaceship never could travel this fast, it mig in theory, be possible to warp the space aroun it, shrinking space ahead and expanding it behind. The snag is that distorting space in this way would require at least a million times the energy locked up in the Sun!

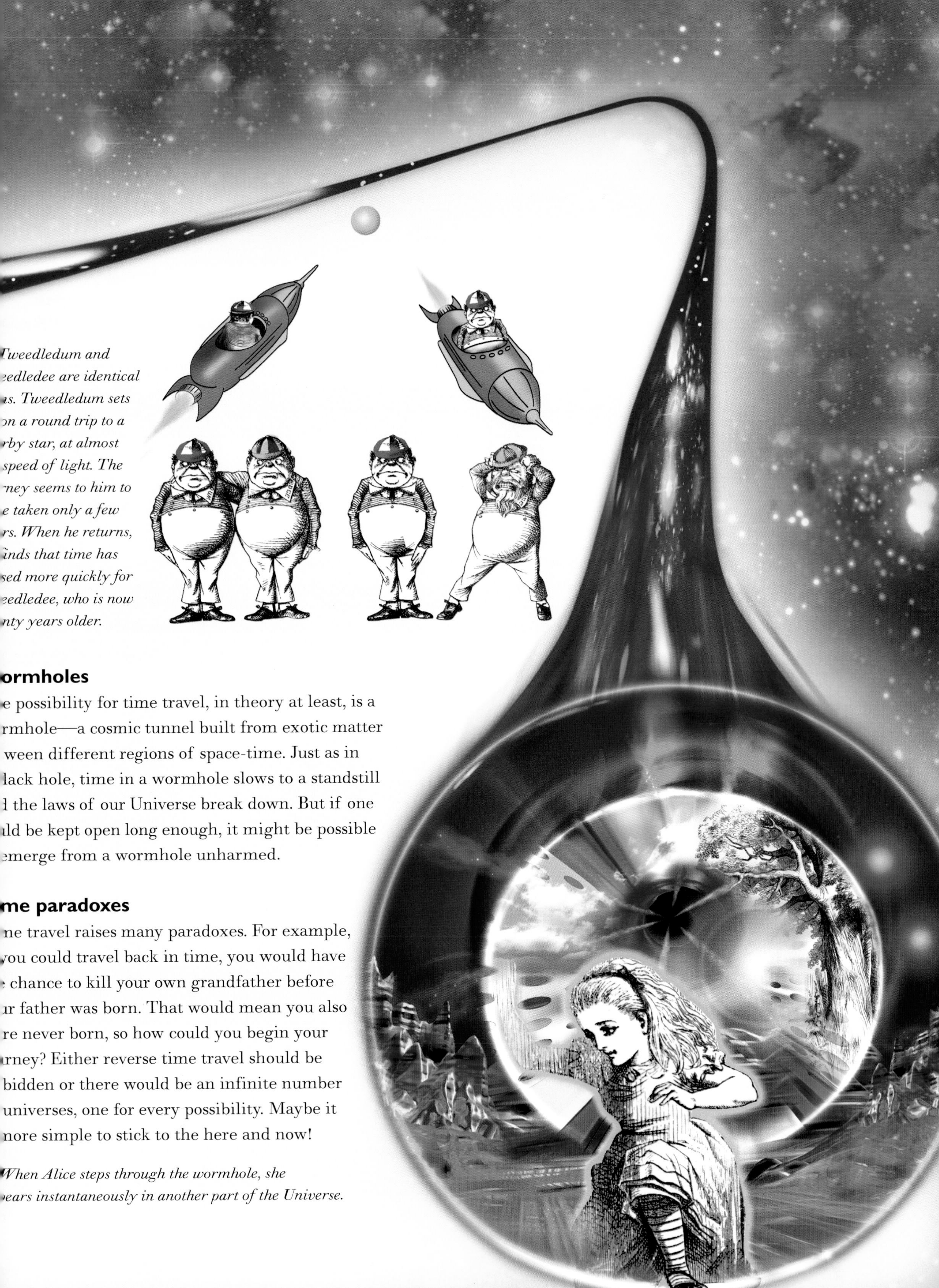

Tweedledum and ɛedledee are identical ɪs. Tweedledum sets ɔn a round trip to a rby star, at almost speed of light. The ney seems to him to e taken only a few rs. When he returns, inds that time has sed more quickly for ɛedledee, who is now nty years older.

ormholes

e possibility for time travel, in theory at least, is a rmhole—a cosmic tunnel built from exotic matter ween different regions of space-time. Just as in lack hole, time in a wormhole slows to a standstill l the laws of our Universe break down. But if one ıld be kept open long enough, it might be possible ɛmerge from a wormhole unharmed.

me paradoxes

ne travel raises many paradoxes. For example, you could travel back in time, you would have chance to kill your own grandfather before ır father was born. That would mean you also re never born, so how could you begin your rney? Either reverse time travel should be bidden or there would be an infinite number universes, one for every possibility. Maybe it nore simple to stick to the here and now!

When Alice steps through the wormhole, she ɪears instantaneously in another part of the Universe.

The Search for E.T.

Are people on the Earth alone in the Universe? As yet, there is no certain evidence of life anywhere else, much less intelligent life. But there are hundreds of millions of stars in our galaxy. If a fraction have habitable planets and a fraction of those developed life, there could be millions of civilizations other than our own. However, the distances between the stars is so great it is unlikely that extraterrestrials—if they exist—have visited our planet. We do not even know exactly how life began on the Earth. The evidence we do have, however, suggests that it takes several billion years of evolution for intelligent life to arise and to develop the technology capable of sending messages to the stars.

△ *The plaque fixed to* Voyager 1 *describes where it comes from and who built it. It also carries a record of natural sounds of the Earth as well as music.*

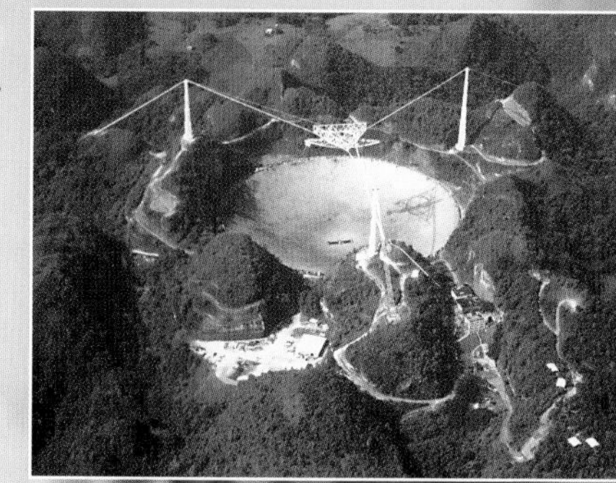

△ *In 1974, the first signal to possible alien life was broadcast from the worl biggest radio dish at Arecibo in Puert Rico. Arecibo has remained the center for the search to identify alien signals*

The search for distant planets

Our best telescopes could never see a distant planet against the glare of its star. But big planets make stars wobble as they orbit, and several wobbling stars have been detected. Most of these stars wobble due to Jupiterlike planets that are inhospitable to humans, but some planets may be far enough away from their stars to be hospitable. Far out in space, telescopes in the future may see distant planets directly. They may even be able to detect gases, such as ozone and water vapor, that may indicate life.

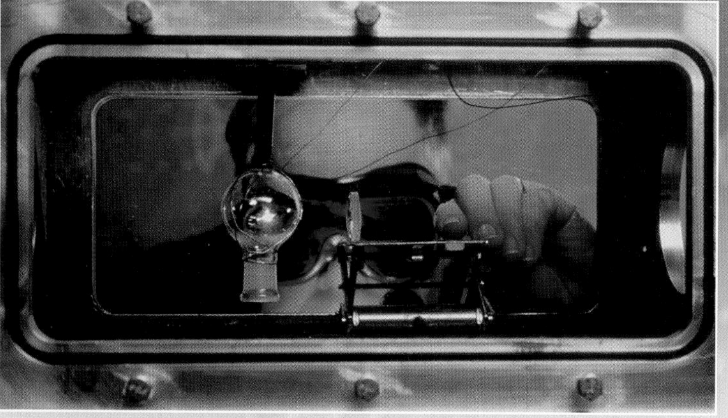

△ *A scientist discharges an electric field across a mixture of water, hydrogen, methane, and ammonia. In this experiment, amino acids—the basis of life on this planet—accumulate after a time, just as they may once have done on the early Earth.*

The search for extraterrestrial intelligence

Since the first radio broadcast, radio signals have been traveling out beyond our planet at the speed of light. The signals have already passed many stars and planets, but unless aliens were listening for them, they would not noti The most powerful radio signal to have left the Earth was sent from a radio telescope at Arecibo, Puerto Rico in 197 It was a brief digital signal describing who and where we and it was directed at a cluster of stars known as M13. Ev at the speed of light, however, it will take 25,000 years to reach its destination. Many teams are taking part in SETI (the Search for Extra-Terrestrial Intelligence). They scan Sunlike star systems with radio telescopes, analyzing milli of radio frequencies by computer in the search for a signa

ıliens look like these mounds
ia? Similar structures may have
ɔng the first inhabitants of the
ore than 3.5 billion years ago.

△ *Alien existence is a subject clouded by fiction and fraud. The "flying saucer" above proved to be a child's toy photographed at close range. Though many people claim to have been visited or abducted by aliens, there is still no evidence of the presence of other beings in the Universe.*

ien life on other planets

ıthere are aliens out there, what are they like?
e on the Earth shows great variety and ingenuity and it
ɔrobable that life on another planet would do the same.
night be based on a different chemistry entirely, with
ron or silicon taking the place of carbon, or with the role
water being played by liquid ammonia. Physically, life
ms will need to do some of the same things as humans.
ey may need to move around, sense their environment,
, and defend themselves. They would probably have a
nt and a back, but eyes, hands, and so on could all be
ɔlaced by other tools, and not necessarily in pairs.

△ *This bright light was photographed over São Paulo, Brazil in 1984. It is one of many so-called UFOs—Unidentified Flying Objects.*

Impossible Questions

Throughout this book, we have seen how astronomers observe our planet, our Solar System, our Galaxy, and some of the billions of other galaxies beyond it. One day, in theory, we could learn every detail of the physical Universe. But there are still so questions that can never be answered with certainty. For example what lies beyond or before our Universe? Why did the Universe begi Why are we here in it? By showing us that the Earth is not the center of the Universe, astronomy has led us to question our own importance in the grand scheme of life. But some of the answers to these big questions could put us at center stage again.

△ *Every culture has proposed a supreme being as the creator of the Universe. Scientists can offer few better explanations for the fundamental laws of the cosmos.*

Beyond the horizon

The farthest galaxies seem to be receding from us so fast that they are approaching the speed of light. We cannot see beyond them. The Universe may be infinite, or it may end just beyond this light horizon. We cannot tell. Perhaps our Universe is just one bubble in a whole foam of universes. Some may not have inflated, while others might have different physical laws or dimensions from our own Universe.

The living Universe

Perhaps, when a black hole forms in our Universe, it gives birth to another universe somewhere else. If the new universe can inherit the ability to make black holes, then universes might evolve and get better and better at making black holes. A universe like our own, which is good at creating black holes, is also good at making stars and ultimately planets and life itself.

▷ *Black holes may give birth to new universes. The colored peaks in this computer simulation are other universes, each with its own physical laws.*

The same force that makes apples fall also 'ds stars together. The same force that makes ngs radioactive blows the elements out from ploding stars to form new stars and planets. e same force that gives us electricity also kes the Universe transparent. It is as if the iverse has been designed for us to study it.

Cosmic coincidences

Life may seem like a lottery, the Universe like a random accident. Perhaps the biggest coincidence of all is that our Universe is just right for life. If, for example, beryllium nuclei, made in the cores of stars, were a different size, they would not go on to form carbon and oxygen, elements essential for life. If the weak nuclear force were slightly different, stars would not explode as supernovae, spewing their elements out to form potential new stars and planets. But if the force of gravity were slightly stronger, all stars would collapse into black holes. The list goes on, raising the question of whether our Universe is meant to be the way it is.

The ultimate question

The final question is: Why we are here? Cosmologists point out how the Universe is finely tuned for complexity and life. This is called the "weak anthropic principle." More controversially, it has also been suggested that this is more than coincidence, and that the Universe *must* produce intelligent observers. Some even argue that observers are necessary to bring the Universe into being, and that ultimately everything that exists must be known. If that is true, astronomy has a bright future and we are back at the center of the Universe.

▽ *On a small, blue planet, the third rock from an average star in a typical spiral galaxy, a life form developed with the potential to understand the Universe. Why?*

Universal Facts

PLANETARY DATA

Equatorial diameter	7,926 miles
Volume	2.6×10^{11} $miles^3$
Mass	1.32×10^{25} lbs.
Density	5.52 of water
Surface gravity	32 $feet/sec^{-2}$
Day length	23.9345 hours
Year length	365.256 days
Axial inclination	23.44^{o}
Age	4,700 million years approx.
Distance from the Sun	Min. 91 million miles Max. 95 million miles
Surface area	197 million $miles^2$
Land surface	57 million $miles^2$
Oceans cover	71% of surface
Atmosphere	Nitrogen 78%, Oxygen 21%, other 1%
Avg. height of land	0.5 miles above sea level
Avg. depth of ocean	2 miles
Continental crust	22 miles avg. thick
Oceanic crust	4 miles avg. thick
Lithosphere	47 miles deep
Mantle	1,800 miles thick
Outer core	1,400 miles thick
Inner core	750 miles thick

MAJOR EARTHQUAKES

Location	Year	Magnitude	Deaths
Turkey	1999	7.8	17,118
N.E. Afghanistan	1998	6.9	4,700+
N. Iran	1997	7.5	1,560
Sakhalin, Russia	1995	7.5	1,989
Kobe, Japan	1995	6.9	5,502
Northridge, CA	1994	6.8	61
Osmanabad, S. India	1993	6.3	9,748
Philippines	1990	7.8	1,621
N.W. Iran	1990	7.7	40,000+
San Francisco, CA	1989	7.1	62
Armenia	1988	7.0	55,000
Mexico City, Mexico	1985	8.1	9,500
N. Yemen	1982	6.0	2,800
S. Italy	1980	7.2	3,000
N.E. Iran	1978	7.8	15,000
Tangshan, China	1976	8.0	255,000
Guatemala	1976	7.5	23,000
N.E. Iran	1968	7.3	12,000
Nan-Shan, China	1927	8.3	200,000
Yokohama, Japan	1923	8.3	143,000
Gansu, China	1920	8.6	200,000
Messina, Italy	1908	7.5	83,000
San Francisco, CA	1906	8.3	500
Calcutta, India	1737	-	300,000
Hokkaido, Japan	1730	-	137,000
Shaanxi, China	1556	-	830,000
Antioch, Syria	526	-	250,000

PROPERTIES OF COMMON MINERALS

Name	Type	Hardness	Crystal	Optical
Talc	Silicate	1	Cubic	Pale green or gray; pearly luster
Graphite	Element	1-2	Trigonal	Gray metallic luster
Gypsum	Sulfate	2	Monoclinic	White to transparent
Calcite	Carbonate	3	Trigonal/Hexagonal	Double refraction
Barite	Sulfate	3-3.5	Orthorhombic	Pale, translucent
Fluorite	Halide	4	Cubic	Many colors, fluorescent
Pyrite	Sulfide	6-6.5	Cubic	Commonly known as "fool's gold"
Quartz	Oxide	7	Trigonal/Hexagonal	Translucent
Garnet	Silicate	7	Cubic	Various forms, often plum red
Tourmaline	Silicate	7-7.5	Trigonal/Hexagonal	Pink and green
Zircon	Silicate	7.5	Tetragonal	Often brown
Beryl	Silicate	7-8	Trigonal/Hexagonal	Many colors, emerald green
Spinel	Oxide	7.5-8	Cubic	Many colors
Corundum	Oxide	9	Trigonal/Hexagonal	Various forms incl. ruby and sapphire
Diamond	Element	10	Cubic	Transparent, sparkles if cut

A mineral's optical properties include nc only its color, but als transparency and lus or shine. Hardness is a scale based on ten minerals. These rang from talc, the softest (to diamond, the hardest (10).

AJOR VOLCANOES

Name	Ht. (ft.)	Major eruptions	Last
Bezymianny, Russia	9,186	1955–56	1984
El Chichón, Mexico	4,426	1982	1982
Mt. Erebus, Antarctica	13,199	1947, 1972	1986
Mt. Etna, Italy	10,617	Frequent	1991
Mt. Fuji, Japan	12,388	1707	1707
Hekla, Iceland	4,892	1693, 1845, 1947–48, 1970	1981
Helgafell, Iceland	705	1973	1973
Kilauea, Hawaii	4,091	Frequent	1991
Klyuchevskaya, Russia	15,912	1700–1966, 1984	1985
Krakatoa, Indonesia	2,684	Frequent, esp. 1883	1980
Mauna Loa, Hawaii	13,687	Frequent	1984
Nyamuragira, Zaire	10,026	1921–38, 1971, 1980	1984
Paricutín, Mexico	10,459	1943–52	1952
Mt. Pelée, Martinique	4,583	1902, 1929–32	1932
Mt. Pinatubo, Philippines	4,797	1391, 1991	1991
Popocatépetl, Mexico	17,989	1920	1943
Mt. Rainier, WA	14,409	1st century B.C., 1820	1882
Ruapehu, New Zealand	9,173	1945, 1953, 1969, 1975	1986
Mt. St. Helens, WA	8,363	Frequent, esp. 1980	1987
Soufrière, St. Vincent	4,042	1718, 1812, 1902, 1971–72	1979
Soufrière Hills, Montserrat	3,002	1995	1998
Stromboli, Italy	3,054	Frequent	1986
Surtsey, Iceland	571	1963–67	1967
Thira, Greece	4,314	Frequent, esp. 1470 B.C.	1950
Unzen, Japan	4,462	1360, 1791	1991
Vesuvius, Italy	4,229	Frequent, esp. A.D. 79	1944

RINCIPAL ORE MINERALS

Ore of	Mineral	Type	Features
Aluminum	Bauxite	Hydroxide	White reddish
Copper	Chalcopyrite	Sulfide	Brassy yellow
	Cuprite	Oxide	Black
	Malachite	Carbonate	Green
Gold	Native	Metal	Golden
Iron	Pyrite	Sulfide	Brassy yellow
	Magnetite	Oxide	Black
	Hematite	Hematite	Black/reddish
	Siderite	Carbonate	Orange
Lead	Galena	Sulfide	Metallic black
Silver	Native	Metal	Silver
Tin	Cassiterite	Oxide	Black/brown
Titanium	Ilmenite	Oxide	Black opaque
Uranium	Uraninite	Oxide	Dull brown/black
Zinc	Sphalerite	Sulfide	Black

GEOLOGICAL TIMELINE

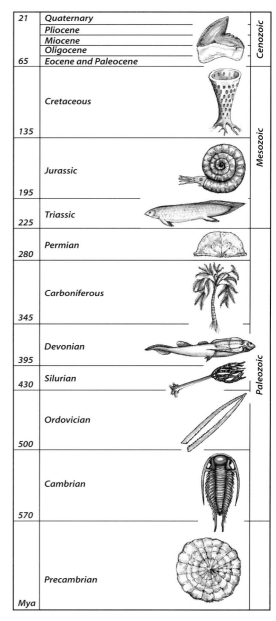

Mya	Period	Era
21	Quaternary	Cenozoic
	Pliocene	
	Miocene	
	Oligocene	
65	Eocene and Paleocene	
135	Cretaceous	Mesozoic
195	Jurassic	
225	Triassic	
280	Permian	Paleozoic
345	Carboniferous	
395	Devonian	
430	Silurian	
500	Ordovician	
570	Cambrian	
Mya	Precambrian	

Mya stands for millions of years ago.

The changing fossil record *(above)* provides an effective means of dating rocks. So-called zone or index fossils have been picked as key markers for each time. The fossil record goes back to the Precambrian era, which began 600 million years ago.

THE PLANETS OF THE SOLAR SYSTEM

Name	Distance from Sun (Miles)	Diameter (Miles)	Mass (Earth=1)	Rotation	Year	Moons
Mercury	35,980,000	3,031	0.055	58.66 days	87.97 days	0
Venus	67,230,000	7,521	0.81	243.01 days	224.7 days	0
Earth	93,000,000	8,000	1.00	23.93 hrs	365.26 days	1
Mars	141,600,000	4,223	0.11	24.62 hrs	686.98 days	2
Jupiter	483,600,000	88,846	318	9.92 hrs	11.86 years	16
Saturn	888,200,000	74,898	95.18	10.67 hrs	29.46 years	23
Uranus	1,786,400,000	31,763	14.50	17.23 hrs	84.01 years	18
Neptune	2,798,800,000	30,800	17.14	16.12 hrs	164.79 years	8
Pluto	3,666,200,000	1,430	0.0022	6.375 days	248.54 years	1

BRIGHTEST STARS (in order of apparent brightness)

Name	Type	Location	Distance (Light years)	Apparent magnitude	Absolute magnitude
Sirius	White Major	Canis	8.6	-1.46	1.4
Canopus	Yellow Giant	Carina	1200	-0.72	-8.5
Alpha Centauri	Yellow	Centaurus	4.3	-0.27	4
Arcturus	Orange Giant	Botes	36	-0.04	-0.2
Vega	White	Lyra	25	0.03	0.5
Capella	Yellow	Auriga	43	0.08	-0.7
Rigel	Blue Giant	Orion	900	0.12	-7.1
Procyon	Yellow Minor	Canis	11	0.38	2.6
Achernar	Blue Giant	Erudanus	85	0.46	-1.6
Betelgeux	Red Giant	Orion	310	0.5	5.6
Agena	Blue Giant	Centaurus	460	0.61	-5.1
Altair	White	Aquila	17	0.77	2.2
Acrux	Binary	Southern Cross	360	0.83	-3.9
Aldebaran	Orange	Taurus	68	0.85	-0.3
Antares	Red Giant	Scorpius	330	0.96	-4.7
Spica	Blue Giant	Virgo	260	0.98	-3.6
Pollux	Orange Giant	Gemini	36	1.14	0.2
Fomalhaut	White	Piscis Australis	22	1.16	2.0
Deneb	White Giant	Cygnus	1800	1.25	-7.5
Beta Crucis	Blue Giant	Southern Cross	425	1.25	-5.0
Regulus	Blue	Leo	85	1.35	-0.6

Note: The lower the value of the magnitude, the brighter the star.

Apparent magnitude is how bright the star seems from the Earth.

Absolute magnitude is how bright it would seem if all the stars were the same distance from the Earth.

Firsts in astronomy

1600 B.C. Babylonian star catalogs compiled

270 B.C. Aristarchos proposes that the Earth revolves around the Sun

230 B.C. Eratosthenes measures the Earth's circumference

135 B.C. Hipparchos discovers that the Earth's axis wobbles

A.D. 127 Ptolemy develops the Earth-centered theory of the Univers

1054 Chinese observe the Crab supernova

1543 Copernicus revives the idea of a Sun-centered Universe

1609 Kepler describes the orbits of planets

1609 Galileo is first to use a telescop for astronomy

1655 Huygens discovers Saturn's rin

1668 Newton makes first reflecting telescope

1687 Newton publishes Theory of Gravitation

1705 Halley recognizes that comets orbit the Sun

1781 Herschel discovers Uranus

1838 Bessel measures the distance of a star

1846 Adams and Leverrier predict existence of Neptune

1912 Leavitt discovers Cepheid variable stars

1920 Slipher discovers that nebulae are receding

1923 Hubble shows that receding nebulae are galaxies

1938 Bethe and Weizsäcker suggest stars are powered by nuclear fusion

1963 Schmidt discovers the first quasar

1965 Penzias and Wilson discover microwave background radiati

1967 Jocelyn Bell discovers first puls

1992 *COBE* satellite identifies rippl in the microwave background

MAJOR TELESCOPES—Optical/infrared

Name	Location	Diameter (feet)	First light
Gemini	Hawaii	19.7	1999
VLT	Chile	52 ft. equivalent	1998
Keck	Hawaii	2 x 32	1990
Mt. Hopkins	Arizona	21.3	1999
Zelenchukskaya	Russia	19.6	1976
Hale	California	16.4	1948
Herschel	Canary Islands	13.7	1987
Cerro Tololo	Chile	13	1976
Mayall	Arizona	12.4	1973
Anglo-Australian	Australia	12.7	1975
U.K. InfraRed	Hawaii	12.4	1978
Hubble	Space	7.8	1990

MAJOR PLANETARY PROBES

Name	Nation	Launch	Target	Result
Mariner 2	U.S.A.	1962	Venus	First flyby
Venera 3	U.S.S.R.	1965	Venus	Crushed during descent
Mariner 4, 6, & 7	U.S.A.	1964, '69, '69	Mars	Flybys
Venera 7	U.S.S.R.	1970	Venus	Landed. Survived 23 minutes
Mars 2 & 3	U.S.S.R.	1971	Mars	2: Orbiter, dropped flag 3: Orbiter and lander
Mariner 9	U.S.A.	1971	Mars	Orbiter
Pioneer 10	U.S.A.	1972	Jupiter	Flyby 1973
Pioneer 11	U.S.A.	1973	Jupiter and Saturn	Jupiter flyby 1974 Saturn flyby 1979
Viking 1 & 2	U.S.A.	1975	Mars	Orbiters and landers
Voyager 1	U.S.A.	1977	Jupiter and Saturn	Jupiter flyby 1979 Saturn flyby 1980
Voyager 2	U.S.A.	1977	Grand Tour	Flybys: Jupiter 1979, Saturn 1981, Uranus 1986, Neptune 1989
Pioneer Venus	U.S.A.	1978	Venus	Orbiter
Venera 13	U.S.S.R.	1981	Venus	Landed, lasted 2 hours
Venera 15	U.S.S.R.	1983	Venus	Radar mapper
Vega 1	U.S.S.R.	1984	Venus	Lander and balloon, plus Halley's Comet flyby
Magellan	U.S.A.	1989	Venus	Radar mapper
Galileo	U.S.A.	1989	Jupiter	Orbiter plus probe
Pathfinder	U.S.A.	1996	Mars	Lander and rover
Global Surveyor	U.S.A.	1996	Mars	Mapping orbiter
Cassini	U.S.A./ Europe	1997	Saturn	Orbiter and Titan probe

Firsts in space

1957 *Sputnik 1* (U.S.S.R.) first satellite launched

1958 *Explorer 1* (U.S.A.) discovers Van Allen radiation belts

1959 *Luna 1* (U.S.S.R.) escapes Earth's gravity

1959 *Vanguard 2* (U.S.A.) takes first photos of the Earth

1959 *Luna 2* (U.S.S.R.) hits the Moon

1959 *Luna 3* (U.S.S.R.) returns first pictures of far side of the Moon

1960 *TIROS 1* (U.S.A.) first weather satellite

1960 *ECHO 1* (U.S.A.) first communications satellite

1961 *Vostok 1* (U.S.S.R.) first manned orbital flight

1962 *Aerobee* (U.S.A.) X-ray satellite launched

1963 *Vostok 6* (U.S.S.R.) carries first woman in orbit

1965 *Early Bird* (U.S.A.) commercial geostationary communications satellite

1965 *Gemini 6* (U.S.A.) manned rendezvous in space

1966 *Luna 9* (U.S.S.R.) soft Moon landing

1969 *Apollo 11* (U.S.A.) manned lunar landing

1975 Apollo/Soyuz first international linkup

1978 Launch of *International Ultraviolet Explorer* (U.S.A./Europe)

1981 *Columbia* (U.S.A.) first space shuttle flight

1986 Launch of *Mir* space station

1990 *Hubble Space Telescope* (U.S.A./Europe) launched

1998 Launch of first component of *International Space Station*

1999 Launch of *Chandra X-ray Observatory* and *XXM-Newton X-ray Observatory*

Glossary

Abyssal plain The flat floor of an ocean basin below a continental slope. Its surface consists of a layer of sediment covering uneven rock.

Accretion disk A disk of matter that builds up around a dense object as material spirals down toward it. It is believed that accretion disks often form around black holes.

Antarctic The region south of the Antarctic Circle, or the cold region around the South Pole—Antarctica and surrounding far southern parts of the Atlantic, Indian, and Pacific oceans.

Antimatter A form of matter, such as an opposite electrical charge, that shares properties with the fundamental particles of matter, but in reverse.

Arctic The region north of the Arctic Circle, or the cold region around the North Pole. It includes the Arctic Ocean and surrounding far northern parts of Europe, Asia, and North America.

Ash The fine, powdery material that is blown out by gas during a volcanic eruption. Ash can spread for thousands of miles and fall to form layers many inches thick.

Asteroid A rocky object, anything from a few feet to a few hundred miles across, in orbit around the Sun. Most asteroids are in the asteroid belt between the orbits of Mars and Jupiter, but some come into the inner Solar System and, every million years or so, one collides with the Earth.

Astronomical unit The average distance between the Earth and the Sun (927,506 miles). It is a useful unit for expressing distances in the Solar System.

Atmosphere The thin layer of air, composed mostly of nitrogen and oxygen, that is held in place around the Earth by gravity.

Atoll A ring-shaped coral reef surrounded by open sea and enclosing an area of shallow, sheltered water called a lagoon. Atolls grow on the rims of volcanic islands.

Atom The smallest component of an element that retains its chemical properties. Even the biggest atom is only two hundred millionths of an inch.

Aurora The display at high latitudes that looks like colored curtains of light, and is caused by energetic particles from the Sun streaming toward the Earth's magnetic poles and striking atoms in the atmosphere.

Basalt One of the most common rocks in the Earth's crust. It is created by partial melting of the mantle and erupts as a runny lava from volcanoes. It is dark, dense, and fine-grained.

Basin A depression in the Earth's surface containing an ocean. It also refers to the part of the ocean floor more than 6,500 feet below sea level.

Billion One thousand million (1,000,000,000).

Binary star A pair of stars in orbit around the common center of gravity between them (i.e., around each other).

Biodiversity The full range of plant, animal, and microorganism species found in a particular habitat. The health of an ecosystem can be measured by the degree of its diversity.

Bivalves Soft-bodied animals living in a pair of hinged shells that they can open and close. Bivalves include clams, mussels, and oysters.

Black hole A region of space-time where there is such a concentration of matter, and consequently gravity, that not even ligh can escape. Black holes ca form when massive stars collapse. Others lie at the heart of active galaxies.

Bony fish A fish with a bony skeleton. Bony spec such as herring and tuna outnumber cartilaginous (gristly) species, such as sharks and rays, by more than thirty to one.

Brown dwarf A small star of such low mass (les than 8 percent of the Su mass) that nuclear fusion reactions cannot begin. A brown dwarf shines on because of the faint heat released as it contracts.

Canyon A deep valley or gorge, often with near vertical sides. A canyon is carved by a river running through an arid, mountainous region.

Cartilaginous fish A fish with a cartilaginous, or gristly, skeleton. Cartilaginous fish includ sharks and rays. Unlike bony fish, they lack a swim bladder—if they stop swimming, they sink

Cepheid variable A star that varies its brightness a regular period of betw one and fifty days.

Cs An abbreviation chlorofluorocarbons—emicals once widely ed in aerosol sprays and rigerators. When released o the atmosphere, CFCs nage the ozone layer. eir use is now limited by ernational agreement.

uster A group of stars galaxies affecting each er by their gravitational raction.

met An object made of , dust, and other material. ere may be billions of nets beyond the orbit of ito. Some come nearer Sun, on elliptical orbits, ving spectacular tails gas and dust.

nstellation A grouping stars in the same ection in the sky, though t necessarily associated th each other.

ntinent A great landmass the surface of the Earth. ere are seven continents.

ntinental crust The rth's crust forming the ntinents.

ntinental rise A gentle pe formed by sediment the foot of a continental pe.

ntinental shelf The n of a continental dmass. It slopes gently wn to about 590 feet and ends at the continental slope.

Copepod A tiny, shrimplike creature forming part of the zooplankton.

Core The innermost 4,300 miles of our planet, composed mostly of iron with traces of nickel and other minerals. The central 1,500 miles is solid, but the outer core is molten and slowly circulating. Electric currents within the core generate the Earth's magnetic field.

Corona The outer atmosphere of the Sun, extending many millions of miles above the visible surface. The corona can reach 3,600,000°F and is visible during eclipses.

Cosmic background radiation Microwave radiation coming from all directions in the sky and thought to be the cooled remnant of the fireball of the Big Bang, in which the Universe began.

Cosmology The study of the structure and origin of the Universe.

Crater A circular depression on a planet, moon, or asteroid, usually resulting from the impact of another body.

Current An ocean current is water flowing through the sea. Winds drive surface currents. Deep-sea currents occur where dense water sinks and spreads over the seabed.

Dark matter Matter known to exist, but mostly invisible. It might be normal matter in the form of brown dwarfs or black holes, or it could be ghostly, unidentified particles.

DNA An abbreviation of deoxyribonucleic acid—the chemical that carries the genetic code of life. It is made up of a long chain that forms a double helix or spiral structure.

Earthquake An often violent shaking of the Earth caused when two of the plates that make up the Earth's crust crack as they scrape past each other. Earthquakes are most frequent along plate boundaries.

Echinoderm A spiny-skinned marine invertebrate such as a sea urchin, starfish, or sea cucumber.

Eclipse A shadow cast by one celestial object on another. For example, the Earth's shadow falling on the Moon causes a lunar eclipse. The Moon's shadow falling on the Earth is seen as a solar eclipse.

El Niño The Spanish name given to the warm ocean current that occasionally flows toward the coast of Peru, disrupting fisheries and wildlife and bringing droughts to some parts of the world and storms and floods to others.

Epicenter The point on the Earth's surface directly above the focus of an earthquake the place where the ground cracks.

Erosion The process by which rocks are worn away over time, usually as a result of the action of water, wind, or ice.

Escape velocity The velocity that a projectile must reach if it is to escape from the gravity of an astronomical object without further propulsion.

Estuary The place where a river widens and slows as it flows out into the sea. As the water slows, it can deposit the sediments it is carrying to form a delta.

Event horizon The boundary of a black hole, beyond which neither matter nor radiation can escape.

False-color Color added by computer to enhance the details of an image.

Fault A crack in the Earth's crust that forms during an earthquake due to stresses within the rock.

Fold A region of rocks that have been deformed or bent by movements in the Earth's crust.

Fossil The traces of a prehistoric plant or animal preserved within rocks or sediment. Fossils can be made up of the original hard parts of the organism, or they can be replaced by other minerals.

Fossil fuel Fossil fuels include coal, oil, and natural gas, all produced from the decay, burial, and fossilization of organic remains. Fossil fuels have taken millions of years to form, but humans have used much of them up in just a few centuries.

Galaxy A celestial city of millions or billions of stars, gas, and dust bound together by their gravitational pull.

Gamma rays The most energetic radiation in the electromagnetic spectrum.

Glacier Literally, a river of ice that builds up in a mountain valley as a result of the compression of snow. A glacier can flow slowly downhill, gouging out a deep, U-shaped valley.

Global warming A general warming of the Earth's climate brought about by increasing levels of so-called greenhouse gases, such as carbon dioxide, in the atmosphere. It is predicted that human activity will result in global warming of several degrees over the next century.

Globular cluster A spherical cluster of between a few thousand and a million stars. Globular clusters form the halo of our galaxy and contain very ancient stars.

Gondwanaland The name given to the great southern continent that resulted from the breakup of the supercontinent Pangaea. It included present-day Africa, South America, Australia, Antarctica, and India.

Granite A crystalline, igneous rock produced by the upwelling, or intrusion, of molten crustal rocks. It contains the minerals quartz, mica, and feldspar.

Gravitational lens A region of mass, such as a cluster of galaxies, that bends light from more distant objects.

Gravity The force that makes objects attract one another. It holds us on the surface of the Earth and keeps the Moon in orbit around our planet and the Earth in orbit around the Sun.

Greenhouse effect A phenomenon caused by atmospheric gases, such as water vapor and carbon dioxide, that allow sunlight into the Earth's surface but prevent the escape of heat. As a result, the gases act like a blanket, keeping the planet warm in the same way as the glass in a greenhouse keeps plants inside warm.

Hotspot A place on the Earth's surface above an upwelling plume of hot mantle material. Hotspots are often the site of intensive, long-term volcanic activity. Examples include Hawaii and Iceland.

Hubble constant The rate at which the Universe is expanding. As the galaxies move farther apart, this causes redshift, which can be used to measure the rate of expansion.

Hurricane A tropical Atlantic storm with winds up to 100 mph. The Pacific Ocean's typhoons and the Indian Ocean's cyclones are similar storms.

Hydrothermal vent Where volcanic forces rise beneath the ocean crust, for example along the mid-ocean ridges, they can heat groundwater so that it jets out of underwater springs or vents.

Ice age A prolonged period during which the Earth's climate cools and ice sheets and glaciers spread from the poles. It may be triggered by periodic variations in the Earth's orbit around the Sun. There have been four ice ages in the last two million years, and there may be more to come.

Iceberg A mass of ice broken off a land-based glacier or ice sheet and floating in the sea. Most icebergs come from Antarctica and Greenland.

Igneous Igneous rocks are produced by the melting of material deep within the Earth's crust or upper mantle. There are two main types—extrusive igneous rocks, which come out of volcanoes and cool quickly, so they are usually fine-grained, and intrusive igneous rocks, which bulge up in large masses within a continent. These cool more slowly and as a result are sometimes crystalline.

Infrared radiation Electromagnetic radiation with a longer wavelength than red light, but less than radio.

vertebrate An animal .thout vertebrae—the nes forming a backbone. iimals with a backbone e known as vertebrates.

rill Small, shrimplike ustaceans. Krill teem in lar seas, where they form uch of the food consumed various baleen whales.

urasia The great rthern continent formed om the breakup, 200 illion years ago, of the percontinent Pangaea. It as made up of present-day rope, North America, eenland, and Asia.

va The molten rock that ws out of a volcano and en solidifies.

ght year The distance at light travels in one ar (5,865,634 miles).

ocal Group The grouping about 30 galaxies in nich our own galaxy found.

agma Molten rock ider the Earth's surface. metimes it rises within a lcano to flow out as lava.

agnetometer A highly nsitive instrument used geologists to measure e Earth's magnetic field.

agnetosphere The agnetic bubble around the rth or another planet in which ionized gas is controlled by the planet's magnetic field.

Main sequence The range of temperature and brightness at which the majority of stars spend most of their lives.

Mantle The thick layer of dense silicate rock that forms the bulk of the Earth beneath the thin crust and above the iron core. Although virtually solid, it carries heat from the interior of the planet and produces volcanic activity on the surface.

Metamorphic Metamorphic rocks have been changed by heat and pressure. They can be derived from either igneous or sedimentary rocks. The heat and pressure can turn shale into slate, limestone into marble, and sandstone into quartzite.

Meteor A brilliant streak across the sky caused by objects, such as specks of dust or rocks, burning up as they enter the Earth's atmosphere. Meteors are popularly known as shooting stars.

Meteorite A lump of rock or metal that has fallen to the Earth from space. The largest meteorites create craters on impact.

Mid-ocean ridge The long range of underwater mountains that runs down the centers of many of the world's oceans. It forms lines of undersea volcanoes from which new ocean crust is spreading.

Mineral A naturally formed chemical substance with a precise molecular structure. Minerals are the building blocks of rocks. Mined natural substances, such as coal and oil, are also known as minerals.

Mollusk A soft-bodied invertebrate, usually with one or two shells. Mollusks include gastropods, such as sea slugs and whelks; cephalopods, such as squid and octopuses; and bivalves, such as mussels and oysters.

Moraine The lines and piles of stones and mud deposited along the sides and at the end of a glacier.

Nebula A cloud of gas or dust in space.

Neutrino A particle with no charge and little or no mass.

Neutron star A star that has been so compressed that electrons and protons have been squashed together to make neutrons. It has the mass of a star, but is much smaller.

Ocean The salt water covering two-thirds of the Earth, or one of its four major divisions—the Atlantic Ocean, Indian Ocean, Pacific Ocean, or Arctic Ocean.

Oort Cloud A cloud of millions or even billions of dormant comets thought to lie beyond the orbit of Pluto.

Ooze Soft, wet mud on the deep ocean floor. The contents of deep-sea oozes include dust and the remains of billions of tiny planktonic organsims.

Orbit The path of one body around another, such as the Moon around the Earth or the Earth around the Sun. It may be circular or, more often, elliptical.

Ore A mineral rich in a particular useful substance, such as a metal, used in commercial quantities for producing that material.

Ozone A form of oxygen molecule that contains three oxygen atoms. It forms naturally in a thin layer in the stratosphere, about 12 miles above us, where it filters out potentially damaging ultraviolet radiation from sunlight. However, it is destroyed by chemicals such as CFCs.

Pangaea The supercontinent containing all the world's landmasses. It existed between about 250 and 200 million years ago and broke up to form Gondwanaland and Laurasia, with the Tethys Ocean between them.

Parallax The apparent motion of an object against a more distant background caused by a changing viewpoint. It provides a basis for calculating the distances to nearby stars.

Perihelion The closest point to the Sun in the orbit of a body such as a comet or planet.

Permian The geological period between about 280 and 225 million years ago. Some of the first large reptiles lived during the Permian period. However, it ended abruptly with the extinction of many species.

Photon The smallest particle of energy that can be carried as light.

Pillow lava Deposits of volcanic lava shaped like a series of pillows. They erupted underwater and were quickly quenched and solidified by the water before they could flow far.

Planet A body in orbit around the Sun or another star, shining in reflected light only. Bodies over 620 miles across are normally considered to be planets. Smaller objects are called minor planets.

Planetary nebula A cloud of gas that can look like a planet, but really consists of expanding shells of gas thrown off by a star close to the end of its life.

Plankton The various tiny organisms that drift near the surface of sea water. Plankton provides the food that most marine creatures depend on, directly or indirectly.

Plate A unit of the rocky lithosphere—the crust and hard top to the mantle—that can slide intact over the Earth's surface as a result of continental drift.

Polar Relating to the world's far north or far south—the regions around the North Pole or the South Pole.

Polyp A sea anemone, coral, or other form of coelenterate. These organisms have a stalklike body fixed at one end to a rock or other underwater object. The other end has a mouth surrounded by a ring of tentacles.

Predator An animal that preys on others.

Protostar An early stage in the formation of a star before nuclear fusion has begun.

Pulsar A spinning neutron star emitting bursts of radiation, often many times a second.

Pyroclastic flow A deadly flow of lava, ash, superheated steam, and gas that can race downhill from a volcanic eruption, scorching everything in its path.

Quasar The energetic core of an active galaxy. Quasars give out as much energy as a big galaxy from a region no bigger than our Solar System. Quasar is short for quasistellar object.

Red dwarf A small, dim red star with a surface temperature of between 4,500°F and 9,000°F.

Red giant A bright red star up to 100 times the diameter of the Sun and thought to be near the end of its life.

Redshift The stretching of light from an object, such as a galaxy, that is moving away from us. Because the Universe is still expanding, the higher the redshift, the more distant the object.

Ridge A long, narrow, raised, steep-sided area of the Earth's crust. Spreadir ridges on the ocean floor are formed where the Earth's plates diverge.

Rift A valley formed whe a mass of rock slid down between two plates that were moving apart. Rift valleys can also be found along the crest of a mid-ocean ridge.

Satellite Any object in orbit around another obje The term is normally applied to a moon or an artificial craft orbiting around a planet.

Sea ice Ice formed from frozen seawater.

Sediment Loose particles deposited by water or wind. Inshore sediment includes gravel and boulders. Deep-sea sediment is mainly made up of fine clays.

Sedimentary Sedimentar rocks are rocks laid down, usually in layers, by water or by wind, ice, and vegetation. They are most formed from the erosion o other rocks; these so-callec clastic rocks include shale and sandstone. Others are chemical deposits such as limestone and gypsum.

Seismic wave A wave running through the Earth, usually produced by an earthquake.

smograph An rument for measuring mic waves.

cate One of the group ninerals containing :on and oxygen atoms nd to other elements h as metals. Silicates the main rock-forming ıerals of the planet.

elting The process in ich an ore is heated to ract a metal from it.

ar wind The stream electrically charged ticles blowing from Sun. When it strikes lecules of air in the th's atmosphere, it duces an aurora.

ice-time The nbination of the three ıensions of space plus of time. Space-time kes up the fabric of Universe.

ectrum The rainbow ıd of electromagnetic iation of different velengths. The light m a star or galaxy, split into wavelengths of ferent colors.

ring tide A tide when difference between high l low water is greatest.

lactite A deposit calcium carbonate ıging like an icicle m the roof of a cave.

Stalagmite A column of calcium carbonate rising up from a cave floor, often beneath a stalactite and formed by a similar process.

Submarine canyon A deep, narrow, steep-sided, underwater valley created by a slide of sediment.

Subatomic physics The study of the fundamental particles that make up atoms, and the forces that act between them.

Submersible A manned or remotely operated submarine designed for research in deep water.

Sunspot A dark spot on the surface, or photosphere, of the Sun, caused by a magnetic disturbance. A sunspot is slightly cooler than the surrounding area.

Supercluster A grouping made up of clusters of galaxies. Superclusters can be hundreds of millions of light years across.

Supernova An exploding, massive star torn apart by an intense flash of radiation. This happens when the core of a star collapses.

Tide The regular rise and fall of sea level caused by the gravitational pulls of the Moon and the Sun on the Earth.

Tornado A small but extremely violent storm in which a funnel-shaped column of cloud rotates rapidly as warm air rises within it. Tornadoes can reach speeds of several hundred miles per hour and are common in parts of the United States and Australia.

Trench A deep, narrow trough in the ocean floor.

Tsunami Sometimes known as a tidal wave, a tsunami can be triggered by an underwater earthquake or landslide. In open ocean it may be only an inch or so high, but it can travel great distances and, as it reaches the shore, can build into a wall of water tens of feet high.

Ultraviolet radiation Electromagnetic radiation of shorter wavelength than the blue end of the visible spectrum.

Universe Space-time and everything contained within it. In theory, there might be universes other than our own, but we could not have direct knowledge of them, or they would be part of our own Universe.

Van Allen belts Belts of radiation around the Earth caused by charged particles trapped in the Earth's magnetic field.

Vertebrate An animal with a backbone. Vertebrate species include fish, amphibians, reptiles, birds, and mammals, as well as humans.

Volcano A place where molten magma rises to the surface of the planet and is released, often with violent results. A volcano can build into a mountain thousands of feet high.

Water cycle The continual flow of the Earth's water. Water vapor from the sea and the land rises into the atmosphere, becoming rain, hail, or snow. These fall on the sea or fill rivers flowing to the sea.

Wavelength The distance between successive peaks (or troughs) in a wave, such as electromagnetic radiation.

White dwarf A hot, compact star no heavier than 1.4 times the mass of the Sun. With most of its nuclear fuel used up, the star contracts until it is very dense and hot.

X rays Electromagnetic radiation of shorter wavelength than ultraviolet radiation.

Zooplankton The animals forming part of the plankton. They feed on single-celled algae called phytoplankton.

Index

Acknowledgments

The publishers would like to thank the following illustrators for their contributions to this book: Julian Baker, Julian Baum, Jim Burns, Tom Connell, Debbie Cook, Anthony Duke, Tim Duke, James Field, Gary Hinks, Richard Holloway, Rob Jakeway, Dave Kesarisingh, John Lawrence, Ceri Llewellyn, Kevin Maddison, Mark Preston, Bernard Robinson, David Webb, ZAP ART.

Key: b = bottom, *c* = center, *l* = left, r = right, t = top;
The publishers would like to thank the following for supplying photographs:
8-9 *b* The Bridgeman Art Library, London, New York/Vatican Museum & Galleries, Rome **9** *b* The Bridgeman Art Library, London, New York/San Marco, Venice/Francesco Turino Bohm **10** *tl* SPL/NASA GSFC/Gene Feldman, *bl* SPL/CNES, 1995 Distribution Spot Image **10-11** SPL/Royal Observatory, Edinburgh, *c* Powerstock/Zefa/Panther **11** *c* SPL/U.S. Geological Survey, *cr* SPL/NASA, *bc* SPL/Space Telescope Science Institute/NASA, *br* SPL/NASA **12** *tr* SPL/NASA **13** *tr* PEP/ Georgette Douwma **14** *tl* Mary Evans Picture Library **15** *tr* Robert Harding Picture Library **16** *cl* OSF/Matthias Breiter, *br* SPL/David Parker **17** *cl* Robert Harding Picture Library, *br* SPL/David Parker **18** *tl* Mary Evans Picture Library **19** *tr* National Geographic Society/ Cartographic Computer Lab/INGS Image Collection **20** *tl* Jean-Loup charmet, *bl* SPL/NASA **21** *br* Geoscience Features Picture Library **23** *tr* SPL/Pekka Parviainen **24** *tl* SPL/Simon Fraser, *bl* SPL/Simon Fraser **24-25** *b* Tony Stone Images/Wayne Eastep, **25** *tr* FSP/NASA/Liaison/*b* B. Ingalls **26** *tl* AKG London, *bl* Martin Redfern **27** *br* FSP/Gilles Bassignac **28** *tl* Werner Forman Archive/British Museum, London, *cl* Robert Harding Picture Library/D. Peebles **29** *tc* FSP/B. Lewis/ *tr* PEP/Bourseiller & Durieux, *c* FSP/A.P.I., *cr* PEP/ Verena Tunnicliffe **30** *tl* PEP/Bourseiller - I & V **30-31** Katz Pictures/Alberto Garcia/SABA **31** *tr* FLPA/USDA Forest Service, *cr* FLPA/USDA Forest Service, *br* FLPA/ USDA Forest Service **32** *tl* Topham Picture Point, *tr* Popperfoto/Reuters/Ted Aljibe, *cl* ET Archive/Royal Society, *bl* PEP/Bourseiller - I & V **33** *tl* Corbis U.K./Library of Congress, *tc* Corbis UK/Library of Congress, *tr* Corbis U.K./Library of Congress, *cr* FSP/Kevin West, *br* PEP/ Krafft - I & V **34-35** *c* TRH/U.S. Navy **35** *cl* SPL/David Parker, *c* Popperfoto/Reuter, *bc* Popperfoto/Reuters/Reinhard Krause **36** *t* Rex Features/Sipa Press, *tl* Peter Newark's Pictures, *clt* John Frost Historical Newspaper Service, *cl* John Frost Historical Newspaper Service, *bl* Popperfoto/Reuter, *br* Popperfoto/Reuter **36-37** *t* Popperfoto/Reuter **37** *tr* Tony Stone Images/Warren Bolster, *b* Tony Stone Images/Ed Pritchard **38** *tl* SPL/Science Museum **38-39** *b* Popperfoto **39** *br* SPL/David Parker **40** *tl* SPL/Martin Bond, *bl* Tony Stone Images/Monica Dalmasso **42** *tl* Tony Stone Images/Gary Irving, *cr* Corbis U.K./Library of Congress **43** *tl* FSP/Shamsi-Basha, *tr* FSP/Gamma/ Schofield /Liais, *cl* OSF/M.P.L. Fogden, *cr* NHPA/Jany Sauvanet, *br* Sygma/Palm Beach Post/Waters **44** *tc* OSF/Scott Camazine, *tr* Popperfoto/Reuters/Peter Morgan, *cl* SPL/NASA, *bl* SPL/NASA **45** *tr* OSF/E.R. Degginger, *cl* The Met Office, *br* Sygma/Bleibtreu/John Hillelson Agency **46** *tl* Rex Features/Sipa/Oliver Monn, *bl* SPL/Pekka Parviainen **46-47** Popperfoto **47** *br* FLPA/Martin B Withers **50** Image Bank/Mancle Isy Stewart, *tl* Tony Stone Images **48-49** *c* PEP/J.P. Nacivet, *bc* Tony Stone Images/Frans Lanting **49** *br* NHPA/Anthony Bannister **50** *tl* SPL/Dr Jeremy Burgess, *bl* SPL/NASA **51** OSF/Paul Franklin **52** *tl* Tony Stone Images/Glen Allison, *bl* Tony Stone Images/Demetrio Carrasco **53** *c* Tony Stone Images/Cameron Davidson **54** *bl* Panos Pictures/Liba Taylor **55** *c* SPL/Earth Satellite Corporation, *cr* SPL/Earth Satellite Corporation **56** *tl* Mary Evans Picture Library, *bl* Tony Stone Images/Tom Bean **57** *tr* Tony Stone Images/Arnulf Husmo, *br* PEP/John Lythgoe **58** *tl* NHPA/George Bernard, *bl* PEP/Jon & Alison Moran **58-59** *c* SPL/Martin Dohrn **59** *bc* FSP **60** *tl* Mary Evans Picture Library, *c* The Royal Geographical Society **61** *tl* Corbis UK/Jim Sugar Photography, *cr* NHM, London, *br* Auscape International Photo Lib. **62** *cr* Corbis UK/James L. Amos **63** *cl* Simon Conway Morris University of Cambridge **64** *tl* PEP/Steve Hopkin **64** *tc (background)* SPL/Kaj R. Svensson **64** *bl* PEP/A.S. Edwards **64-65** *t* OSF/Manfred Kage **64-65** *b (background)* SPL/Kaj R. Svensson **65** *tc (background)* SPL/Kaj R. Svensson **65** *tr* SPL/Sinclair Stammers **65** *br* OSF/Marshall Black **66** *tr* PEP/Peter Scoones **67** *cl* PEP/Ken Lucas **68** *cl* NHM, London, *cr* SPL/Sinclair Stammers **69** *cl* SPL/Sinclair Stammers **70** *c* SPL/Vaughan Fleming **71** *cr* The Ronald Grant Archive, *bc* NHM, London **72** *tl* SPL/Geological Survey of Canada/Mark Pilkington, *bl* SPL/NASA **75** *cl* Alessandro Montanaii **77** *cl* Corbis U.K./Ecoscene/Sally A. Morgan, *cr* NHM, London **78** *tl* Novosti **79** *cl* NHM, London, *cr* NHM, London **78** *tl* Powerstock/Zefa, *tr* NHM, London **79** *tl* Powerstock/Zefa/Bond, *c* NHM, London, *cr* NHM, London, *bc* NHM, London, *br* NHM, London **80** *cl* SPL, *bl* SPL **81** *cl* SPL, *br* SPL **82** *tl* SPL/KAJ R. Svensson **82-83** *t* SPL/Rosenfeld Images Ltd **83** *br* Tony Stone Images/Lester Lefkowitz **84** *tl* SPL/Vaughan Fleming, *cr* NHM, London, *br* The Bridgeman Art Library, London, New York/Derby Museum & Art Gallery **85** *c* NHPA/Anthony Bannister, *cr* Popperfoto/W.U.W. **86** *tl* Martin Redfern, *bl* Tony Stone Images/Philip H. Coblentz **88** *tl* Tony Stone Images/David Woodfall **89** *tr* Tony Stone Images/David Woodfall, *cl* Tony Stone Images/Robert Van Der Hils.Pages *co* The Bridgeman Art Library/British Library, London **92** *tr* SPL, *bl* SPL **92-93** *c* SPL **94** *b* SPL **96** *l* OSF **97** *tc* Images Colour Library, *cr* Images Colour Library, *bc* NHPA **98-99** *b* Image Bank **99** *b* Hulton Getty **100** *tl* BBC Natural History Unit Picture Library, *cl* OSF, *cr* Natural Science Photos **100-101** *b* NHPA **101** *t* Fred Bavendam, *cl* PEP, *cr* PEP **102** *t* Natural Science Photos, *cr* PEP, *bl* Natural Science Photos, *br* BBC Natural History Unit Picture Library **103** *t* Ardea London, *cl* PEP, *cr* Image Bank, *br* Bruce Coleman Collection **104** *tl* OSF, *c* PEP **105** *tc* (reef) FLPA, *tc* (snake) PEP, *tr* (reef) PEP, *cl* (lionfish) PEP, *c* (corals) OSF, *c* (reef) Robert Harding Picture Library, *cr* (nudibranch) Linda Dunk, *cr* (starfish) Bruce Coleman Collection, *bl* (grouper) PEP, *bl* (reef) NHPA, *bl* (sponges) NHPA, *bc* (corals) NHPA **106** *tl* OSF, *b* PEP **107** *tl* PEP, *tc* OSF, *tr* OSF, *cl* NHPA, *c* OSF, *cr* PEP, *bl* NHPA **108** *tr* PEP, *bl* Art Dire & Trip Photographic Library, *br* PEP **108-109** *c* PEP **109** *t* PEP, *cr* FLPA, *bl* PEP, *br* **110** *cl* OSF, *bl* OSF, *br* OSF **110-111** *c* PEP **111** *c* Bruce Coleman Collection, *bl* OSF, OSF, *br* PEP **112** *t* Tim Severin **113** *cr* Rex Features, *b* Rex Features **114** *l* Corbis, *c* Mary Evans Picture Library **115** *tr* Mary Evans Picture Library, *bl* Natural Science Photos **116** *t* Michael Holford, *bl* Mary Evans Picture Library, *br* The Bridgeman Ar Library **117** *tl* Bridgeman Art Library, *tr* Michael Holford, *c* The British Museum, *b* Picture Source Ltd, *br* The Bridgeman Art Library **118** *tl* The Art Archive, *cr* The R Grant Archive, *bl* Michael Holford/Victoria & Albert Museum **118-119** *t* Metropolita Museum of Art, **119** *cr* Bruce Coleman Collection, *bl* Superstock, *br* The Art Archive *t* FSP, *c* PEP **121** *tl* OSF, *tr* Still Pictures **122** *tl* NHPA, *bl* FSP, *br* Hulton Getty **122-** T Rex Features **123** *bl* NHPA, *br* Sygma **124** *tl* PEP, *tr* PEP, *bl* PEP, **125** *l* PEP **126** Powerstock/Zefa, *tr* SPL/Jean-Loup Charmet, *cr* The Bridgeman Art Library/British Library **127** *cl* SPL/Hale Observatories, *c* Corbis **128** *tl* Science & Society Picture Li *tl* Scala/Biblioteca Nazionale, Firenze, *c* Mary Evans Picture Library **128-129** backgr Hulton Getty, *t* SPL/Peter Menzel, *b* Carnegie Institute of Washington **129** *tr* SPL, FSP/Gamma **130** *t* PEP, *cr* NASA/Univ. of Washington/B. Balik, *bl* European Space Agency/PPARC **131** *tl* NASA/KSC, *cr* European Space Agency, *br* European Space Agency **132** *l* PEP, *tl*, The Art Archive, *tr* Popperfoto, *cr* Corbis/Bettmann/UPI **133** Novosti, *tc* SPL/Novosti *cr* FSP/Gamma **134** *bl* NASA/Portfolio Pictures, *bc* FSP/Gamma **135** *c* Genesis Photo Library, *cr* Genesis Photo Library/NASA **136** *tl* FSP/Gamma, *bl* Telegraph Colour Library **136-137** *c* FSP/Gamma, **137** *cl* SPL/Nov *c* European Space Agency, *br* SPL/NASA **138** *tl* SPL, *cl* SPL/NASA, *bl* NASA, *br* Nov **138-139** *t* NASA/Portofolio Pictures **139** *tr* NASA/Portofolio Pictures, *c* SPL/NASA, SPL/NASA, *br* SPL **140** *tr* Popperfoto, *cr* European Space Agency, *bl* SPL, *bc* Popperf *b* Popperfoto **141** *tl* NASA, *tc* NASA, *tr*, NASA, *cr* NASA, *b*l European Space Agency, *b* PEP, *br* Tony Stone Images **142** *tl* European Space Agency, *c* SPL, *bl* SPL/ESA **142-1** SPL **143** *cl* SPL, *c* PEP, *cr* FSP/Gamma **146** *tl* SPL/NASA, *cl* SPL **147** *tr* (insert) SF **148** *tl* SPL/NASA, *cl* SPL/Novosti, *cr* SPL/NASA **148-149** *c (background)* SPL/NASA/David Anderson **149** *tr* SPL/NASA, *cl* SPL/NASA, *c* SPL/NASA **150** *t (background)* PEP, *tl* SPL, *c* PEP **150-151** *c* SPL/NASA **151** *b (background)* NASA *tl* SPL/NASA, *cl* SPL/NASA, *bl* SPL/NASA **152-153** PEP *c*, SPL/U.S. Geological Su **153** *tl* PEP, *tc* SPL, *tr* NASA, *c* SPL/NASA, *cr* SPL/U.S. Geological Survey, *br* PEP **15** SPL, *b (background)* SPL/NASA **155** *t (background)* The Ronald Grant Archive, *tl* P *tr* SPL/NASA, *c* SPL **156** *cl* SPL/Novosti, *bl* SPL/Geological Survey of Canada, **157** Powerstock/Zefa, *tr* National Air Library of Canada, *cl* (3) SPL, *cl* (1) NHM, London, (2) SPL, *cl* (4) NHM, London, *bc* NHM, London, **158** background SPL, *cl* SPL/NASA/STSI, *bl* Jet Propulsion Lab/NASA, *br* SPL/J.Tennyson & S.Miller, Unive College, London, **159** *tl* Jet Propulsion Lab/NASA, *tr* PEP, *cr* Jet Propulsion Lab/NAS SPL **160** *cr* PEP, *bl* PEP **161** *cl* PEP, *cr* SPL, *bc* SPL **162** *tl* PEP, *tr* SPL/STSI/NASA SPL, *br* SPL/STSI/NASA **163** *tl* SPL/NASA, *b* Jet Propulsion Lab/NASA **164** *tl* SPL/NASA, *tr* (2) SPL/NASA, *tr* (4) Jet Propulsion Lab, *tr* (3) SPL/NASA **165** *tr* (1) SPL/NASA *tr*, (5) SPL/NASA **166** *tl* Telegraph Colour Library, *cl* SPL, *cr* SPL, *bl* SPl **167** *tl* SPL, *tr* (3) SPL/NASA *tr*, (2) SPL/NASA, *tr* (1) SPL/NASA, *cl* SPL **168** *tl* SPL SPL, *bc* SPL **169** *cr*, SPL/NASA **170** *tl* SPL/NASA/STSI, *cl* SPL **171** *cl* SPL, *bl* PEF **172** *tl* Ann Ronan/Image Select, *tr* The Art Archive, *cl* SPL/David Parker, *c* SPL/ESA SPL, *bc* SPL/Gordon Garradd **173** *br* SPL/Steven Jay **174** *cl* SPL/Pekka Parviainen, SPL/George Post **175** *tl* SPL/Jisas/Lockheed, *c* SPL/Dr. Douglas Gorgh, *br* SPL/Da Parker **176** *c* Telegraph Colour Library, *b* SPL/NASA **177** *tl* Martin Redfern/Smithsonian Institute, *tr* SPL/Hale Observatories **178** *cl* SPL, *cr* Martin Redfern/NASA, *bl* SPL **179** *cl* Martin Redfern/NASA/Jeff Hester, Paul Scowen, *br* Martin Redfern/Protoplanetary Disks/C.R. O'Dell **180** *cr* SPL/ESA, *bl* SPL **181** *l* SPL/Luke Dodd, *br* Martin Redfern/NASA **182** *tl* SPL/STSI/NASA, *cr* NASA/Harv Smithsonian Center of Astrophysics/Peter Garnavich, *bl* SPL/STSI/NASA **182-183** b ground Martin Redfern/Royal Observatory/Photolabs, *t* Martin Redfern/NASA/STS **183** *tr* SPL/STSI/NASA, *cl* SPL/STSI **186** *tl* SPL/Dennis Di cicco/Peter Arnold Inc. SPL/NASA **187** *tr*, PEP, *c* SPL/Max Planck Inst. for Radio Astronomy, *cr* SPL/NASA Martin Redfern/Smithsonian Institute **188** *c* & *cr* SPL/STSI, *tc* SPL/Harvard Colleg Observatory **188-189** *t* SPL, 189 *t* SPL, *c* SPL **190-191** *t* Department of Astrophysics, Oxford University/University of Oxford **191** *cl* SPL, *cr* Department of Astrophysics, Oxford University **192** *tl* SPL/Dr. Martin England, *cr* SPL/U.S. Naval Observatory, *bl* SPL, *br* Martin Redfern **193** *tl* Martin Redfern/Smithsonian Institute, *cl* Martin Red *cr* Martin Redfern/NASA **194** *bl* SPL **195** *tr* SPL, *c* SPL **196** *tc* SPL, *bl* Zap Art **196** *c* PEP **197** *br* SPL/AT & *t* bell Labs./R.Wilson & A.Penzias **198** *cl* Corbis **200** *bl* SPL Martin Redfern/NASA **204** *tl* Martin Redfern/NASA/JPL, *cr* PEP, *bl* SPL/Peter Me **204-205** *t* SPL/John Reader **205** *bl* Fortean Picture Library **206** *c* Corbis **206-207** Pi International Ltd

(NHM Natural History Museum; FSP Frank Spooner Pictures)

The publishers would also like to thank the following: Clarissa Claudel, Peter Clayman, Dougal Dixon, Jo Fletcher-Watson, Ian Graham, Dr. Paul Murdin, Pauline Newman, Robin Redfern, Dr. Denise Smythe-Wright, Marc Wilson.